094115
D0756501

GCSE HISTORY

FOR WJEC SPECIFICATION A

IN-DEPTH AND OUTLINE STUDIES OF ASPECTS OF WELSH/ENGLISH AND WORLD HISTORY

PAUL BARNES, R. PAUL EVANS, PERIS JONES-EVANS

Heinemann is an imprint Pearson Education Limited, a company incorporated in England and Wales, having its registered office at Edinburgh Gate, Harlow, Essex, CM20 2JE. Registered company number: 872828

Heinemann is a registered trademark of Pearson Education Limited

© Paul Barnes, R. Paul Evans and Peris Jones-Evans, 2003

Copyright notice

All rights reserved. No part of this publication may be reproduced in any material form (including photocopying or storing it in any medium by electronic means and whether or not transiently or incidentally to some other use of this publication) without the prior written permission of the copyright owner, except in accordance with the provisions of the Copyright, Designs and Patents Act 1988 or under the terms of a licence issued by the Copyright Licensing Agency Ltd, 90 Tottenham Court Road, London W1T 4LP. Applications for the copyright owner's written permission to reproduce any part of this publication should be addressed to the publisher.

First published 2003

ISBN: 978 0 435 30802 5
09
10 9 8

Designed, illustrated and typeset by hicksdesign
Printed and bound in China(EPC/08)

Photographic acknowledgements

The authors and publisher would like to thank the following for permission to reproduce photographs:

AKG: 140A, 143D, 150C, 156, 160D, 164A, 210A, 211B, 213C; Archive Photos: 240C; Archiv Gerstenberg: 159B; Bildarchiv Preussischer Kulturbesitz: 162H; Birmingham (Alabama) Public Library: 251E; Cadw Photographic Library: 13A; Camera Press: 180, 182B; Centre for the Study of Cartoons and Caricature (University of Kent): 226B, 227D, 263F; Christies Images: 213D; Corbis: 122I, 175B, 207I, 234A; Corbis/AFP: 229E; Corbis/Bettmann: 103D, 106G, 116, 118B, 127E, 219J, 239B, 247L, 252G, 253I; Corbis–Bettmann/UPI: 113C; Corbis/David Turnley: 189C; Corbis/Henry Diltz: 245I; Corbis/Hulton-Deutsch Collection: 6B, 57A, 98; Corbis/Underwood & Underwood: 123; Daily Mail: 169B, 259C; David King: 60C, 66C, 70F, 78H, 81A, 86C, 87D, 90F, 90A, 92A; Hampton University Museum, Hampton, Virginia: 170D; Hulton: 8C, 26, 38C, 44B, 49B, 50C, 51F, 53H, 58B, 67D, 71G, 76E, 77G, 97D, 119D, 125C, 137C, 144E, 145F, 161F, 174, 270; Illustrated London News: 74C, 162G; Imperial War Museum: 21C; Mary Evans Picture Library: 112B, 153F, 153G; Mayibye Centre: 177E; National Library of Wales: 11F, 12, 29B; National Museums & Galleries of Wales: 16D, 40B, 62; Novosti: 64A; Peter Newark: 30D, 100A, 105E, 107A, 120E, 121F, 126D, 149A, 243G, 249B; Philip Sauvain: 230; Pictorial Press: 244H; Popperfoto: 46D, 89E, 231 (both); Popperfoto/Reuters: 187A; Punch: 23E, 48, 201E, 209K; Reuters/Bettmann: 179G, 191D; Robert Hunt: 157A; Rugby Relics: 32F; Sam Nzima: 178F; Solomon Andrews collection at Caernarfon Record Office, Gwynedd Archives Service: 40E; Solo Syndication: 55A; Topham Picturepoint: 32A, 68E, 73A, 80J, 95C, 105F, 147, 172F, 189B, 242F, 269 (both); Ullstein Bilderdienst: 217H; Wiener Library:155I

Cover photograph: © The Art Archive (see also page 53)

Picture research by Liz Moore

Written source acknowledgements

The authors and publisher gratefully acknowledge the following publications from which written sources in the book are drawn. In some sentences the wording or sentence structure has been simplified:

C. Bielenberg, *The Past is Myself* (Chatto & Windus, 1968): 164I; W. Carr, *The History of Germany, 1815–1945* (Edward Arnold, 1979): 139D; J. Charmley, *Churchill: The End of Glory* (Hodder & Stoughton, 1993): 56D; J. Davies, *A History of Wales* (Penguin Books, 1993): 15C, 19D; H. Fairlie, *The Kennedy Promise* (Methuen, 1973): 241E ; T. Fiehn et al, *The USA Between The Wars, 1919–41* (John Murray, 1998): 121G; R. Graves, *Goodbye to All That* (London, 1929): 30C; W. Guttman & P. Meehan, *The Great Inflation: Germany, 1919–23* (Farnborough, 1975): 138A; J. Hakim, *History of USA: War, Peace and All That Jazz* (New York, 1999): 107H, 122H; T. Herbert & G. Elwyn Jones (eds), *Wales Between The Wars* (University of Wales Press, 1988): 41D; A. Horner, *Incorrigible Rebel* (London, 1960): 19C; P. Ingram, *Russia and the USSR, 1905–56* (CUP, 1997): 76F; R.W. Johnson, *How Long Will South Africa Survive?* (Macmillan, 1982): 172G; J. Jones, *Unfinished Journey* (Hamish Hamilton, 1937): 27A; Y. Kukushkin, *History of the USSR* (Moscow Progress, 1981): 82D, 91D; K. Morgan, *Rebirth of a Nation: Wales 1880–1980* (Clarendon, 1981): 31E; A. Owings, *Frauen: German Women Recall the Third Reich* (Penguin, 1993): 142C; W. Paynter, *My Generation* (Allen & Unwin, 1972): 33C; R. Radway, *Germany 1918–45* (Hodder & Stoughton, 1998): 165D; E. S. Reddy, *The Anti-Apartheid Movement* (Anti-Apartheid Movement Archives Committee, 1999): 186C; M. Spring Rice, *Working Class Wives* (Harmondsworth, 1939): 37B; S. Roberts, *The House That Hitler Built* (London, 1939): 149B; H. Salisbury, *Russia in Revolution, 1900–30* (London Deutsch, 1978): 91B; L. Schapiro, *1917: The Russian Revolutions and the Origins of Present-Day Communism* (Hounslow, 1984): 80I; W. Shirer, *Berlin Diary* (London, 1941): 152E; R. Turvey, *Wales and Britain 1906–51* (Hodder & Stoughton, 1997): 33D; J. Vick, *Modern America* (University Tutorial Press, 1985): 130D; H. Ward, *The USA from Wilson to Nixon* (1998): 108D; M. Wolff-Monckeberg, *On the other side to my children: from Germany, 1940–45* (London Owen, 1979): 165B; N. Worden, *The Making of Modern South Africa* (Blackwell, 1994): 193D; N. Wynn, *The Afro-American and the Second World War* (Elek, 1976): 250C

Tel: 01865 888058 www.heinemann.co.uk

CONTENTS

IN-DEPTH STUDIES

OUTLINE STUDIES

1 THE EDWARDIAN ERA AND THE FIRST WORLD WAR, 1902–19

Although many features of the Victorian Age remained, for many people the new king, Edward VII, and the start of the new century meant a new beginning. Members of the aristocracy were still living a life of ease with their armies of servants. However, an increasing number of surveys and reports were published about the contrast between the lives of the rich and the poor. These circumstances provided the background for the Liberal government's social and political reforms.

Continuing industrial growth meant that Wales produced a significant proportion of Britain's iron, steel, tinplate, non-ferrous metals and roofing slates. It was the coal industry, however, that saw the greatest expansion. The popularity of Welsh coal made Cardiff a seaport and commercial centre of world importance. Coal production reached its peak in 1913, the year of the worst mining disaster at Senghennydd and serious industrial unrest at Tonypandy and Llanelli.

In 1914 people welcomed the outbreak of war, but as they struggled to come to terms with the huge loss of life a large growth in government power occurred. The government's impact on economic life, party politics and social attitudes was greater than in any previous conflict. The war also strengthened the claim of women to be treated equally.

In Wales, Welsh was still spoken by half the population in 1902 but was increasingly threatened by social and educational trends, and by the influx of people caused by the expansion of the coal industry. The role of religion in Welsh life diminished, a tendency which was accelerated by the war. New ways of expressing Welshness were developed in schools, and on the playing field.

TIMELINE OF EVENTS

1903 Foundation of the Women's Social and Political Union (WSPU)

1906 Liberals win a landslide victory in the general election
School meals established

1907 School medical inspections set up

1908 Old age pensions introduced

1909 The People's Budget

1910 Tonypandy riots

1911 The National Insurance Act, Part I

1913 The National Insurance Act, Part II

1914 4 August: Britain declares war on Germany.
Defence of the Realm Act (DORA)

1916 January: Military Service Act introduces conscription for men aged 18–41
David Lloyd George becomes Prime Minister

1917 German U-boat campaign threatens Britain's food supplies: rationing introduced

1918 Representation of the People Act
11 November: Armistice Day – the end of the war

COLEG CYMUNEDOL ABERGELE
ABERGELE COMMUNITY COLLEGE
CANOLFAN ADNODDAU DYSGU
LEARNING RESOURCE CENTRE

To what extent was there a demand and need for social and political reform in the period 1902–14?

LUNCHEON HAMPERS	
(INCLUDING HIRE OF HAMPER, CONTAINING LINEN, PLATES, GLASS, CUTLERY, &C)	
FOR FOUR PERSONS	
VEAL AND HAM PIE, ROAST LAMB AND MINT SAUCE, ROAST FOWL, CUT HAM, SALAD AND DRESSING, BREAD ROLLS, BUTTER, CHEESE, CAKE, PASTRY AND CONDIMENTS &C	£1.87
4 BOTTLES ACHILLE MORAT CHAMPAGNE	£1.00
1 BOTTLE SHERRY OR WHISKY	15
2 BOTTLES RED WINE	20
6 BOTTLES MINERAL WATER	10
	£3.32

SOURCE A From the *Army & Navy Stores Catalogue*, 1902.

THE NATURE AND EXTENT OF POVERTY IN 1902

One unexpected result of the Boer War, which ended in 1902, was a new interest in the welfare of the poorest members of society. The Army Medical Corps shocked the nation and the government when it revealed that about 40 per cent of those examined for military service were physically unfit to fight. The 40 per cent came from the poorest section of the community. At the same time several private studies were being conducted into the standard of living of the poor. Charles Booth had started his studies of the poor of London in the 1880s and the final part of his *Life and Labour of the People of London* was published in 1903. In 1901, Seebohm Rowntree had published *Poverty: A Study of Town Life*, based on a study of the city of York. Yet another study was published in 1905, *Riches and Poverty* by a businessman, Chiozza Money, who was also a Liberal MP.

These studies gave details of thousands of families living on an income of about £1 a week. The rent of a slum house or flat could cost a quarter of that sum, which meant that two parents and several children and often a grandparent as well had to live on less than 15 shillings (75p) a week.

SOURCE B A poverty-stricken couple with their five children, c.1900.

Poor diet and appalling living conditions meant that the poor often fell ill and their suffering was made worse because they could not afford medical treatment. Some households, where the regular wage earner was too sick or too old to work, or was unemployed, had to try to live on even less. For these families, the threat of being taken to the workhouse was a constant worry. As a result of the studies by Booth and Rowntree, an income level of £1 a week for a family of five came to be seen as the 'poverty line', below which it was impossible to live properly. Rowntree estimated that over 30 per cent of the population lived below the poverty line.

Q Questions

1 How useful is Source A as evidence about standards of living during the Edwardian age?

2 Why had the question of poverty become more of a talking point by 1905?

CONSERVATIVE ATTITUDES TO SOCIAL AND POLITICAL REFORM

Apart from the Education Act of 1902 and changes to the licensing of public houses in 1905, Balfour's Conservative government (July 1902 to December 1905) seemed to be more interested in foreign and colonial matters than in tackling problems at home. As members of the Conservative Party were often landowners and important businessmen, they could not be expected to give much thought to improving the lives of the poor, if that meant higher taxation and more power for trade unions.

The Conservative Party was also divided within itself. During the nineteenth century, the two main political parties (Conservatives and Liberals) in Britain had maintained a policy of free trade, allowing goods to be imported and exported without tariffs (taxes). In 1903, however, Joseph Chamberlain resigned as Colonial Secretary so that he could campaign for a policy of tariff reform. Some foreign goods were to have tariffs, but not those goods traded between Britain and the countries of the British Empire. By imposing tariffs the jobs of British people at home and abroad would be protected from foreign competition. Although some business leaders supported this policy, Balfour and the Conservative leadership continued to support free trade. It was these differences within the Conservative Party that led Balfour to resign in December 1905. Henry Campbell-Bannerman took over as the leader of a minority Liberal government until a general election could be held in the New Year.

The Liberal Party won an overwhelming victory in 1906, gaining a majority of 84 seats over all the other parties combined. Nowhere was the political change greater than in Wales, where the Conservative Party, supported by the landowning families, failed to win a single seat.

Party	Seats
Liberals	377
Conservatives	157
Irish Nationalists	83
Labour	53

The results of the 1906 general election.

THE NATURE AND IMPACT OF THE LIBERAL SOCIAL REFORMS

Children's health

The new Liberal government wasted no time in introducing a programme of reform. In 1906 the Education (Provision of Meals) Act was passed: it enabled local authorities to provide poor children with school meals. By 1914, when it was made compulsory, the service provided 150,000 children with a midday meal, which in many cases was their only real meal. At a time when many families could not afford to pay for medical care, the School Medical Inspection Service, set up in 1907, was a great improvement, especially with the addition of clinics providing free treatment for school-age children in 1912.

SOURCE C The first person to draw an old age pension, 1909.

Old age pensions

In 1908 Herbert Asquith became Prime Minister and David Lloyd George became Chancellor of the Exchequer. Lloyd George began to prepare an Old Age Pensions Bill. People over 70 years of age, whose annual income was no more than £21, would receive a payment of 5 shillings (25p) a week. The bill became law on 1 August 1908 and the first pensions were paid on 6 January 1909. At the end of the first full year, the total number of pensioners was nearer 700,000 and the cost £8.5 million. That, according to the opponents of state pensions, was the cost of four of the new dreadnought battleships being built for the Royal Navy at the time! Old people could hardly believe their luck and it was said that many had tears in their eyes as they collected their 'Lloyd George' from the local post office.

SOURCE D

We've often thought it would be best for us to die, for we were just a burden to our children who kept us. But now we want to go on living for ever, because we can give them our ten shillings a week, and it pays them to have us with them.

The husband of a couple aged over 90 talking about the introduction of old age pensions.

National insurance

Illness and unemployment remained major causes of poverty for many families. The National Insurance Act, which first came into force in 1911, provided health insurance for male workers earning less than £160 a year. Those workers would receive 'free' medical attention and a sickness payment or a disability payment. Later, unemployment cover for some workers was added. To qualify, every working man had to contribute 4 old pence (about 1.5p) a week by means of a National Insurance stamp; employers and the government added another 5 old pence (2.5p).

THE 1909 BUDGET AND THE CONSTITUTIONAL CRISIS

Lloyd George had to find the money to pay not only for pensions and other social reforms but also for the new battleships being built for the Royal Navy. He proposed to do this by raising taxes, including a new super-tax on incomes above £3000.

Lloyd George introduced his budget to the House of Commons on 29 April 1909. The proposals to raise heavier taxes on the rich shocked many. The Conservatives knew that the large Liberal majority would ensure that the budget would be passed in the House of Commons. However, the House of Lords, with its enormous Conservative majority, would be a different matter. Lloyd George toured the country, making a series of speeches attacking rich landlords and especially the members of the House of Lords.

SOURCE E

The capitalist risks his money; the engineer puts his brains in; the miner risks his life ... Yet when the Prime Minister and I knock at the doors of these great landlords, and say to them: 'Here, you know these poor fellows who have been risking their lives, some of them are old and can work no more. Won't you give us something towards keeping them from the workhouse?' they scowl at us. We say, 'Only a ha'penny.' They retort, 'You thieves!' And they turn their dogs on us.

Part of Lloyd George's 'Limehouse speech', given in a poor area of London on 30 July 1909.

Q Questions

1 To what extent were poor people better off as a result of the Liberal government's reforms, 1908–13?

2 Why was the budget of 1909 so controversial at the time?

The general election January 1910 and the Parliament Act 1911

The People's Budget, as it was now known, was passed by the Commons on 4 November, but was rejected by the Lords on 30 November 1909. There was now a constitutional crisis, with the rich, represented by the House of Lords, preventing the will of the people, as represented by the elected House of Commons. The people had to express their will once again in a general election, which was held in January 1910. Some described the election as 'peers against people'. Although the Conservatives increased their vote, the Liberals still had a majority and the budget was finally passed in April 1910.

A Parliament Bill was now drawn up to reduce the power of the House of Lords. It would prevent the Lords from rejecting a money bill and only allow them to postpone other measures sent from the House of Commons. A second general election and the king's threat to create new peers persuaded a majority of the House of Lords to vote for the Parliament Act, which became law in August 1911. The reduction in the power of the Lords meant that the House of Commons had become more democratic. In addition MPs were to be paid, which meant that ordinary men, without a private income from land or business, could now afford to stand as an MP.

THE RISE OF THE LABOUR PARTY

Throughout the nineteenth century, trade unions had been growing in strength and influence. It was becoming normal for trade union officials to negotiate wage rates and working conditions with employers on behalf of their members and they could legally take part in peaceful industrial action. After the Reform Act of 1884, some trade union officials began to stand for Parliament under the banner of the Liberal Party. In the House of Commons they soon became known as Lib-Lab members.

In 1893 at a meeting held in Bradford, chaired by James Keir Hardie MP, a new political party for working men, the Independent Labour Party (ILP), was established. In 1900 a conference of trade unions established the Labour Representation Committee (LRC) to secure wider representation for working men in Parliament. The LRC received financial support from the trade unions by means of a 'political levy' (tax). After the 1906 general election the name 'Labour Party' was officially adopted by the 29 successful candidates. By 1918 there were 59 Labour MPs.

Results

The new party had to campaign forcefully to assert rights. After a strike on the Taff Vale Railway in South Wales in 1900, the railwaymen's union was forced to pay damages of £32,000 to the company. Another problem arose in 1908 when the Osborne judgment (a legal decision) declared that the political levy paid by trade unions to the Labour Party was illegal. The Trade Disputes Act of 1906 and the Trade Union Act of 1913 eventually restored the right of trade unionists to strike without being sued and let them make financial contributions to the Labour Party.

Although working men's rights were slowly being improved, there were many during this period who thought that progress was too slow. For many workers, wages remained low and job security uncertain. 'Syndicalists' among trade union members thought that working men should take over their own industries by means of frequent strikes and violent protest if necessary. There were some successes – such as the 1912 strike by miners, dockers and transport workers – which forced the government to agree to a minimum wage.

VOTES FOR WOMEN

At the beginning of the twentieth century, although thousands of mainly younger women worked in domestic service and in some industries, the majority of women were expected to devote their time to their homes and families. In political affairs it was felt that women could be represented by their fathers or husbands.

Suffragists

Gradually some more educated and mainly middle-class women began to establish societies to demand for women the right to vote in elections on the same terms as men. They became known as suffragists, from the word 'suffrage', meaning the vote. By the 1890s, women in New Zealand and some of the states in the USA had already won the right to vote. Since the government in Britain seemed to pay little attention to women's demands, in 1897 Millicent Fawcett formed the National Union of Women's Suffrage Societies (NUWSS).

SOURCE F Demonstration of the National Union of Women's Suffrage Societies in Wales, 1907.

The new NUWSS published pamphlets and organised peaceful meetings and demonstrations to support the demand for 'votes for women'.

Suffragettes

Impatient with the lack of progress made by the NUWSS, the Women's Social and Political Union (WSPU) was set up in 1903. The leading members were Mrs Emmeline Pankhurst and her daughters. While the WSPU started peacefully, by 1909 its members began to use more violent methods to attract publicity. The campaign of 'deeds not words' had begun.

Up to 1914, the suffragettes interrupted meetings, chained themselves to railings, poured acid on golf courses, broke shop windows and set fire to public buildings. When they were imprisoned, the suffragettes would continue their protest by going on hunger strike. The prison authorities would then try to force-feed them. The government passed the 'Cat and Mouse Act' in 1913 which allowed the suffragettes to be released until they were fit enough to be returned to prison!

The height of the suffragettes' campaign was in 1913 during the Derby horse race at Epsom. Emily Davison attempted to interrupt the race and was knocked down and killed by the king's horse, Anmer. Her funeral turned into a huge demonstration. While it was unclear whether Emily Davison had deliberately tried to make herself a martyr, she certainly gained a great deal of publicity for the cause.

Q Questions

1. How did trade unions develop after 1884?
2. What were the aims of the new Labour Party?
3. How did the methods of the Suffragettes differ from those of the Suffragists?
4. To what extent did the 'votes for women' campaign achieve its aims before 1914?
5. Describe the important social and political reforms of the Edwardian era.
6. Which groups benefited from the social and political reforms of the Edwardian era?
7. Which groups did not benefit from these reforms?

1 EXAM PRACTICE

These questions test Section B of the examination paper.

POLITICS DURING THE PERIOD 1902–14

Study the information below and then answer the questions which follow.

INFORMATION

Megan Lloyd George with a poster about her father's budget.

EQ Exam Questions

1 **a** Describe *one* of the main causes of poverty at the beginning of the twentieth century. [2]

b Explain why the establishment of old-age pensions was important. [4]

c How important was the 'People's Budget' of 1909? [5]

2 **a** Describe the growth of the Labour Party during this period. [3]

b Explain the contribution of the Pankhurst family to the Suffragette movement. [4]

3 How successfully did the government deal with the demand and need for social and political reform during the period 1902–14? Explain your answer fully. [7]

Was the period 1902–14 a golden age of Welsh heavy industry?

SOURCE A The Navigation colliery at Crumlin; its surface building, contained the most modern machinery available at the time.

THE SCALE OF WELSH HEAVY INDUSTRY IN 1900

In 1900 industries situated in Wales made up a significant proportion of British trade.

Coal, iron and steel

Coal remained the most important source of heat and energy for industry and transport. The clean-burning 'steam coal', found in the South Wales coalfield, had long been recognised as the best type of fuel for this purpose. The shipping companies required coal 'bunkers' to be established in every major port throughout the world and these had to be replenished regularly with supplies of Welsh steam coal.

By 1900, the coal industry, with its 140,000 miners, had become a larger employer than the iron and steel industry. In 1900 South Wales produced about 10 per cent of Britain's iron. Some was made into steel, but by this time Welsh supplies of iron ore had run out. The Welsh steel industry now depended on imported ores and the only profitable plants were those on the coast, such as the East Moors works in Cardiff.

Other industries

The tinplate industry in the Swansea area produced steel sheets, galvanised (coated) with tin. The tin coating prevented the steel from rusting and the tinplate was used in the manufacture of food cans. In 1900 the Welsh tinplate industry was still suffering from the effects of the McKinley Tariff imposed in 1891 by the USA on tinplate imports. The tinplate trade remained localised and Welsh in character, relying on the skilled labour of the Welsh-speaking women of west Wales.

The unique contribution of North Wales to the industrial age was the vast slate quarries of Snowdonia. In 1900 about 18,000 quarrymen were employed. The slates produced were used as roofing material in the growing towns of England, and they were also exported to Europe.

THE PENRHYN LOCKOUT

The North Wales Quarrymen's Union was established in 1874, but the quarry owners disliked negotiating wages and working conditions with union officials.

Lord Penrhyn, the owner of the Penrhyn quarry at Bethesda, claimed that wage rates and conditions were his responsibility alone, and that the men could 'take it or leave it'.

In October 1900, Lord Penrhyn and his manager tried to introduce new working practices into the quarry, but refused to meet officials of the union to negotiate terms. This led to the sacking of 26 quarrymen and, when their fellow workers stopped work in sympathy, the manager closed the quarry.

The results of the lockout

In May 1901 it was announced that the quarry would reopen to any quarryman who rejected the union and accepted the owner's terms. Those who accepted received a gold sovereign. The union men, still on strike, called it *Punt y Gynffon* (the Blacklegs' Pound).

By the winter of 1902, the strikers and their families were suffering hardship and feelings became increasingly bitter. The strikebreakers were abused and often attacked on their way to and from work. Police reinforcements and soldiers were sent to Bethesda to keep order and court cases followed. Some strikers left the district to seek work elsewhere; others joined choirs and went on countrywide tours to raise funds.

i D. A. THOMAS AND THE CAMBRIAN COAL COMBINE

David Alfred Thomas, born in 1856, made a fortune from the expanding coal trade of Aberdare and the Cynon valley. Although David had 16 brothers and sisters, his family was well-off enough to enable him to go away to school and college. After graduating from Cambridge in 1883, he returned to Wales to learn about mining and the coal trade. He worked underground and soon became an expert in every aspect of coal mining and marketing.

Thomas was elected to Parliament in 1888 and remained an MP, for Merthyr Tydfil and later Cardiff, until 1916, when he entered the House of Lords as Lord Rhondda. For a time he worked closely with Lloyd George in the *Cymru Fydd* movement, campaigning for Welsh Home Rule. Thomas, who saw himself as the political leader of industrial South Wales, viewed Lloyd George with suspicion.

Thomas later devoted more of his energies to his business interests. He bought a number of smaller companies and by 1908 had created the huge Cambrian Coal Combine. It was partly his hardline attitude towards trade unions and wage negotiations that caused the dispute which led to the Tonypandy riots in 1910.

During the First World War his relations with Lloyd George improved and he was sent to the USA to represent British industry and later proved a great success as Controller of Food during the 1917 crisis. His position in government meant that he had to retire from business which included the directorships of more than 30 industrial concerns in Wales and overseas. The strain of overwork eventually took its toll and he died at his mansion, Llanwern House, near Newport, in July 1918.

By the autumn of 1903, large numbers of quarrymen had returned to work on Lord Penrhyn's terms and the strike was officially called off on 11 November 1903. It had been a disaster. The three-year stoppage led to the loss of markets for slates at home and abroad and replacement products, such as roofing tiles made of clay or cement, were developed. The great days of the slate industry were over.

Q Questions

1 Describe the main Welsh industries in 1900.

2 What were the causes of the Penrhyn lockout?

3 What do Sources B and C show about the way the coal industry was developing in the Edwardian age?

CARDIFF AS A PORT AND TRADING CENTRE

Although it depended on one trade only (coal), in terms of tonnage handled Cardiff was the largest port in the world by 1900. The Cardiff Coal Exchange was established in 1886 to enable merchants to buy and sell coal in bulk. Since a large proportion of South Wales coal was exported, the prices paid at Cardiff set the worldwide price of coal. The market was dominated by Cardiff-based companies such as Cory Brothers, who owned coaling stations or bunkers in every important port. Some of the profits of the coal trade were used to build a new City Hall and other grand public buildings in Cathays Park. As a result, Cardiff was given city status in 1905. By the census of 1911, its population had grown to 182,000.

The Cambrian Combine in 1910

Company	Collieries	Miners employed
Naval Colliery Co. Ltd	Ely	939
	Nant Gwyn	821
	Anthony and Pandy	340
Cambrian Collieries Ltd	Cambrian Navigation No 1	701
	Cambrian Navigation No 2	1498
	Cambrian Navigation No 3	1855
Glamorgan Coal Co. Ltd	Llwynypia No 1	1712
	Llwynypia No 2	1539
	Llwynypia No 6	656
	Sherwood	537
	Total	**10,598**

SOURCE B Data from *The South Wales Coal Annual*, 1909–10.

SOURCE C

By 1913, the Powell Duffryn Company was employing 13,600 men, while D. A. Thomas, of the Cambrian Combine, was the owner of an industrial empire with a value of over £2 million. The coal companies were generous to their shareholders: in 1911, the Ocean Coal Company gave a bonus of 50 per cent and, between 1910 and 1912, Powell Duffryn paid an annual dividend of 20 per cent.

Extract from *A History of Wales* by John Davies, 1993.

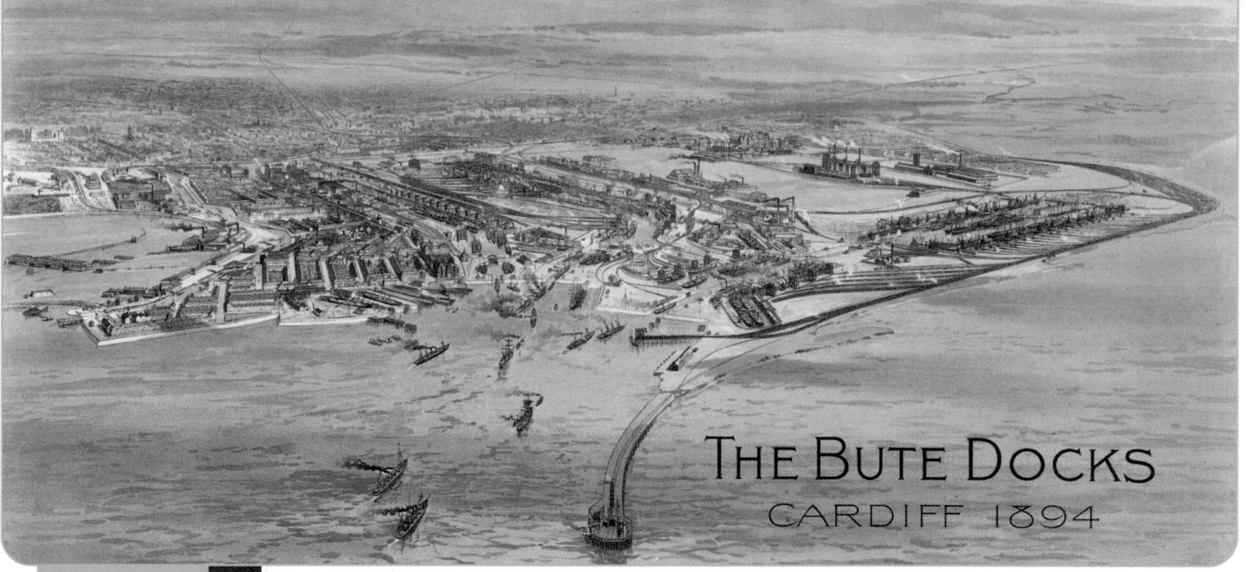

SOURCE D Cardiff docks in 1894.

RIOTS IN TONYPANDY AND LLANELLI

The first decade of the twentieth century was a period of increasing unrest, not only in the South Wales coalfield but in the whole of Britain and Ireland. The new large-scale enterprises – such as D. A. Thomas's Cambrian Combine and the older Powell Duffryn and Lewis Merthyr companies – were very unpopular with the miners and their families. Greater competition was driving down the price of coal and the Eight Hours Act of 1908 reduced working hours. For these reasons, mine owners were reluctant to increase wages, even though the cost of living was rising. Some members of the South Wales Miners' Federation (SWMF) believed that only large-scale strikes and other forms of industrial action could persuade the mine owners to pay better wages and improve working conditions.

Matters came to a head in the Rhondda valley in the autumn of 1910. Eighty miners in a dispute at the Ely Colliery, owned by the Cambrian Combine, were sacked and the others locked out. Miners in other collieries stopped work in support and by November 30,000 miners were on strike.

i THE MINERS AND THEIR TRADE UNION, THE SWMF

The South Wales Miners' Federation (SWMF) was established in 1898 when a number of local trade unions joined together. The coal industry was expanding and thousands of workers were moving into the mining valleys where the population grew rapidly. The local unions, led by the Welsh-speaking William Abraham (1842–1922), better known as *Mabon*, were willing to co-operate with the mine owners. Since the 1870s, a sliding scale had been in use to calculate pay scales and wages were linked to the price of coal. Some younger miners' leaders thought the sliding scale was unfair to the workers and demanded its abolition. These leaders, often from a non-Welsh background, demanded that the new union take a more militant and active role against the mine owners. The sliding scale was abolished in 1903, and although *Mabon*, who was also a Liberal MP, remained President of the SWMF, the real leadership passed into the hands of people who were more likely to support the new Labour Party.

Tension increased when Cambrian Combine unsuccessfully tried to bring 'blackleg labour' from other areas to break the strike. A protest meeting outside the Glamorgan Colliery on 7 November ended with serious clashes between miners and the police. The following day about 60 shops were attacked and looted in Tonypandy. The Home Secretary, Winston Churchill, sent soldiers to Pontypridd as well as police reinforcements from the Metropolitan Police. Mounted troops and police continued to patrol the area throughout the winter as the strike continued. Hunger and misery eventually forced the miners to return to work on 1 September 1911.

Meanwhile in Llanelli striking railwaymen threatened to stop trains. The government, determined to defend the movement of people and goods, responded by sending in 600 troops. On 19 August 1911, during a bad-tempered exchange, the troops opened fire on a crowd of onlookers and two people were killed. In the riot which followed, almost 100 railway trucks were destroyed and a further four people were killed.

SOCIALISM AND SYNDICALISM

Some newspapers suspected that the industrial unrest of 1910–11 was planned. Some younger members of the SWMF, such as Noah Ablett from Porth in the Rhondda valley, thought that the union leadership was too moderate. Ablett was a socialist who believed that workers and poor people should take action to improve their lives. He argued that unions should hold frequent strikes which would eventually enable them to take control of the mining industry. These ideas became known as 'syndicalism', from *syndicat*, the French word for a trade union.

An Unofficial Reform Committee was established to plan changes to the SWMF and published the famous booklet, *The Miners' Next Step*, in 1912.

SOURCE E

A centralised British union of mineworkers shall organise political action, both local and national, on the basis of complete hostility to all capitalist parties ... Steps are to be taken to bring all workers into one national and international union to work for the taking over of all industries by the workmen themselves. A Central Production Board shall co-ordinate all production and distribution according to need, leaving the men themselves to decide under what conditions and how the work should be done.

Part of *The Miners' Next Step*, a booklet published by the Unofficial Reform Committee in 1912.

The syndicalists were a tiny minority, but their ideas horrified both the Liberal government and the Conservatives. This could explain the government's readiness to use force against protesting workers in places such as Tonypandy and Llanelli.

THE CLIMAX OF THE WELSH COAL INDUSTRY, 1913

1913 was a significant year for the Welsh coal industry when coal production reached its maximum: 46 million tons, of which 37 million were exported. 1913 was also marked by the worst single disaster in the history of the South Wales coalfield. At the Universal Colliery at Senghennydd, part of the Lewis Merthyr combine, 439 miners were killed in an explosion on 14 October. The problem of 'firedamp' here was well known: 81 miners had been killed in a gas explosion in 1901.

Enquiries into the disaster continued well into 1914 and the surviving miners accused the management of ignoring safety regulations in order to maximise production.

The situation in 1914

As the First World War approached in 1914, the situation in the industrial areas of Wales remained tense. The bitterness caused by industrial disputes and the loss of life in accidents continued. The great expansion in coal output had been achieved by employing more miners, and not by introducing more efficient means of production. In 1913 almost all the coal was still cut by hand and productivity (output per man) had actually declined since 1900. The golden age of Welsh heavy industry was becoming a memory.

Q Questions

1. Why were mine owners reluctant to increase wages between 1900 and 1910?
2. Why did riots break out in Tonypandy in 1910 and Llanelli in 1911?
3. Use the information box, Source E and your own knowledge to explain the importance of the SWMF.
4. Why has 1910–11 become known as the period of 'the Great Unrest' in Wales and Britain?
5. Was the period 1902–14 a golden age of Welsh heavy industry? Explain your answer.

1 EXAM PRACTICE

These questions test Section A of the examination paper.

ECONOMIC DEVELOPMENT AND INDUSTRIAL RELATIONS IN SOUTH WALES

Study Sources A–D and then answer the questions which follow.

SOURCE A A drawing to commemorate the visit to Cardiff by King Edward VII and Queen Alexandra in 1907, when she opened and named the Queen Alexandra Dock.

SOURCE B

I have provided men with the means to pay for food and clothing for themselves and their families. I have contributed more to the happiness and well-being of Welsh colliery workers than all the miners' leaders combined. The only value of wealth is the influence and power it places in the hands of its possessor to do good.

The words of D. A. Thomas, as reported in the newspaper, *The South Wales Daily News* in 1916.

SOURCE C

When I reached Tonypandy, the rioting had been going on all through the night. It had begun after the owners had attempted to bring blackleg labour to man the colliery. I saw in action that day the vicious alliance of the government and the coal owners backed by police and armed troops against the miners. I never forgot that lesson.

From the autobiography of the trade union leader Arthur Horner, published in 1960.

SOURCE D

Although the amount of the unrest was striking, it is easy to exaggerate its importance. In considering day-to-day life in industrial Wales, too much attention can be given to riots, politics and trade unionism. There were more people present at a boxing match in Tonypandy on 8 November 1910 than took part in the riot there that night.

A modern historian, John Davies, writing in *A History of Wales* (1993).

EQ Exam Questions

1 What information does Source A give about the development of Cardiff? [3]

2 Use the information in Source B and your own knowledge to explain the importance of D. A. Thomas. [4]

3 How useful is Source C as evidence to an historian studying industrial relations in the South Wales coalfield up to 1914? Explain your answer using the source and your own knowledge. [5]

4 In Source D the author is saying that the importance of the unrest in industrial Wales in 1910–11 has been exaggerated. Is this a valid interpretation?
In your answer you should use your own knowledge of the topic, refer to the other relevant sources in this question, and consider how the author came to this interpretation. [8]

What were the effects of the First World War on the people?

THE OUTBREAK OF WAR

On 3 August 1914, Sir Edward Grey, the British Foreign Secretary, realised that Britain would have to go to war and said: 'The lamps are going out all over Europe. We shall not see them lit again in our lifetime.' Not everyone was so sad. The British army and navy had won victories all over the world and many people thought that the challenge of a war in Europe would help the country. Thousands of people came out on to the streets of London to celebrate the declaration of war, as they did in many other European cities. Many believed that the war would be over by Christmas.

What did people think they were fighting for?

Since the government had declared war in the king's name, most people thought it was their duty to remain loyal to the crown. People were very proud of the British Empire, which the Germans were seen to be threatening.

The German Schlieffen Plan to attack France involved sending German troops across Belgian territory. This would violate Belgium's neutrality, which had been guaranteed by Britain since the Treaty of London of 1839. As part of this treaty Britain had promised to defend Belgium if it were attacked.

SOURCE A

We were fighting for king, country and empire and for 'gallant little Belgium'. The British Empire was the greatest empire the world had ever known. Its greatness was due to the superior qualities of the British.

Ulric Nisbet, who joined the army in 1914 as a junior officer, speaking after the war.

SOURCE B A propaganda postcard, issued in 1914, showing the British bulldog defending Belgium. The Kaiser was said to have referred to the Treaty of London of 1839 as 'only a scrap of paper'.

DORA AND THE IMPACT OF WAR ON CIVILIAN LIFE

New wartime conditions changed many aspects of life, which the government had not been involved in before. The Defence of the Realm Acts (DORA), the first of which was passed in August 1914, gave the government sweeping powers to help fight the war and to control many aspects of people's lives.

- Daylight working hours were extended by the introduction of British Summer Time in 1916.
- Restrictions were placed on pub opening hours to reduce drunkenness; even the beer was watered down.
- The government took control of some essential jobs, such as coal mining, farming and transport.
- To avoid strikes in industry, arbitration (the settlement of a dispute by a third party) was made compulsory.
- The trade unions were compelled to allow women and other unskilled workers to perform jobs previously reserved for craftsmen. This policy was known as dilution.

Propaganda

- Controls were also imposed on the way the war was reported. Newspapers were not allowed to publish photographs of dead soldiers or accounts of battles with heavy casualties. As a result some fantastic rumours circulated, especially during the early part of the war. One popular story in 1914 involved large numbers of Russian troops who were said to have landed in Scotland. People claimed to have seen them travelling by train through England on their way to the Western Front, with the snow still on their boots!

Questions

1 Describe popular attitudes towards the war in 1914.

2 Describe the changes brought about by DORA to improve Britain's war effort.

RECRUITMENT

The British Expeditionary Force (BEF) was sent over to France and Belgium in September 1914 to meet the advancing German army. The British army, unlike other European armies, had traditionally relied on volunteers. The government decided that voluntary recruitment was to continue, backed by an official recruitment campaign.

September 1914	436,000
December 1915	55,000

Monthly recruitment figures, 1914–15.

At the beginning of the war the numbers of young men volunteering to fight were so great that the army found difficulty in accommodating and training them all. However, by the end of 1915 the figures had fallen drastically. The scale of losses on the Western Front could not be hidden from the public. Thousands of families received telegrams from the War Office informing them that their son, brother or husband had been killed, wounded or was missing; newspaper readers could not avoid reading the many obituaries. The government had to consider whether to introduce conscription (compulsory military service).

Government propaganda

During the First World War, the government issued a series of posters urging people to support the recruitment campaign and the war effort. Many of these posters were aimed at women, who were encouraged to persuade sons, boyfriends and, later, husbands to join the army. Women themselves were encouraged to work in munitions factories or to work in agriculture as part of the 'Land Army', or in other voluntary organisations.

SOURCE C Lord Kitchener, Secretary of State for War, urging men to join the army in a British army recruitment poster of 1914.

Conscription and conscientious objectors

Because of the heavy casualties on the Western Front, and the fall in recruitment figures, the government feared that voluntary recruitment would not produce enough soldiers to replace those killed and wounded. The Military Service Act was passed in 1916, bringing conscription into force for men aged 18–41. Some men, for religious or political reasons, thought that war was wrong and refused to enlist. These men were usually called to appear before a tribunal, where most were registered officially as 'conscientious objectors'. Some served as stretcher-bearers in the army but those who refused were sent to prison where, as 'conchies', they suffered a great deal of hardship. Young men in civilian clothes were often suspected of being 'conchies' and were sometimes shouted at by women and presented with a white feather, the sign of cowardice.

To the No-conscription Fellowship
Heartiest greetings!
Keep the flag flying outside!

We in here are in the highest spirits, and are determined to stand firm to the end, come what may. In the cause of freedom it is a small sacrifice temporarily to give up one's personal liberty ... Surely the cause for which we strive is worthy; and in a worthy cause no sacrifice is too great.

Comrades, we are with you in the fight for freedom and the cause of international peace and brotherhood.

NB Written with a needle and a little ink in the lid of a salt pot.

SOURCE D This letter by Harold Bing, a conscientious objector, was smuggled out of Wormwood Scrubs prison, 1916.

Q Questions

1 How successful was the government's recruitment campaign during 1914 and 1915?

2 Why were conscientious objectors willing to face unpopularity and punishment?

INTRODUCTION OF COALITION GOVERNMENT

The fighting in the trenches on the Western Front used up more ammunition than ever before, and shortages began to occur. This presented the government with its first real crisis of the war. The Liberal Prime Minister, Herbert Asquith, was criticised for not doing his best to tackle the problem. In May 1915 Asquith decided to invite members of the opposition to join his government and so form a coalition. David Lloyd George, seen by many as the most energetic minister in the government, was put in charge of armaments production. The Munitions of War Act of 1915 introduced strict regulations for munitions factories and under his leadership the production of shells soon increased.

SOURCE E A *Punch* cartoon of 1915 showing Lloyd George 'Delivering the goods'.

THE IMPACT OF WAR ON THE WORKFORCE

The miners

Not all workers were willing to obey every government order. The miners, who produced the coal needed to power factories and ships, had long-standing complaints dating back to the years before the war (see page 16). Knowing that their work was essential, miners in South Wales went on strike in July 1915 and, although troops were sent to threaten them, the government gave way and the miners won most of their demands.

i DAVID LLOYD GEORGE (1863–1945)

David Lloyd George was born in Manchester, but after the death of his father, his mother returned to her home village of Llanystumdwy in North Wales. A fiery and determined character, David was elected Liberal MP for Caernarfon Boroughs and campaigned hard for Welsh Home Rule as a leader of the Welsh nationalist group within the Liberal Party.

As Chancellor of the Exchequer in the 1906 Liberal government, he was responsible for a number of social and political reforms. Many poor people regarded him as a hero but the rich viewed him often with hatred and suspicion.

His success as Minister of Munitions paved the way for his appointment as Prime Minister in December 1916, the first and only Welshman to hold that office to date. As he was prime minister for the rest of the war his supporters always saw him as 'the man who won the war'. However, the divisions within his own party over his appointment as prime minister, and a number of scandals in which he was involved, eventually led to his fall from power in 1922 and the end of the Liberals as a party of government.

Women in employment

The high number of men recruited into the armed forces created labour shortages, especially in those key industries essential for the war effort. The government realised that women could fill many of the vacant jobs in the factories, and DORA had already provided the powers necessary to control the labour market. Some of the suffragette leaders, who had campaigned unsuccessfully for the vote before the war, saw an opportunity to co-operate with the government and perhaps advance their cause. To reflect this desire to help the war effort, the suffragettes changed their slogan from 'The Right to Vote' to 'The Right to Serve'.

Although women had been employed for many years in the cotton mills of northern England and the tinplate works of west Wales, during the First World War they were recruited into areas of employment previously closed to them. The war gave many women new experiences and a sense of independence, although they were hardly ever paid the same rates as men, as they had been promised.

	July 1914	July 1918
Metal trades	170,000	594,000
Chemical industries	40,000	104,000
Food, drink and tobacco	196,000	235,000
Government service	2,000	225,000
Timber trades	44,000	79,000

The number of women in employment in Britain, 1914–18.

The new opportunities given to women during the war led to many social changes.

- Fashions changed and skirts became shorter and corsets and other restrictive garments were abandoned.
- Behaviour that would have been considered shocking before the war was increasingly seen as normal (see Source G).
- Older people were shocked when, in 1918, Dr Marie Stopes published two books about birth control, *Married Love* and *Wise Parenthood*. By giving women information about family planning and choosing the size of their families, this marked the beginning of a revolution in the role and status of women.

SOURCE F Women working in a munitions factory in 1916.

SOURCE G

I felt embarrassed one night in a pub. Some factory girls were also present and, when I put my hand into my pocket to pay, one girl said, 'You keep your money, Corporal. This is on us.' With no more ado she pulled up her frock and produced a roll of notes. Many of the girls earned ten times my pay as a full corporal.

Written by a soldier, rifleman H.V. Shawyer, in 1916.

In 1918, many people recognised the huge contribution that women had made to the war effort and the Representation of the People Act finally gave women the vote. However, women were not given the vote on equal terms with men (only some women over 30 could vote).

Q Questions

1 How did the government deal with the problem of ammunitions shortages in 1915?

2 How important was the war in changing the role of women?

LLOYD GEORGE AS PRIME MINISTER

Lloyd George became prime minister on 7 December 1916. His first act was to set up a coalition government of just five ministers, who met daily to deal with the war. This War Cabinet consisted of one Liberal, one Labour and three Conservative politicians. Winning the war was their number one priority.

War Socialism

In 1917 Lloyd George introduced his policy of 'War Socialism', by which the government took control of the resources of the country.

- → The **railway network** was taken over so that transport could be co-ordinated more effectively. This enabled troops and war materials to be moved round Britain more quickly.
- → All **coalmines** were taken over, to provide power for trains and most ships. In 1917, coal production reached an all-time high; wages rose and safety records also improved.
- → **Shipyards** were taken over and all merchant ships became government property. From 1916, the German navy had begun to sink all ships sailing to British ports. Lloyd George ordered merchant ships to sail in convoys for protection and forced the Royal Navy to provide escorts. From October 1917, the number of ships sunk by German U-boats fell.
- → **Food production** was taken over. German U-boats were sinking many of the ships carrying food supplies to Britain, so it became essential to avoid waste, to grow more food at home and to ensure that it was shared equally. More young women were encouraged to join the Women's Land Army to help with farming. Rationing was introduced in November 1917, limiting the amount of certain foods that people could buy each week. In 1914 Britain produced about 60 per cent of its food supply only, but by 1918 this figure had increased to more than 90 per cent.

WALES AND ENGLAND AT THE END OF THE WAR

The end of the war came in November 1918 when the Germans asked for an armistice (ceasefire) on the Western Front. The guns fell silent at 11 am on 11 November and Allied governments, supported by the newspapers, claimed that a great victory had been won over German aggression. Services of thanksgiving were held in churches and chapels. There were also scenes of wild celebration in London and major towns. Some people, reflecting on the hundreds of thousands of men killed and wounded, wondered whether the price of victory had been too high.

SOURCE H

Although the war resulted in the deaths of many thousands and left still more disabled, there was an overall improvement in people's diet and a decline in the death rate, especially in infant deaths. The explanation for this appears to be that many of the poor found themselves in permanent employment for the first time and wages generally kept up with wartime inflation.

From an article by a modern historian, Clive Emsley, in 1996.

Q Questions

1 What changes did Lloyd George make as prime minister?

2 How valid is the argument in Source H that the war led to improvements in people's lives?

I EXAM PRACTICE

These questions test Section B of the examination paper.

LIFE ON THE HOME FRONT, 1914–18.

Study the information below and then answer the questions which follow.

INFORMATION

The First World War changed the lives of most people, such as the woman seen here checking shells in a munitions factory.

EQ Exam Questions

1 **a** Describe how people reacted to the declaration of war in 1914. [2]

b Explain the role of government propaganda during the war. [4]

c How important was the appointment of David Lloyd George as prime minister? [5]

2 **a** Describe how the government controlled trade and industry during the war. [3]

b Explain why the war helped to change the role and status of women. [4]

3 Did the effects of the First World War improve the lives of all the people at home?
Explain your answer fully. [7]

How and why did people's attitudes and values change in the period 1902–19?

POPULATION GROWTH AND ITS EFFECTS ON THE WELSH LANGUAGE AND CULTURE

When the first reliable figures about the number of people able to speak the Welsh language were published after the 1891 census, it was found that 54.5 per cent could do so. During the early 1900s, the total population of Wales was growing rapidly and thousands of people, mainly from England, were moving into the industrial areas of Wales. Bert Coombes, who moved to Resolven in 1912, was typical. He was brought up on a farm in Herefordshire where, as he wrote later, his friend told him, 'Up there beyond the Brecon Beacons, in the works, is the place for a young feller. Shorter hours and good money, not like as it be hereabouts.' Although Bert Coombes himself learned to speak Welsh, Welsh speakers were declining in number and as a percentage of the total population.

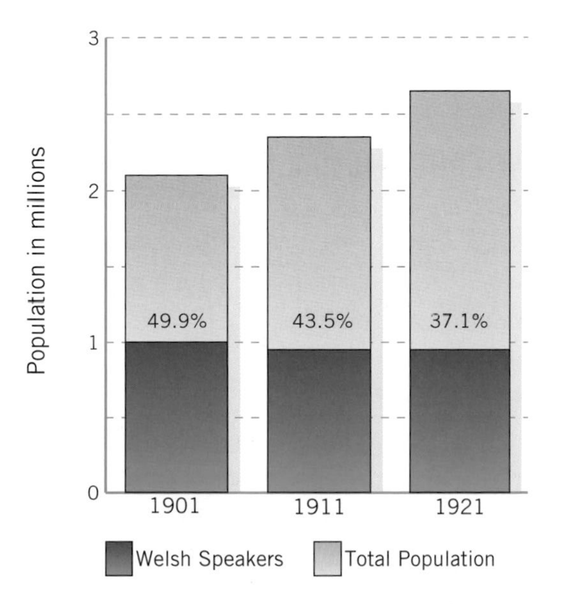

Population and percentage of Welsh speakers 1901–21.

Migration from England was not the only reason for the decline of the Welsh language at the time. Many parents believed that speaking English was essential for their children to 'get on'. These attitudes were supported by most businessmen and school teachers, many ministers of religion and the leaders of the growing trade unions and Labour Party, who knew that most Welsh speakers supported the Liberal Party. A further decline in the Welsh language occured during the First World War (see page 30).

SOURCE A

The Welsh were in a minority in our street, where they mixed with English, Irish and Scotch people. At first I only knew Welsh from my parents and grandparents, but as I went on playing with the Scott, Hartley, Ward and McGill children, I became more fluent than in my native tongue. Dad was annoyed when I started replying in English to what he had said in Welsh, but our Mam said in Welsh: 'Oh, let him alone. What odds anyway?'

Memories of his childhood in Merthyr Tydfil, by the novelist Jack Jones, *Unfinished Journey*, 1937.

CHURCH AND CHAPEL: RELIGIOUS LIFE IN WALES

At the beginning of the twentieth century, religion played a very important part in the life of most people in Wales. Membership of the main Christian denominations ran into many thousands. The majority of Welsh speakers and a significant number of English speakers attended one of the chapels of the main nonconformist denominations – the Independents, the Methodists or the Baptists.

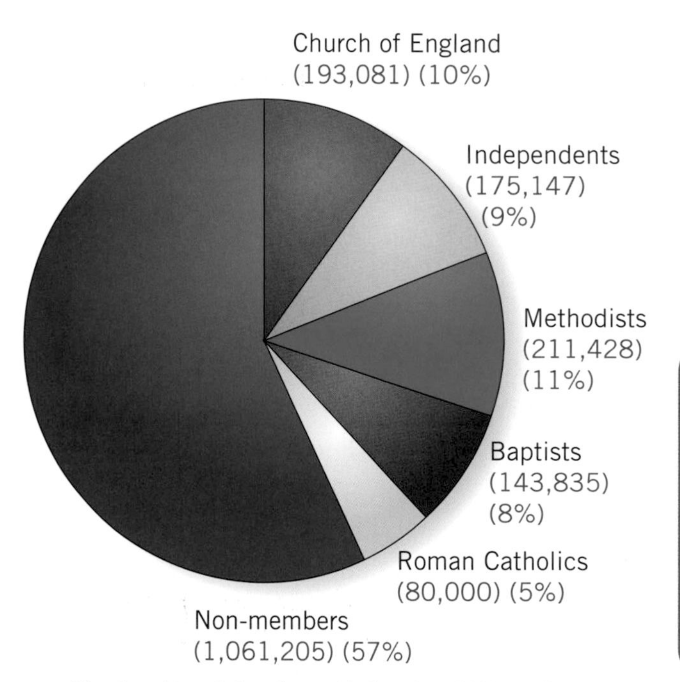

Membership of churches and chapels in Wales, 1905.

The social and cultural activities associated with the chapels – choirs, study groups, newspapers and *eisteddfodau* – were in many ways as important as the religious services. They helped to maintain Welsh culture at a time when it had little official support. The Church of England, on the other hand, was usually suspected of giving little support to Welsh culture. Before 1920 all the Protestant churches in Wales belonged to the Church of England. However, after a long campaign, led mainly by the nonconformists, the Anglican Church of Wales was disestablished (no longer given status and privileges) and separated from the Church of England.

The nonconformist chapels were originally established as a result of a religious revival in the eighteenth century. Further revivals occurred during the nineteenth century. In 1904 Evan Roberts, a young preacher from Loughor, drew large crowds by his powerful sermons. His services would often continue for hours as individual members made public confessions; hymns were sung with fervour and miracles were recounted. The enthusiasm spread to many parts of Wales, and services were even held in quarries and coal mines. The revival lasted for over a year and its influence affected some people for the rest of their lives.

Q Questions

1. Explain the changing position of the Welsh language during the early years of the twentieth century.
2. How important was religion in the lives of the people of Wales during this period? Explain your answer.

NEW EDUCATIONAL OPPORTUNITIES

In 1902 the Conservative government passed an Education Act which made local education authorities, usually the education committee of the county council, responsible for the schools of the area. Education had long been a matter of debate in Wales. By the turn of the century it was compulsory for all children to attend elementary (primary) school. By 1900 every county in Wales had opened a number of county (secondary) schools, for the more fortunate children, whose parents could pay the fees, to continue their education up to the age of 16 or 18. As a result the percentage of children entering secondary education was higher than it was in many parts of England. The 1902 Act, however, was far from popular in Wales because it allowed church schools to be supported from public funds. When the Liberals passed a new act in 1907, secondary schools were forced to make one-quarter of their places free for pupils who were successful in the 11-plus entrance examination.

Although educational opportunities for Welsh children were extended, this was achieved at the expense of the Welsh language and its culture. The new county schools were modelled on their English equivalents and soon came to be known as 'grammar schools'. With their uniforms and English curriculum, they sometimes ignored their links with the local community, but they did enable the brightest pupils to go to university and to take up better-paid occupations.

Q Questions

1. How were educational opportunities improved during this period?
2. Read the information box below. To what extent was the career of Sir Owen M. Edwards successful?

THE IMPACT OF WAR

Loss of life

In spite of the anti-war attitudes of the Welsh chapels and trade unions, the outbreak of war in 1914 was greeted with enthusiasm in Wales. Much of this was due to the loyalty of many Welsh people towards David Lloyd George, who claimed that Britain had entered the war to save small countries, such as Belgium, from the aggression of Germany and the Central Powers.

i SIR OWEN M. EDWARDS (1858–1920)

Owen Morgan Edwards was born in Llanuwchllyn and went to the village school. He eventually became a history tutor at Oxford but his heart remained in Wales and he considered it his life's work to make the Welsh language and culture more popular. He did this by writing a series of travel books in Welsh and by establishing several successful magazines.

In 1907 he was appointed the first Chief Inspector of Schools in Wales. He now used his influence to strengthen the position of the Welsh language in Welsh primary and secondary schools. He was only partially successful – some areas did allow some Welsh language teaching and Welsh was recognised as an examination subject, but English remained the dominant language in all the schools of Wales, especially the grammar schools, for many years. It was not until the second half of the twentieth century, with the growth of Welsh-medium education, that some of his ideas were put into practice.

SOURCE B

Sir Owen M. Edwards.

280,000 Welshmen served in the armed forces, representing almost 14 per cent of the population, a slightly higher proportion than the equivalent figure for the rest of the United Kingdom. Of these, 40,000 were killed.

SOURCE C

The chapels held soldiering to be sinful, and in Merioneth the chapels had the last word. However, Lloyd George became Minister of Munitions in 1915, and persuaded the chapels that the war was a crusade, and we had a sudden tremendous intake of Welshmen.

From the early autobiography of the poet and novelist Robert Graves (1895–1985), *Goodbye to All That*, 1929. His family had a holiday home in Harlech and he enlisted in the Royal Welsh Fusiliers in 1914.

Decline of the Welsh language

The war dealt yet another blow to the Welsh language. The armed forces discouraged the use of any language other than English. Since the latest reports of the war could only be seen in the English daily newspapers, Welsh readers turned to them in increasing numbers. Sales of Welsh-language weekly newspapers declined rapidly and many went out of business.

Opposition to war

As the war continued and the losses mounted, some began openly to criticise the war. About 1000 Welshmen were registered as conscientious objectors (see Source D on page 22), but opposition to the war never drew more than a minority of supporters.

The influence of the English-language war poets, whose poetry often described the horrors of war in graphic detail, was not really felt until afterwards. And although the death of Hedd Wyn in 1917 made a great impact on Wales, it did not significantly alter people's attitude towards the war.

i WILFRED OWEN (1893–1918)

Wilfred Owen, often regarded as the greatest of the English 'war poets', was the son of a railway clerk from the Welsh border country near Oswestry.

Although he had considered himself to be a pacifist, he joined the army in 1915 and was sent to the trenches. He was wounded and, when recovering in hospital, met Siegfried Sassoon and Robert Graves, who encouraged him to continue writing.

It was then that he wrote his most famous poems, 'Anthem for Doomed Youth' and 'Dulce et Decorum Est'. After his return to active service in France in August 1918, he was awarded the Military Cross for bravery. He was killed at the age of 25 on 4 November 1918. The telegram telling his parents of his death arrived on 11 November, as the bells were ringing to celebrate the end of the war.

SOURCE D

Wilfred Owen.

i HEDD WYN (1887–1917)

Ellis Humphrey Evans was born on a remote farm in the Trawsfynydd area of North Wales. He helped run the family farm, but his main interest was always Welsh poetry. Under his bardic name, Hedd Wyn (a name which means peace), he began to win acclaim. When he joined the Royal Welsh Fusiliers in 1917, he had already started to write his entry for the National Eisteddfod to be held at Birkenhead. He posted his poem, 'Yr Arwr' (The Hero), from France. On 6 September, he was declared the winner of the bardic chair but immediately it was announced that he had been killed one week earlier, during the Battle of Pilkem Ridge. With Lloyd George himself on the stage, the shocked audience saw the chair draped with a black cloth and the Birkenhead Eisteddfod became known as the Black Chair Eisteddfod.

Politics and religion

By the end of the First World War in Wales, as elsewhere, there were signs that major changes were taking place. The Liberal Party, for long the most powerful political party in Wales, was in disarray due to divisions within the party and following a number of scandals. The Labour movement was growing, but was not yet strong enough to win power.

As the war progressed and with divisions among religious leaders becoming ever more obvious, the Welsh people's support for their churches and chapels began to decline. There was also a decline in belief as people struggled to come to terms with the extreme loss of life during the First World War.

SOURCE E

The factors that had weakened the chapels before the war – debt, over-expansion in rural areas and lack of support from non-Welsh-speakers and industrial workers in the south – became stronger after the war. In many ways, the new post-war world was bringing in new challenges, to which the chapels were finding difficulty in responding.

Taken from a modern history book.

Q Questions

1 How did Welsh people react to the outbreak of war in 1914?

2 What were the reasons for the decline of the chapels in Wales after the First World War?

POPULAR ENTERTAINMENT AND SPORT

In Welsh-speaking areas traditional forms of entertainment, principally the eisteddfod, remained popular. In the industrial areas, however, newer pastimes and entertainments were gaining ground. In 1909, the newly opened Empire Theatre of Varieties in Tonypandy brought music hall entertainment to the people of the Rhondda valley. The Carlton cinema in Swansea opened in 1914, and was the first of many purpose-built cinemas in Wales.

Although frowned upon by the religious and the upper classes, organised sport continued to grow in popularity. Rugby in Wales developed into a popular sport with a large following, especially in South Wales.

This was especially true after 1905 when the Welsh team unexpectedly defeated the New Zealand All Blacks at Cardiff. Between 1900 and 1912 the Welsh team won the triple crown no fewer than six times. Football was equally popular at a local level, although the Welsh national side was not as successful as its rugby-playing counterparts.

In the First World War and the changes in the fields of sport, pastimes and popular entertainment which followed, many aspects of twentieth-century life can already be recognised.

SOURCE F The Welsh rugby team which defeated the New Zealand All Blacks, 1905.

1 EXAM PRACTICE

These questions test Section A of the examination paper.

SOCIAL, CULTURAL AND RELIGIOUS CHANGE, 1902–19.

Study Sources A–D below and then answer the questions which follow.

SOURCE A An early cinema c.1915.

SOURCE B

A good number of our Welsh parents cannot persuade their own children to learn Welsh in their own homes. I admit that it is a difficult matter in a town like Pontypridd where the English tongue is so strong among all classes. Even in the Welsh chapel we find that as soon as the service is over, most of the conversation takes place in English.

From a letter published in *The Glamorgan Free Press*, 26 April 1902.

SOURCE C

I remember coming home from the pit one afternoon to find the minister waiting for me. I was tired and hungry and in no mood to have a discussion on religion. He tried his best to get me to return to the chapel. Finally he got down on his knees. I became very angry and told him I would never respond to such methods.

From the autobiography of a trade union leader, Will Paynter (1972).

SOURCE D

After the First World War, the chapels were in decline. The bloodshed and suffering caused by the war had turned many against the idea of religion. The world was changing but to many people the chapels and churches seemed slow or incapable of adapting.

From a school textbook written by Roger Turvey, *Wales and Britain 1906–51* (1997).

EQ Exam Questions

1 What information does Source A give about the way popular entertainment was changing during this period? [3]

2 Use the information in Source B and your own knowledge to explain the changing position of the Welsh language at the beginning of the twentieth century. [4]

3 How useful is Source C as evidence to an historian studying attitudes towards religion in Wales? Explain your answer using the source and your own knowledge. [5]

4 In Source D the author is saying that it was the war that caused the decline of the chapels. Is this a valid interpretation?
In your answer you should use your own knowledge of the topic, refer to the other relevant sources in this question, and consider how the author came to this interpretation. [8]

2 DEPRESSION, WAR AND RECOVERY, 1930–51

The worldwide effects of the Wall Street Crash of October 1929 depressed British heavy industry even further than before, causing thousands of workers to be laid off. Whole communities in Wales and northern England lived on unemployment benefit. Although protest marches were held, the government took little notice. New industries, producing consumer goods, grew in the Midlands and southern England. As people moved there from Wales and the North, these more prosperous areas developed rapidly.

Looking back, the road to war in 1939 was the most significant development of the decade, though many people tried to avoid another world conflict at the time. As the Nazi leaders repeatedly broke the Versailles settlement, many in Britain tried to find reasons to justify their behaviour. This policy became known as appeasement and is particularly associated with Prime Minister Neville Chamberlain. Appeasement reached its peak at Munich in 1938 when it was agreed to let the Germans occupy part of Czechoslovakia. Thereafter people came to see war as inevitable and when Hitler invaded Poland in 1939, there was no real opposition to the government's declaration of war on Germany.

The Second World War affected civilians more than any previous conflict. Women were encouraged to make a positive contribution to the war effort. Winston Churchill maintained people's morale when Britain stood alone against Nazi Germany.

The Labour Party was elected to power in 1945 and introduced far-reaching reforms with the establishment of the Welfare State. The policy of nationalisation, bringing the main industries into public ownership, proved less popular. This, and the continuation of wartime rationing, led to Labour's fall from power in 1951.

TIMELINE OF EVENTS

1929 Ramsay MacDonald becomes Labour prime minister

1933 Hitler becomes chancellor of Germany

1934 The Special Areas Act introduced

1936 The Jarrow Crusade
German troops reoccupy the Rhineland
Spanish Civil War

1938 *Anschluss* (union) between Austria and Germany
Munich Conference

1939 Britain declares war on Germany

1940 The Battle of Britain
Start of the Blitz

1941 German invasion of Russia
USA enters the war

1944 6 June: Allied forces land in Normandy on D-day

1945 May: VE Day (Victory in Europe)
August: Atomic bombs dropped on Hiroshima and Nagasaki
September: VJ Day (Victory in Japan) – the end of the Second World War

1946 National Insurance Act passed

1948 The National Health Service established

In what ways and to what extent did changes in the economic fortunes of Wales and England affect people's lives in the 1930s?

THE CHANGING DEMAND FOR COAL AND STEEL AND ITS CONSEQUENCES

At the end of the First World War there was a short-lived economic boom, but the people of Britain soon realised that it would not be possible to return to the conditions of trade that had existed before 1914. The Welsh coal industry, which depended on the export trade, now faced a series of problems. Record production figures before the war had been achieved simply by employing more miners and not by investing in coal-cutting machines or modernising working practices. Welsh coal was becoming more expensive.

Countries which had imported coal from Wales before the First World War, now preferred to buy their coal more cheaply from Poland and the USA. The 1919 peace settlement declared that Germany should pay reparations for causing the First World War, so the victorious powers were able to receive coal from Germany in place of reparations payments. At the same time oil was taking the place of coal as the main fuel for ships. Coaling stations around the world, which had been supplied with Welsh coal, therefore saw a large decline in their trade.

Similar problems affected the iron and steel industry in Wales and the rest of Britain. During the First World War other countries, such as Poland and the USA, had modernised their industries so that they were able to produce steel and other metals more cheaply than Britain. Industrial disputes, such as the General Strike in 1926, only made matters worse.

The collapse of the US stock market, known as the Wall Street Crash, in October 1929 led to a further slump in world trade. As US industries closed down and millions became unemployed, it became obvious that Europe would soon be suffering the same kind of problems – the Great Depression of the 1930s was about to begin.

As one of the regions worst affected, South Wales was officially declared a 'depressed area'. By the mid-1930s, the number of miners employed in the Rhondda valleys had fallen by more than half in less than ten years. For most of the 1930s it remained an employment 'black spot', with an unemployment rate of over 40 per cent.

Year	Tonnage produced	Tonnage exported	Miners employed
1929	48.1 million	29.9 million	175,000
1934	35.1 million	19.5 million	126,000
1939	35.2 million	20.0 million	136,000

Production, trade and employment figures for the South Wales coalfield, 1929–39.

The closure of the old iron and steel works in the Merthyr area created another 'black spot', with similar rates of unemployment. However, although the ports of South Wales were hard hit by the decline of the coal trade, the greater variety of work available in Cardiff and the coastal towns saved those areas from the worst effects of the Depression.

Unemployment rates in Wales and England 1928–38.

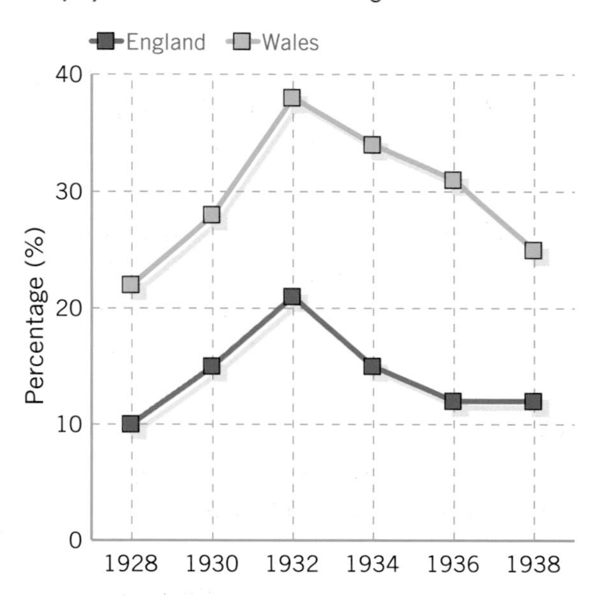

SOURCE A Women from Wales taking part in a hunger march, 1934.

UNEMPLOYMENT, POVERTY AND THE DOLE

In the areas which had depended for so long on coal and steel, the social effects of the Depression were devastating. Skilled miners and steelworkers, who had been regarded as the backbone of British industry, were reduced to claiming unemployment benefit or living 'on the dole' as it became known. From 1934, the dole was managed by the Unemployment Assistance Boards (UAB) and the sum paid to each family was subject to a means test. Families with some savings or a small additional income found that their dole was reduced.

The National Unemployed Workers' Movement (NUWM) was established with support from the Communist Party to organise protests against mass unemployment. These protests often took the form of organised marches, which became known as 'hunger marches'. However, the government's position remained unchanged.

Local protests were also staged against the dole and the means test. When the government threatened to cut benefits in February 1935, large-scale marches were held in Rhondda, Aberdare and Pontypool. The UAB offices in Merthyr Tydfil were attacked and ransacked by a large group of women.

In many deprived communities, with their menfolk idle, it was often the women who suffered most. Mothers would go without as they struggled to feed their families and 'make ends meet'. Mothers would eat the smallest portions at meal times, and generally neglect their own health and well-being. Throughout the 1930s, official reports confirmed that the figures for deaths in childbirth and women's illnesses generally were higher in Wales than in the rest of Britain.

SOURCE B

[A woman from Caerphilly] says she is on her feet for 16.5 hours a day. 'After my children go to bed, I gets two hours rest, I am mending my children's clothes and tidying in those few hours I get.'
[A woman from Cardiff] says she was a housemaid in private service before and was never ill. She is now 39, with six children all living at home, in a house with no bathroom or hot water. She has bad backache, palpitations and heart pains, but has not seen a doctor; she listens to the wireless talks on health.

An extract from M. Spring Rice, *Working Class Wives: Health and Conditions* (1939).

GOVERNMENT MEASURES TO DEAL WITH THE DEPRESSION

The Conservative government, with its policy of reducing public spending, found it very difficult to provide any real help for those areas worst affected by the Depression. The Special Areas Act of 1934 appointed a government commissioner to oversee each of four 'special' or 'distressed' areas, including south-east Wales. Following the closure of the local steelworks in 1936, King Edward VIII visited Dowlais, with its 73 per cent unemployment rate. Having witnessed the poverty for himself he said, 'Something must be done', but not much actually was. The Special Areas Act was strengthened when £1 million was provided to encourage employers to set up new factories in the special areas. Plans were made to build a number of factories together on one site to form a 'trading estate'. The largest of these was the Treforest Trading Estate between Pontypridd and Cardiff. Employers, however, proved very reluctant to move from the more prosperous areas of the Midlands and the London area to Wales, and by September 1939 only 2500 workers were employed at Treforest.

More encouraging was the decision to locate a new steelworks at Ebbw Vale. When production began in 1938, Wales had at least one up-to-date steelworks.

Q Questions

1. Why did the demand for British coal fall after the war?
2. How did the Depression affect women living in the distressed areas?
3. How successful were government measures to deal with the Depression?

HOW SIMILAR WERE THE EXPERIENCES OF WALES AND ENGLAND IN THE 1930S?

The old industries

England in the 1930s was a country of contrasts. The areas which still depended on old industries – coal mining, steel making, ship building and cotton manufacture – were situated mostly in the north and suffered from the same problems as Wales.

The coal and steel industries of England suffered from the same lack of demand. The cotton mills of Lancashire, which before 1914 had supplied about 65 per cent of the world market, now saw their share reduced to less than half of that figure.

As world trade declined, too many shipyards were competing for the limited amount of work available. Shipping companies could no longer hope to order new ships. The shipyards of Merseyside, north-east England and Clydeside in Scotland, laid off thousands of workers. One of the worst affected areas was Jarrow, on Tyneside, 'the town that was murdered', according to the local MP Ellen Wilkinson. The town's main employer, Palmer's shipyard, closed and the town's unemployment rate soared to 68 per cent. The protest march to London in 1936, known as the Jarrow Crusade (see Source C), became the most famous of the hunger marches held in Wales and England during the 1930s. Nevertheless, it still had no success in getting government aid to solve the town's problems.

SOURCE C Marchers on the Jarrow Crusade, 1936.

The growth of new industry

Although the 1930s were the decade of the Great Depression, a great deal of industrial expansion was taking place and some people found that their standard of living was rising. Mass production techniques, first adopted by the Ford Motor Company in the USA, were now being used to manufacture a range of goods from cars and aircraft to electrical goods and branded foods. New chemical processes led to the manufacture of new textile fibres, such as rayon, and plastics, such as Bakelite.

More and more houses now had mains electricity and although the poor could only afford electric lights, wealthier families were buying vacuum cleaners, refrigerators and cookers. By 1937 over half the households in Britain, even in the poorer areas of Wales, had a radio.

The new 'light' industries were largely powered by electricity and not by coal. By 1933, the government's plan to establish a National Grid, linking all generating stations and supplying electrical power to all regions, was complete. Factories no longer had to be built on or near coalfields. The new factories, producing consumer goods, could now be located near their customers in areas of high population, with a skilled labour force nearby. For these reasons the new consumer goods were mainly produced in the Midlands and south-east England. The flourishing businesses of the 1930s included motor companies such as Austin of Birmingham, Morris of Oxford and Ford of Dagenham, and Hoover, making vacuum cleaners at Isleworth, west London. Among branded foods, the chocolate products made by the Cadbury Company at Bourneville,

Birmingham, and Mars at Slough were produced for a nationwide market.

Migration from Wales to England

Thousands of unemployed workers and their families moved from Wales to the more prosperous areas of England. Some took advantage of an official government scheme to find work and accommodation in England for unemployed workers from Wales. However, sometimes they were not welcomed in their new communities (see Source D). Having experienced long-term unemployment, some Welsh workers were willing to work for the lowest pay rates.

Because of the war no census was held in Britain in 1941, so accurate figures for the changes in population that took place in the 1930s are not available. It is estimated, however, that about 430,000 people left Wales during the 1920s and 1930s. Merthyr Tydfil, which lost 17,000 people during the 1920s, lost a further 10,000 during the 1930s and the figures for the Rhondda valleys were even greater

SOURCE D

The Oxford people didn't want the Welsh, because when a new housing estate was being built in 1933–4, it was built by Welshmen who worked for a shilling (5p) an hour. When I went to live there, the hatred against the Welsh was terrible.

Arthur Excell, who found work at the Morris car factory in Oxford after moving there from Beddau, near Pontypridd, recalls his experiences.

Q Questions

1 Did the Depression affect all of England and Wales? Explain your answer.

2 Give examples of the new 'light' industries.

3 Why were the new industries located in the Midlands and south-east England?

Popular culture and entertainment

Sport and popular entertainment helped people to cope with the hardships caused by the Depression. As people had less money to spend on leisure, professional football, which depended on large crowds, suffered. Amateur sport, including Rugby Union, did better; in 1935 the Welsh rugby team beat both England and the New Zealand All Blacks. The Glamorgan cricket team also enjoyed a number of successful seasons. The greatest sporting hero of the 1930s was undoubtedly the boxer Tommy Farr, from the Rhondda. His unsuccessful world heavyweight championship bout in 1938 against the American, Joe Louis, became a legend.

During the 1930s radio came of age – crystal sets and headphones were replaced by radio sets with loudspeakers. In Wales, the establishment of the BBC Welsh Region in 1937 gave radio a boost, with more programmes being made in Welsh and in English. In 1936 the first television programmes were broadcast from Alexandra Palace to viewers in the London area. When the service was suspended in 1939, the total number of viewers was estimated at no more than 50,000.

The most popular form of entertainment in the 1930s was the cinema. Since the turn of the century, silent films had been shown. Towards the end of the 1920s, films were given a sound track and became 'talkies'. People flocked to see the new films. New luxury cinemas were built in many towns (see Source E) and low admission prices meant that even the unemployed could afford an occasional night out. Most of the films shown were American and the film stars Clark Gable, Greta Garbo and Errol Flynn became household names. One of the few films made with a Welsh background was *Proud Valley*, released in 1939, starring the black American singer and actor Paul Robeson.

SOURCE E An advertisement for the new Palladium Cinema at Pwllheli in 1936.

2 EXAM PRACTICE

These questions test Section A of the examination paper.

LIFE DURING THE DEPRESSION

Study Sources A–D below and then answer the questions which follow.

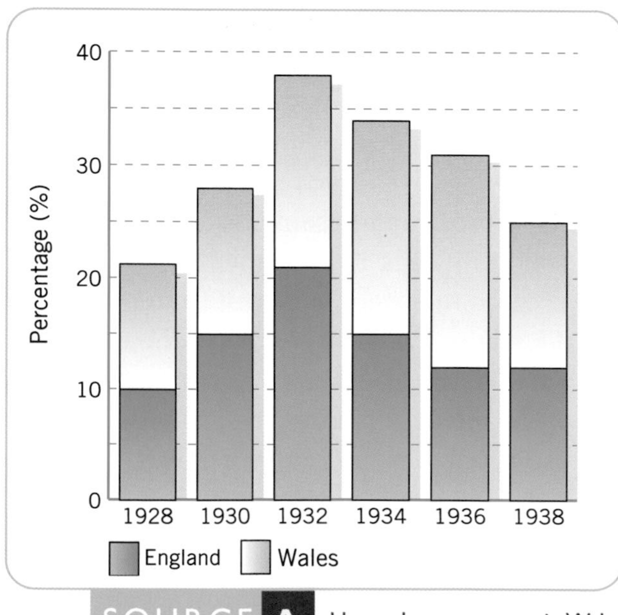

SOURCE A Unemployment rates in Wales and England 1928–38.

SOURCE B A government-funded clothing factory being built in the Rhondda valley, 1938.

SOURCE C

Once I was living in Wales and could see much more clearly the humiliating and terrible effects of unemployment on people. Men were standing on street corners, not knowing what to do with themselves and people were really hungry. You had to take part in any activity which would make people feel at least that they were fighting back and get other people to understand the seriousness of the situation.

From an interview given in 1985 by Mrs Dora Cox, who took part in the hunger march of 1934.

SOURCE D

Even though the image of Wales in the 1930s is one of general misery, our historical common-sense tells us that it cannot have been like that all the time, for everyone, and everywhere. In the late 1930s, there were more radio sets in Cardiff per head of population than in Slough and more cars than in Luton and a study of the local press suggests that these may not have been bad times at all.

A modern historian, Deian Hopkin, writing in *Wales Between The Wars* (1988).

EQ Exam Questions

1 What information does Source A give about the Depression? [3]

2 Use the information in Source B and your own knowledge to explain how the government tried to deal with the Depression. [4]

3 How useful is Source C as evidence to an historian studying the Depression in Wales? Explain your answer using the source and your own knowledge. [5]

4 In Source D the author is saying that in many ways things were improving in Wales during the 1930s. Is this a valid interpretation?
In your answer you should use your own knowledge of the topic, refer to the other relevant sources in this question, and consider how the author came to this interpretation. [8]

Why did Britain go to war with Germany in 1939?

SOURCE A

> How horrible, fantastic, incredible it is that we should be digging trenches and trying on gas-masks here because of a quarrel in a far-away country between people of whom we know nothing.
>
> Neville Chamberlain speaking in a radio broadcast in 1938 just before the Munich Conference with Hitler.

While historians looking at the 1930s recognise a series of events as 'the causes of the Second World War', for British people of the time the picture was far less clear. Most people could remember the First World War and the memories of the loss of loved ones were still fresh; many hoped never to go through the experience of war again. Also, issues of peace and war were far removed from the thoughts of large sections of the population. For people in the depressed areas of Wales, northern England and central Scotland, the main issue was unemployment, the dole and the means test, and the inability of the government to bring about any real improvement.

Families in the more prosperous areas of the Midlands and southern England were often more concerned with their jobs and their ability to pay for their new houses, cars and consumer goods. Many people were beginning to think that things could only get better.

GERMAN AGGRESSION IN THE 1930S

After the surrender of Germany in November 1918, the victorious Allies met in the Palace of Versailles near Paris to discuss the terms to be imposed on Germany. The main terms of the Treaty are outlined below. The German government was not allowed to take part in the peace negotiations and the terms of the Treaty of Versailles were not well received in Germany. Over the next 20 years, German resentment of the Treaty of Versailles contributed to the tension which eventually led to the outbreak of the Second World War in 1939.

THE MAIN TERMS OF THE TREATY OF VERSAILLES, 1919

- Germany blamed for starting the war.
- Germany to pay reparations (£6600 million) to the Allies for the losses and damage caused by the war.
- Alsace and Lorraine returned to France.
- Poland and Czechoslovakia set up as independent republics.
- Many German speakers were ruled by non-German governments.
- Germany and Austria not allowed to unite (the *Anschluss*).
- The Rhineland to be a demilitarised zone.
- The German army restricted to 100,000, without tanks or aircraft.
- The League of Nations established to work towards maintaining world peace.

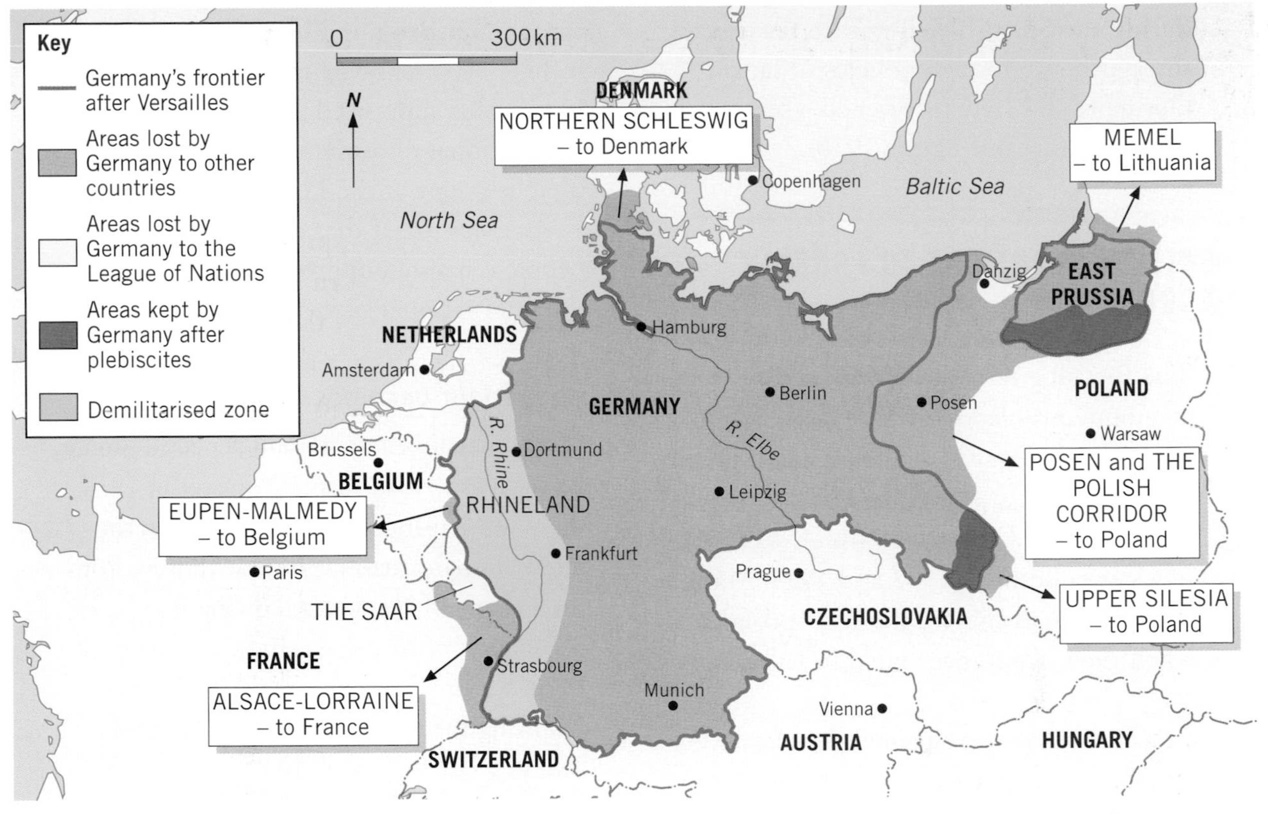

The territorial terms of the Treaty of Versailles, 1919.

Nazi Germany and the Treaty of Versailles

During the 1920s hatred against the 'unfair' Treaty of Versailles developed in Germany. The National Socialist, or Nazi, Party under its leader, Adolf Hitler, became more popular largely because of its promise to undo the terms of the treaty. Hitler and the Nazi Party came to power in Germany in 1933, and secret plans were made to undo many of its terms. Before the end of the year Germany had withdrawn from the League of Nations and was secretly making plans to rearm – something strictly forbidden by the Treaty of Versailles.

The reoccupation of the Rhineland

In March 1936 Hitler ordered the German army to reoccupy the Rhineland, the demilitarised zone in western Germany. Hitler knew that the German army was not yet ready for battle and gave orders that if the French army resisted them, they were to withdraw immediately. However, the French government did nothing. The British Prime Minister, Stanley Baldwin, argued that the Germans were only moving troops within their own territory and tried to convince people that the reoccupation was no threat. By successfully defying the Western powers and dealing another blow to the Treaty of Versailles, Hitler had also increased his power at home.

Gathering clouds in the 1930s

Germany was not the only country to pursue an aggressive foreign policy in the 1930s. Japan occupied Manchuria (a province of China) in 1931 and also left the League of Nations in that year. In 1935 Italy, under its Fascist dictator Mussolini, launched a violent invasion of Abyssinia in East Africa. In 1936, Mussolini sent troops and Hitler sent aircraft and special forces during the Spanish civil war. In these ways, the aggressive foreign policies of Japan, Germany and Italy threatened a second world conflict during the 1930s.

BRITISH REACTIONS TO FOREIGN AGGRESSION

The British government, with serious economic problems at home, was hopeful that a general war could be avoided. British hopes were pinned on the World Disarmament Conference which was held in Geneva between 1932 and 1934. Many people were dismayed, if not surprised, when the Conference ended in failure.

Peace movements remained popular in Britain and especially in Wales during the 1930s. The Welsh Council of the League of Nations Union had been active since 1922. During the early-1930s the League of Nations Union organised a Peace Ballot, based on a house-to-house canvass throughout Britain. The results, published in June 1935, showed that over ten million households supported peace and international disarmament. In 1936 the establishment of the Peace Pledge Union was further proof that large numbers of people remained opposed to war. However, the international situation was worsening.

Chamberlain becomes Prime Minister

When Neville Chamberlain replaced Stanley Baldwin as British Prime Minister in 1937, there was hardly any improvement in the international situation. Italy withdrew from the League of Nations following its occupation of Abyssinia. Italy, Germany and Japan became known as the Axis Powers following the signing of the Rome–Berlin Axis in 1936, which allowed the three countries to work more closely together. Britain was still reluctant to consider the possibility of war, but an Air Raid Precautions Act was passed in December 1937 and plans were made to protect the population from air attack.

i NEVILLE CHAMBERLAIN (1869–1940)

SOURCE B

Neville Chamberlain.

Chamberlain was elected to parliament in 1918 and held a number of important cabinet posts, dealing mainly with home affairs. He became Prime Minister in 1937 and having lived through the First World War, he was determined to avoid a second world conflict. He thought that war could be prevented if the democratic powers agreed to 'reasonable' demands made by potential enemies. Chamberlain's policy of appeasement, which involved attempts to negotiate terms with Germany, was popular for a time, but public opinion changed as it became clear that Hitler had no intention of keeping his promises.

The declaration of war, which Chamberlain announced in a radio broadcast on 3 September 1939, was for him a disaster. After Britain's failure to stop the Nazi occupation of Norway in the spring of 1940, Chamberlain was forced to resign. He died before the end of the year.

THE BRITISH POLICY OF APPEASEMENT

The Anschluss, 1938

As an Austrian, Hitler had personal reasons for hating the ban that had been imposed at Versailles on any *Anschluss*, or union, between Austria and Germany. German nationalists had long dreamed of *Grossdeutschland*, one great German-speaking state in central Europe. Hitler thought that this dream could now be achieved without any real opposition (see Source C).

SOURCE C

> Germany has to reckon with two hate-filled enemies, Britain and France, and Germany's problems can only be solved by means of force ... Our first objective must be to overthrow Czechoslovakia and Austria. Britain, almost certainly, and probably France as well, has already written off the Czechs. Problems with the Empire and reluctance to enter a long European war are decisive reasons why Britain will not take part in a war against Germany.
>
> Hitler speaking in November 1937.

Austrian Nazi supporters were well organised and were already staging demonstrations in favour of the *Anschluss* with Germany. A meeting was hurriedly arranged between Hitler and the Austrian Chancellor, Schuschnigg, on 12 February 1938, in which Schuschnigg gave in to Hitler's demands. On 11 March Hitler demanded that Seyss-Inquart, a Nazi supporter, replace Schuschnigg. Schuschnigg resigned and Seyss-Inquart took over as Chancellor. The next day, 12 March 1938, German troops crossed the Austrian frontier. They met with no resistance. The *Anschluss* had been successful.

Britain and France protested, as they had over the reoccupation of the Rhineland, but no action was taken. In Britain, the Foreign Secretary, Anthony Eden, resigned at the end of February because of disagreements with Chamberlain over the aggressive policies of Germany and Italy. His replacement was Lord Halifax, who supported the idea that war could only be avoided if German grievances were solved. Appeasement – giving in to a potential enemy in order to keep the peace – was now the official government policy.

After the *Anschluss*, the western part of Czechoslovakia was surrounded on three sides by German territory. Within this area a large German-speaking minority, totalling about 3.5 million, lived in many areas along the border. These areas, known as the Sudetenland, had belonged to Austria–Hungary up to 1919; the people therefore had never been German citizens. Encouraged by Nazi propaganda, however, some Sudeten Germans began to protest in favour of union with Germany.

Throughout the spring and summer of 1938, Hitler laid claim to the Sudetenland in ever more aggressive speeches. After secret discussions, Britain and France concluded that nothing could really be done to save the Sudetenland, or Czechoslovakia itself, from suffering the same fate as Austria.

Q Questions

1. Describe the steps which Hitler took to achieve the *Anschluss*?
2. How useful is Source C as evidence about relations between Britain and Germany during 1937–8? Explain your answer.

Chamberlain and the Munich Agreement

Chamberlain believed that international differences could be solved by talks between leaders. On 15 September 1938 he flew to Munich and met Hitler at Berchtesgaden. Hitler was told that Britain had no objection to the transfer of the Sudetenland to Germany. It was only a question of persuading the Czech government to agree. Chamberlain and Hitler met a second time at Godesberg a week later, when further German demands were made.

A further conference was arranged at Munich between Chamberlain and Hitler, this time with Mussolini and the French Prime Minister, Daladier. It was agreed that the Sudetenland should be given to Germany and the Czech representatives were called in to be told. Britain and France guaranteed to protect the new Czech frontiers and Hitler promised that it would be his last demand in Europe.

On his return to London, Chamberlain waved the paper signed by himself and Hitler and declared, 'I believe it is peace for our time'. Chamberlain was welcomed by cheering crowds, and was invited to appear with the king and queen at Buckingham Palace.

Popular attitudes to appeasement

Chamberlain's policy of appeasement was initially popular with the British public.

- Memories of the horrors of the First World War were strong, and people wanted to avoid a second world conflict.
- Many people felt sympathy for Germany and thought that Hitler's demands were justified. They believed that the terms of the Treaty of Versailles had been too harsh, and that Germany had a right to be treated fairly and regain lost lands.
- People were struggling to deal with the effects of the Depression and didn't think that Britain was strong enough to afford the costs of rearmament.

SOURCE D Chamberlain waves the Munich Agreement on his return from Munich, 30 September 1938.

CZECHOSLOVAKIA AND POLAND

Czechoslovakia's defences had been weakened by the Munich Agreement. Poland and Hungary now took the territory they wanted from Czechoslovakia and internal rivalry threatened to destabilise the Czech government. In its weakened state, Czechoslovakia didn't stand a chance against further German aggression. Ignoring the Munich Agreement, the German army moved in to occupy the rest of Czechoslovakia on 15 March 1939.

Germany then turned its attention eastwards towards another problem caused by the Treaty of Versailles. The 'Polish Corridor', or West Prussia, had been given to Poland in 1919, thereby separating East Prussia and the free city of Danzig from Germany. Since Danzig and the corridor were still populated mainly by German speakers, many began to push for union with Germany.

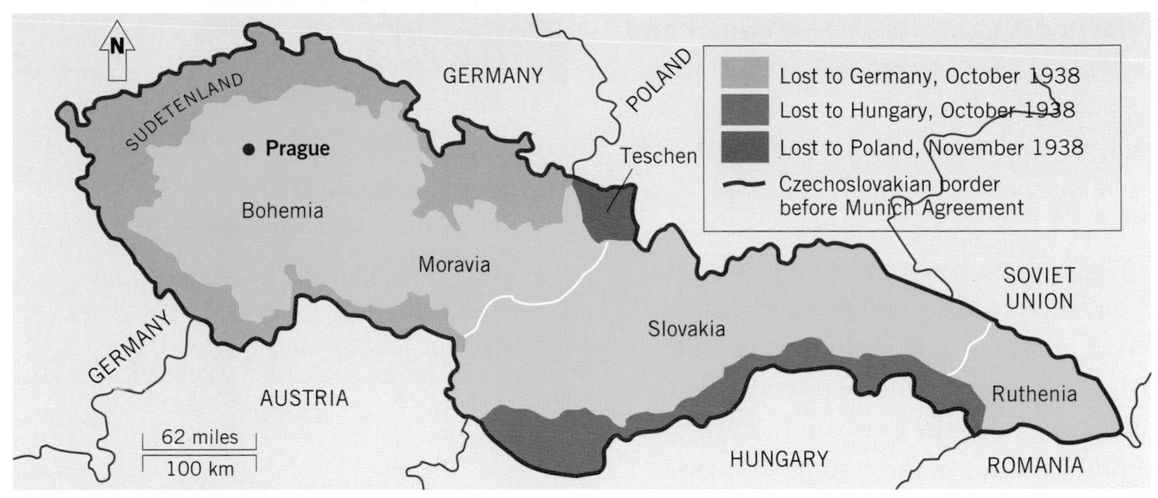

Czechoslovak territorial losses from the Munich Agreement in 1938.

Changes in British policy

The winter of 1938–9 had been a period of reflection for the British government and people, and attitudes towards Germany began to harden. Poland was not to be sacrificed as Czechoslovakia had been. On 31 March 1939, Chamberlain wrote a letter to the Polish government stating that 'if their independence were threatened, His Majesty's Government and the French Government would at once lend them all the support in their power'. This statement showed that Britain was prepared to go to war against Germany over Poland.

The Nazi–Soviet Pact

On 23 August 1939 an agreement known as the Nazi–Soviet Pact was announced between Germany and the Soviet Union. As part of this pact, Poland was to be shared between Germany and the Soviet Union. The pact was the single most important short-term cause of the Second World War. Knowing that the Soviet Union would not prevent an attack on Poland, Hitler ordered his forces to cross the Polish frontier at 4.45 am on 1 September 1939.

Two days later Britain, in accordance with the guarantee given to Poland, sent an ultimatum to Germany which would expire at 11 am on 3 September 1939. No reply was received and later that day Chamberlain announced that Britain was at war with Germany.

HOW READY WAS BRITAIN FOR WAR?

British rearmament and defence preparations

By giving in to Hitler's demands, the Munich Agreement at least gave the British people an extra 12 months to prepare for war. In September 1939 the British people were prepared to make a stand against Hitler's attempts to dominate Europe.

The British navy was reasonably well equipped and large enough to protect Britain from any invasion. The RAF's fighter planes – the Hurricane and the Spitfire – were the best in the world. Radar enabled the RAF to detect approaching enemy aircraft and guide the defending fighters towards their targets. The RAF's bombers were not as modern, but they did provide some means of retaliation against an enemy.

The British army was the least prepared for modern warfare. Conscription was introduced in May 1939 but when war broke out, the army was seriously short of trained soldiers, modern transport and tanks.

In 1939 there was a five-fold increase in expenditure on air raid precautions and large public air raid shelters were built. More hospital beds were provided and plans made for the evacuation of children from the cities to the countryside, away from the threat of bombing raids.

Q Questions

1. Why did Britain and France sign the Munich Agreement in 1938?
2. Was Chamberlain right or wrong to follow a policy of appeasement?
3. How important was the Nazi–Soviet Pact in starting the Second World War? Explain your answer fully.

2 EXAM PRACTICE

These questions test Section B of the examination paper.

BRITAIN AND THE THREAT OF GERMANY

Study the information below and then answer the questions which follow.

INFORMATION

A cartoon published in 1938 showing Chamberlain, the peacemaker, flying to Germany.

EQ Exam Questions

1. a Describe the aims of the peace movement in Britain during the 1930s. [2]
   b Explain why Britain accepted the German reoccupation of the Rhineland. [4]
   c Why was the appeasement policy popular up to 1938? [5]
2. a Describe Britain's role at the Munich conference. [3]
   b Explain why Britain declared war on Germany in 1939. [4]
3. How well was Britain prepared for war in 1939? Explain your answer fully. [7]

How did people in Wales and England cope with the experience of the Second World War?

THE ATTITUDES OF THE GOVERNMENT AND PEOPLE TO WAR

SOURCE A

I am speaking to you from the Cabinet Room of 10 Downing Street. This morning the British ambassador in Berlin handed the German government a final note stating that unless we heard from them that they were prepared to withdraw their troops from Poland, a state of war would exist between us. I have to tell you that no such undertaking has been received and that consequently this country is at war with Germany.

Extract from a radio broadcast by Neville Chamberlain on 3 September 1939.

With the outbreak of the Second World War the government's preparations immediately swung into action. The navy and RAF were put on wartime alert and the British Expeditionary Force (BEF) was sent to France to join the French to wait for the expected German attack. Conscription was introduced for men aged between 18 and 41, children from the cities were evacuated to safer areas in the countryside and petrol rationing was introduced.

Bombing raids, a new form of warfare, were greatly feared. Air-raid sirens were installed and tested. Households with gardens were given corrugated iron Anderson shelters to be dug into the ground and large public shelters were hurriedly built. Everybody was issued with a gas mask in case of gas attacks. After dark, a 'blackout' was enforced; all street lights were switched off and blackout blinds or curtains were fitted to windows. Civil defence regulations were strictly enforced by volunteer air raid precaution wardens. Men who were not conscripted into the regular army joined the Local Defence Volunteers, later renamed the Home Guard.

As the Germans were occupied with their campaign in Poland, there was little action in the west during the first six months of the war. This quiet period was nicknamed the 'phoney war'.

SOURCE B A morale-boosting photograph from the early days of the war.

The phoney war came to a sudden end in April 1940 when the Germans invaded Denmark and Norway. British land and naval forces sent to Norway were unable to prevent the German occupation of the country and were hurriedly withdrawn. The failure was blamed on the Prime Minister who faced criticism in the House of Commons on 7 May. Chamberlain resigned two days later and Winston Churchill became Prime Minister of a coalition government.

Q Questions

1 What steps did the government take to prepare people for war?

2 What was the 'phoney war' and how did it come to an end?

Churchill's leadership was very soon put to the test. The Germans launched their *Blitzkrieg* (lightning war) against the Netherlands, Belgium and France.

i WINSTON LEONARD SPENCER CHURCHILL (1874–1965)

SOURCE C

Winston Churchill.

After army service, Churchill first became famous as a war correspondent during the Boer War (1899–1902). He then became a Conservative MP but soon joined the Liberal Party. He was Home Secretary in the Liberal government after 1906, and during the First World War became First Lord of the Admiralty and later Minister of Munitions. After the war he became a Conservative once more.

During the 1930s he opposed the government's appeasement policy and warned of the danger of German expansion. After the declaration of war in 1939, more people came to believe that Churchill was the strong leader that Britain needed, and on 10 May 1940 he succeeded Chamberlain as Prime Minister. His speeches (see Source D) inspired the British people (see page 54).

Churchill was able to co-operate closely with US President Roosevelt and more distantly with Stalin. As US involvement in the war grew, Churchill's power to control events became less. Although he remained a powerful influence on foreign affairs up to 1945, his popularity at home was declining. People began to think that the Labour Party should take charge of Britain in the post-war period, and the Conservatives were defeated in the 1945 election. Churchill retired in 1955. His death in 1965 was marked by a grand state funeral.

SOURCE D

I have nothing to offer but blood, toil, tears and sweat. You ask, what is our policy? I will say: It is to wage war, by sea, land and air, with all our might and with all the strength that God can give us. You ask, what is our aim? I can answer in one word: Victory – victory at all costs, victory in spite of all terror; victory, however long and hard the road may be.

Churchill's first speech as Prime Minister.

SOURCE E A poster of 1940.

This new form of warfare relied on speed and surprise, and the use of air power and fast-moving armoured tanks (the *Panzers*), against which the British and French had no real defence. The British soon found themselves surrounded and retreating towards the port of Dunkirk. Most of the BEF and thousands of French troops were evacuated from the port and the beaches of Dunkirk. Most of the army's heavy guns and equipment were lost, but Churchill managed to portray Dunkirk as a miraculous escape, which could almost be regarded as a victory.

France surrendered to Germany on 22 June 1940 and for the next 12 months Britain stood alone against the Nazis.

After the fall of France, Hitler ordered the *Luftwaffe* (the German air force) to destroy the RAF, after which he planned to invade Britain. The air struggle which followed was named the Battle of Britain. The battle was fought in the skies above south-east England and lasted until September. The RAF eventually won because of its radar cover, the superiority of its Spitfire and Hurricane fighter aircraft, the bravery of their pilots and German mistakes. Churchill expressed the people's appreciation of their heroic role in a memorable speech on 20 August 1940: 'Never in the field of human conflict was so much owed by so many to so few.'

THE BLITZ AND BOMBING OF WELSH AND ENGLISH CITIES

In the autumn of 1940, the Luftwaffe began its bombing campaign on London and other British cities. This became known as 'the Blitz', a shortened form of the German, *Blitzkrieg*. High explosive and incendiary (fire-making) bombs were used.

SOURCE F

The ruins of Coventry Cathedral following the most serious single attack during the Blitz in November 1940. The city centre was destroyed and over 500 people were killed.

COLEG CYMUNEDOL ABERGELE
ABERGELE COMMUNITY COLLEGE
CANOLFAN ADNODDAU DYSGU
LEARNING RESOURCE CENTRE
09415

As the city blazed above them, Londoners took refuge in their Anderson shelters and demanded that the underground stations be opened at night to provide further safe shelter. In this way a wartime spirit of friendship and co-operation was created, which helped people to cope with the hardship and loss of loved ones. Press and radio reports reflected this wartime spirit and always played down any suggestion of panic or a general lack of support for the war effort.

SOURCE G

The press versions of life going on normally in the East End of London are not true. There was no bread, no milk, no electricity, no gas, no telephones. The press version of cheerful, smiling people is a gross exaggeration ...
The people of Southampton are broken in spirit after the sleepless and awful nights. Everywhere I saw men and women, carrying suitcases and bundles, struggling to get anywhere out of the town. Everywhere there was fear.

Contemporary reports of the Blitz.

After Hitler decided to attack the Soviet Union in June 1941, the air raids on Britain were reduced and the Blitz came to an end. Towards the end of the war, however, the people of London and southern England experienced a second Blitz, when the Germans used V1 flying bombs and V2 rockets to attack the city.

Q Questions

1 Explain the term *Blitz*.

2 Describe the impact of the Blitz on British civilians.

EVERYDAY LIFE DURING THE WAR

Rationing

As the war progressed, the government tightened its control over most aspects of everyday life. Price controls were put on goods to prevent profiteering and by 1942 no petrol was available for private cars. From January 1940, basic foodstuffs, meat, butter and sugar were rationed; clothing was added in June 1941. Everyone was issued with books of coupons, without which it was impossible to buy goods. Some people bought from black market traders, known as 'spivs', who sold rationed goods 'under the counter' at high prices, but this was frowned upon by officials and the general public. As the same amount of food was available to everyone, rationing actually improved the diets of some people.

Evacuation

One of the most important effects of the war was the arrival of the evacuees from the cities in the countryside. Whole schools were often evacuated with their teachers and were allowed to share a local school building with local children. Evacuees were also allocated to local families. The experiences of the evacuees were mixed; many were made welcome and lived as full members of the host families, often enjoying a better standard of living than they did at home. Others found that they were resented and in places were expected to work hard on a farm or in other family businesses. The host families in the country were often shocked by the behaviour of some of the evacuees from poor city communities and many stories were told of bed wetting and bad table manners.

In Wales, some Welsh speakers were worried that the arrival of the evacuees would be harmful to the language. In fact many evacuees from Merseyside and elsewhere came to speak Welsh fluently.

SOURCE H Evacuees arriving at a railway station in south Wales in 1939.

Women's contribution to the war effort

The contribution of women to the war effort was far greater than it had been during the First World War. Women were encouraged to enlist in the armed services, the Auxiliary Territorial Service (ATS), the Women's Auxiliary Air Force (WAAF) and the Women's Royal Naval Service (WRNS). Although women did not fight they provided valuable support, from filling sandbags to operating searchlights. Nursing in civilian and military hospitals became an essential and highly-regarded occupation. As men were conscripted into the armed forces many industries, including farming, faced labour shortages. Unmarried women were conscripted to work in factories producing all kinds of war material, including munitions, aircraft and vehicles. By 1943, 57 per cent of workers were women. In Wales, women were the main workforce at the huge munitions complex at Bridgend.

SOURCE I A poster encouraging women to contribute to the war effort.

The shortage of farm labour was met by the creation of the Women's Land Army. Many of the town girls who joined soon became skilled at dealing with livestock and operating farm machinery. The Land Army and the 'Dig for Victory' campaign, which urged people to grow their own food, helped to almost double food production by 1943.

Government propaganda and maintaining morale

The government thought it essential to maintain a positive attitude towards the war to keep morale high – a policy it had followed during the First World War.

Churchill's speeches encouraged the 'bulldog spirit'. The government controlled, or censored, information made available to the press and radio. There was a strong emphasis on 'people's war spirit' bringing out the best in people. Successes such as the Battle of Britain were always well publicised, as were any stories of courage and fighting spirit during the Blitz. Failures, such as the fall of Singapore or shipping losses in the Atlantic, received less attention. The Ministry of Information employed the best artists and designers of the day to produce propaganda posters.

Civilians were told not to speak about their work to prevent any possibility of useful information reaching the ears of enemy spies (see Source J). There were also strict penalties for spreading alarm. Housewives were encouraged not to waste food and to 'make do and mend' instead of buying new clothes. Children were recruited to collect scrap metal for the war effort.

SOURCE J A poster encouraging caution at home.

Q Questions

1. How important was the role that women played in the war effort?
2. How did the government maintain the morale of the British people?

Planning for peace

The people who lived through the Second World War were determined to create a better world for themselves and their children once the war was over. A number of politicians from all three main political parties began planning a better future. Among them were R. A. Butler (Conservative), William Beveridge (Liberal) and Aneurin Bevan (Labour).

The Beveridge Report on improved social security was published in December 1942. The report proposed that the state should look after its citizens 'from the cradle to the grave'. It also explained how the state should attack the 'five giants' responsible for the problems faced by ordinary people – want, ignorance, disease, squalor and idleness. People came to expect that post-war governments would improve national insurance, education, health, housing and employment.

- In 1943 a Ministry of Town and Country Planning was set up to plan the rebuilding needed after the damage caused by the bombing.
- The Education Act was passed in August 1944. Its main aim was to tackle 'ignorance' by providing access to secondary education for all children. The school leaving age was raised to 15 years and, later, to 16 years.

With the end of the war in sight, the Labour Party was increasingly seen as the party most likely to put into practice the promises made.

THE END OF THE SECOND WORLD WAR

After Hitler's suicide on 30 April 1945, the Germans surrendered and the end of the war in Europe was celebrated officially on 8 May 1945 – VE-day. The wartime coalition government ended on 23 May 1945. Churchill then formed a 'caretaker' administration to govern until the general election which was to be held on 5 July 1945. The Labour Party won and Clement Attlee became Prime Minister for the final weeks of the war. After the Japanese surrender, VJ-day was celebrated on 2 September 1945. Britain had been at war for one day short of six years.

Q Questions

1 What were the aims of the Beveridge Report of 1942?

2 How did the British government 'plan for peace'?

3 In what ways did the lives of British civilians change during the Second World War?

4 Describe the different propaganda methods used by the British government during the Second World War.

2 EXAM PRACTICE

These questions test Section A of the examination paper.

LIFE ON THE HOME FRONT, 1939–45

Study Sources A–D (pages 55–6) and then answer the questions which follow.

SOURCE A A cartoon by David Low, 'We're all behind you, Winston', published in the summer of 1940.

SOURCE B

The all clear signal tells us that the bombers have gone. It's just six a.m. London raises her head, shakes the debris of the night from her hair and takes stock of the damage done. The sign of a great fighter in the ring is, can he get up from the floor after being knocked down? London does this every morning. Today the morale of the people is higher than ever before.

A newsreel commentary by Quentin Reynolds, a US journalist, in 1940.

SOURCE C

I expect that the Battle of Britain is about to begin. Upon this battle depends the fate of Christian civilisation. Hitler knows that he will have to break us in this island or lose the war. If we can stand up to him, all Europe may be free. But if we fail, then the whole world will sink into a new Dark Age. Let us therefore brace ourselves to our duties and so bear ourselves that, if the British Empire and its Commonwealth last for a thousand years, men will still say, 'This was their finest hour'.

From a speech by Winston Churchill, delivered in the House of Commons on 18 June 1940 and repeated in the evening on radio.

SOURCE D

In pursuing the slogan 'Victory at all costs', Churchill did not care what the costs might be. By the end of the war, it had become hard to argue that Britain had won in any sense save that of avoiding defeat. Churchill stood for the British Empire, for British independence and for an anti-socialist vision of Britain. By July 1945, the first of these was fading, the second was entirely dependent on America and the third had just vanished in a Labour victory.

A modern historian, John Charmley, writing in his book, *Churchill: The End of Glory* (1993).

EQ Exam Questions

1 What information does Source A give about Churchill's appointment as prime minister? [3]

2 Use the information in Source B and your own knowledge to explain how the people of London and other cities coped with the Blitz. [4]

3 How useful is Source C as evidence to an historian studying Churchill's leadership during the war? Explain your answer using the source and your own knowledge. [5]

4 In Source D the author is saying that Churchill did not achieve his war aims. Is this a valid interpretation?
In your answer you should use your own knowledge of the topic, refer to the other relevant sources in this question, and consider how the author came to this interpretation. [8]

How and to what extent did the economic and social policies of the Labour governments change Wales and England in the period 1945–51?

WALES AND ENGLAND IN 1945

The general election

The result of the 1945 general election surprised many people. Even King George commented that the new prime minister, Clement Attlee, still looked surprised during their first formal meeting.

Labour	393 seats (25 in Wales)
Conservatives	213 seats (3 in Wales)
Liberals	12 seats (7 in Wales)
Others	22 seats

The results of the 1945 General Election.

The people of Wales overwhelmingly supported the new government and two Welsh MPs, Aneurin Bevan (Ebbw Vale) and James Griffiths (Llanelli), were given key positions in Attlee's cabinet as Minister of Health and Minister of National Insurance.

Most people in 1945 could remember the economic problems and depression of the 1920s and 1930s, and their determination that these conditions should not return was one of the reasons for the Labour victory. The Labour government was anxious to make use of the 'wartime spirit' of togetherness to tackle Britain's post-war problems.

i CLEMENT ATTLEE (1883–1967)

SOURCE A

Clement Attlee.

Clement Attlee was born in London to a wealthy middle-class family. Unlike many Labour members at the time, he went to a boarding school and Oxford University. He became a lawyer but spent most of his time doing social work among the poor of London's East End. After becoming an MP in 1922, he was soon appointed a junior minister in the first minority Labour government. By 1931 he was Deputy Leader of the Party and during the war served as Deputy Prime Minister. He became Prime Minister in 1945. Attlee's careful and modest approach was in contrast to Churchill's more dramatic style. Attlee was also a skilled negotiator. After losing the elections of 1951 and 1955 to the Conservatives, he retired to the House of Lords.

The economic position in 1945

The economic position faced by Attlee's government was one of virtual bankruptcy. During the war British overseas investments worth £1000 million had been sold with a resulting loss. The national debt had risen from £760 million to £3355 million and spending abroad was running at £2000 million a year, while earnings were only £350 million. It was no wonder that there were shortages of food and raw materials and that wartime rationing had to be continued. The period came to be known as the 'Age of Austerity'. Further loans had to be obtained from the USA, but economic problems continued for Britain.

THE ESTABLISHMENT OF THE WELFARE STATE

The ideals of the Labour Party

The Labour Party elected in 1945 introduced policies which reflected its ideals about social equality. Labour politicians believed that it was possible to achieve true equality among the people of Britain by sharing the country's wealth and providing equal opportunities. Labour policies therefore focused on providing better public services. These included a free health service; better government support for the elderly, sick and unemployed; cheaper housing and new educational opportunities.

Labour's reconstruction and housing policy: 'homes for all'

After the First World War, Lloyd George had failed to fulfil his promise to provide 'homes fit for heroes'. In 1945 the Labour government began to implement its 'homes for all' policy under the supervision of Aneurin Bevan. This was part of the government's attack on squalor.

i ANEURIN BEVAN (1897–1960)

SOURCE **B**

Aneurin Bevan.

Aneurin Bevan, the son of a miner, was born in Tredegar in South Wales. He left school at 13 and began to work underground. He continued to educate himself by reading library books on economics and politics. He was elected chairman of the local branch of his union, the South Wales Miners' Federation, at the age of 19. He later studied at the Labour College in London and during the 1920s was a local councillor, a county councillor and a leading local activist during the General Strike of 1926. He became MP for Ebbw Vale in 1929 and made a name for himself as a fiery speaker, criticising the government's social and economic policies. After Labour came to power in 1945 he was appointed Minister of Health, with an additional responsibility for housing.

Bevan's greatest achievement was the establishment of the National Health Service in 1948. Bevan believed that health should be free for everyone and in 1951, as Minister of Labour, he resigned over the government's proposal to impose charges for dental and optical services.

Over 800,000 new homes were built between 1946 and 1951, but the policy was hampered by a shortage of money and materials. Four out of five houses were council houses built by local authorities to be rented by working-class families. However, a great shortage of new houses built for sale remained. The total figures never got close to the 350,000 houses per year built during the 1930s, peaking at 200,000 new homes in 1948.

For a time the government had to accommodate homeless people in disused army camps. Prefabricated houses, known as 'prefabs', were also built in some places. Another policy was the building of new towns, such as Stevenage and Harlow in England and Cwmbrân in Wales, to reduce overcrowding in the cities. Some slums were demolished and houses were improved by the installation of bathrooms and hot water systems.

Q Question

1 How successful were the Labour government's housing policies, 1945–51? Explain your answer.

Social Security

Many governments in the past had attempted to deal with 'want', or poverty. Old age pensions had been introduced before the First World War as had sickness and unemployment pay for some workers. Beveridge recommended in his report that the attack on 'want' should be given priority. He felt that it should be the cornerstone of the Welfare State.

Attlee gave responsibility for the sickness and unemployment benefit to James Griffiths, MP for Llanelli who was appointed Minister of National Insurance. Griffiths had been President of the South Wales Miners' Federation and knew all about the problems of working-class people. He was determined to abolish what remained of the Poor Law and the means test.

By the National Insurance Act of 1946 the whole population was insured for sickness benefit, unemployment benefit, retirement pensions, widows' pensions, maternity grants and death grants. A separate act provided a family allowance, payable directly to mothers for every child in a family. A National Assistance Board was added in 1948 to deal with additional payments for people who needed particular help. The scheme was financed by weekly contributions from workers and employers, paid by means of stamps fixed to a National Insurance card.

The NHS and the role of Bevan

Labour's attack on 'disease' had been outlined in the Beveridge Report and set a framework for the National Health Service (NHS). The National Health Service Bill was introduced into the House of Commons in 1946 by Aneurin Bevan. It aimed to provide people with a complete range of medical services 'free at the point of delivery'. The service was to be paid for partly by National Insurance contributions and partly out of general taxation.

In order to function, the NHS had to win the support of doctors. They declared at first that they would not co-operate with a centralised system which threatened to take away their independence. Many doctors worked in private medical practices where they were paid directly by their patients.

MEDICAL SERVICES INCLUDED IN THE NATIONAL HEALTH SERVICE

- Family doctor services.
- Opticians' services, including spectacles.
- Dental care, including dentures.
- District nurse and maternity services.
- Infant and Child welfare services.
- Free drugs and medicines under prescription.
- All hospital treatments, including surgery and after care.

The Conservative Party and the British Medical Association were also against the idea of the NHS.

It was only after lengthy talks, lasting almost 18 months, between Bevan and doctors' representatives that agreement was finally reached. A compromise was agreed whereby doctors were allowed to carry out some private work whilst working mainly within the NHS.

SOURCE C A cartoon of 1946 about the popularity of the NHS. The figure on the left represents the doctors who opposed the measure.

The new NHS was welcomed by the vast majority of people, and was especially popular with those who had traditionally been reluctant to seek medical attention during the days of doctors' bills. In its first year, the cost of the NHS soared beyond the £500 million mark and by 1951 the government had to introduce charges for dental and optical services.

New educational opportunities

The 1944 Education Act stated that all children up to the age of 15, and later 16, were entitled to free secondary education. The old elementary schools, teaching pupils from 5 to 14, were to be abolished. The new secondary system was to be based on three different types of school:

- grammar schools, providing a traditional academic education for those able to pass the 11-plus examination
- technical, teaching vocational skills
- secondary modern schools.

The Act resulted in an increase in the number of pupils staying in secondary education and moving on to colleges and universities. Some Labour MPs, however, thought that all secondary education should be based on comprehensive schools teaching pupils of all abilities together. A lack of resources meant that only a few technical schools were established.

LABOUR'S NATIONALISATION POLICIES

Members of the Labour Party believed that the country's main industries should be owned by the people and not by a small group of owners or shareholders. Most unpopular of all were the coal owners who were accused of profiteering and neglecting the welfare of their workforce.

Since the coal mines, the railways and the docks and canals were old-fashioned and needed large-scale investments if they were to be modernised, the Conservatives allowed these industries to be nationalised. The newly-nationalised industries were run by government-appointed boards and the previous owners and shareholders received financial compensation. Attlee's government had rejected the idea that workers should be given a voice in the running of their industry. In Wales, most of the collieries continued to be managed by men who used to work for the private Ocean and Powell Duffryn coal companies.

The nationalisation of the coal industry under the Labour government was celebrated in the mining valleys; it was welcomed as a victory over the hated coal owners. However, the harsh winter of 1947 exposed the government's financial difficulties, making the shortage of coal and other fuels painfully obvious and causing short-time working and serious disruption across industry in general.

Unlike the railways and the coal mines, many people saw road haulage and iron and steel as relatively modern industries run efficiently under private ownership. When, in 1949, the government proposed to extend nationalisation to the iron and steel industry, Conservative MPs decided that this would be an opportunity to go on the attack and win public approval. The Conservatives managed to delay nationalisation and, during this period, the public began to see that nationalisation was associated with declining industries and centralised government control.

i INDUSTRIES NATIONALISED BY THE LABOUR GOVERNMENT 1945–50

1946	The Bank of England
1947	The coal industry under the National Coal Board (NCB)
	The airlines, BEA and BOAC
	Electricity generation and distribution
1948	Railways
	Docks and canals
	Road haulage
	Gas production and distribution
1949	The iron and steel industry

Q Questions

1 Why was the NHS unpopular with doctors?

2 How successful was the Labour government's nationalisation policy?

REACTIONS TO LABOUR'S POLICIES

After five years in office, Attlee had to call a general election in 1950. The results of the February poll came as a shock to Labour supporters. Their 'landslide' majority of 1945 had been reduced to a single figure. Although Attlee and the Welfare State measures remained popular, people felt that in many ways things had hardly improved since the end of the war.

- Rationing still remained and there was a shortage of many goods and materials.
- Re-armament caused by the Cold War led to a further rise in government spending.
- Inflation represented a threat to middle-class living standards.
- Taxation remained high and was especially resented by the wealthier classes.

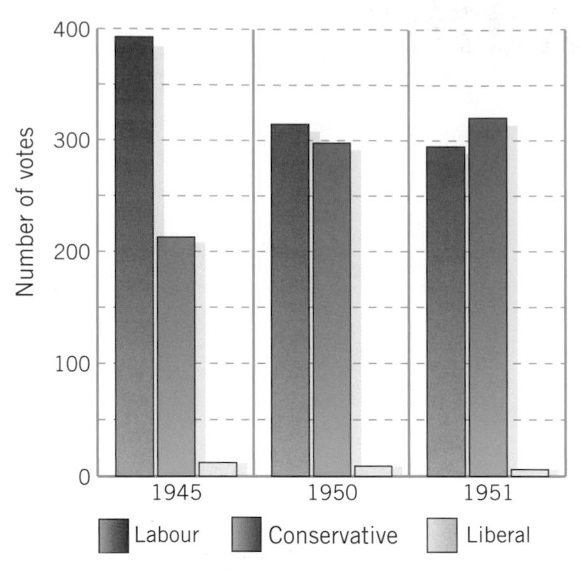

Election results 1945–51.

The Labour government stayed in power for another 18 months. The Conservatives with their policy of opposition to steel nationalisation and rationing were gradually becoming more popular. Divisions within the Labour Party weakened the government still further.

Difficulties in Parliament led Attlee to call another election in October 1951. The Conservatives won the election and Winston Churchill was returned as prime minister. However, the Welfare State and other aspects of Labour's economic and social policies were left intact and remained a powerful influence on life in Wales and England for the rest of the twentieth century.

Q Questions

1 How did the Labour government attack 'ignorance'?

2 Why had Attlee's government lost popularity by 1950?

2 EXAM PRACTICE

These questions test Section B of the examination paper.

WALES AND ENGLAND 1945–51

Study the information below and then answer the questions which follow.

INFORMATION

Port Talbot steelworks, opened in 1951 shortly after the nationalisation of the steel industry.

EQ Exam Questions

1 **a** Describe *one* of the main domestic problems faced by the Labour government in 1945. [2]
b Explain the aims of Clement Attlee as prime minister. [4]
c How important was the establishment of the National Health Service? [5]

2 **a** Describe the educational changes introduced by the Labour governments. [3]
b Explain why Labour's nationalisation policy was supported and opposed. [4]

3 How far had the Labour governments' economic and social policies changed Wales and England by 1951? Explain your answer fully. [7]

3 RUSSIA IN REVOLUTION, 1905–24

Between 1905 and 1924 the Russian Empire went through a period of great change. Spread over a vast landmass the Empire was a mixture of different peoples, languages, cultures and traditions. While the Empire was beginning to industrialise with the growth of cities, the process was slow.

In 1905 Russia was governed by Tsar Nicholas II. The tsar's absolute power was challenged by a Revolution in 1905 and he was forced to grant some limited reform. However, he soon re-established his absolute authority and radicals were either arrested or driven into exile. During the First World War the Russian army was without adequate leadership, training and supplies. This, and increasing hardship in Russia, led to criticism of the tsar and tsarina and demands for change.

In 1917 Russia experienced two Revolutions. The first in February caused the tsar to abdicate in favour of a Provisional Government. In the second revolution in October the leader of the Bolsheviks, Lenin, recently returned from exile and the Bolsheviks seized power in Petrograd. The Bolsheviks then faced the difficult task of spreading their authority over the rest of Russia. Between 1918 and 1920 a Civil War was fought between the Bolshevik (Red) and Tsarist (White) forces – the Reds under the leadership of Trotsky eventually won the war. The drain upon the civilian population resulted in a major famine in 1921.

Between 1921 and his death in 1924 Lenin laid the foundations of the communist state of the USSR. The communists, as his followers were now called, attempted to control all aspects of life including education, religion and culture. The New Economic Policy helped to revive the economy but Lenin's failing health resulted in a power struggle to succeed him, with Stalin eventually winning that battle.

TIMELINE OF EVENTS

1904	Start of Russo–Japanese War
1905	9 January: Bloody Sunday Revolution in St Petersburg
	Tsar issues the October Manifesto
1906	First democratically-elected Duma lasts for just 75 days
	Stolypin becomes Chief Minister
1914	August: Russia enters the First World War
1917	February: Revolution on the streets of Petrograd; Tsar Nicholas abdicates
	Formation of the Provisional Soviet Government Dual Power
	Lenin's April Theses
	The July Days
	The Kornilov Plot
	October: storming of the Winter Palace – Bolsheviks seize power
1918	Treaty of Brest–Litovsk Civil War between the Whites and the Reds
	July: murder of the Romanov royal family
1920	Red victory
	Russo–Polish War
1921	The Kronstadt Rebellion
	Introduction of the NEP
1924	Death of Lenin

Why did revolution break out in 1905 and what consequences did it have on the tsarist rule of Russia?

RUSSIA IN 1905

The nature and structure of Russian society

The Russian Empire covered one-sixth of the world's land surface and its vast size made it very difficult to govern. The 1897 census recorded a population of 125 million including 55 million Russians, the other 70 million consisting of different nationalities such as Ukranians, Belorussians, Poles, Jews, Tartars and Germans. The official policy of 'Russification' meant that these national groups had to become Russian, using the Russian language in business and in schools.

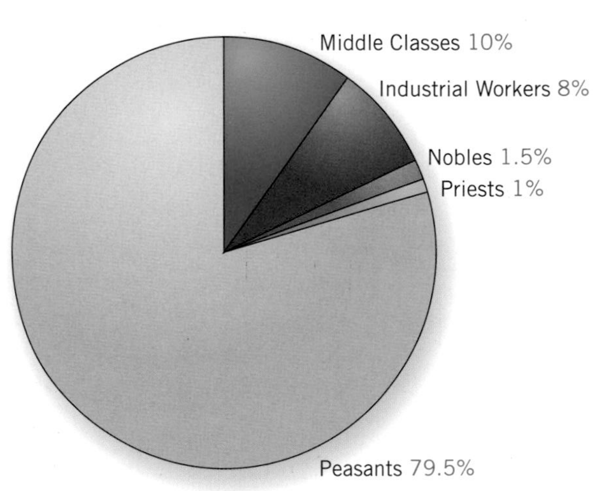

The structure of Russian society in 1905.

Russian society was very rigid and at the top of the pyramid stood the tsar. He was an autocrat and his power was absolute which meant he could make laws and govern as he wished. There was no parliament and political parties were banned. The tsar received advice from a Committee of Ministers chosen from the rich nobles by himself. Newspapers and books were censored and opposition was dealt with by the secret police, the Okhrana. Their job was to get rid of opposition groups to the Tsar. They used ruthless tactics and sent people who tried to oppose the Tsar to prison camps in Siberia.

Below the tsar were the nobles. They formed about 0.1 per cent of the population yet owned over 25 per cent of the land. They were very wealthy and influential. A middle class, the bourgeoisie, began to emerge following rapid industrialisation at the close of the nineteenth century. These people increasingly began to demand a say in how the country was governed.

Nearly 80 per cent of Russia's population were peasants. Despite the abolition of serfdom in 1861 the majority were still very poor and were restricted in what they

SOURCE A The home of a wealthy Russian noble complete with servants in 1905.

did by the village commune or *mir* which made all major decisions. Primitive farming methods and poor agricultural land meant that there were few crops and food shortages were common. Living conditions were terrible, with whole families often living in a single room.

SOURCE B

They receive miserable wages, and generally live in an overcrowded state, very commonly in special lodging houses. It is common to see ten or more persons living in one room and four sleeping in a bed ... The normal working day is eleven and a half hours of work, exclusive of meal times.

An account of the conditions experienced by Russian workers by Father Gapon (1905), a Russian priest who attempted to organise a trade union to help the workers.

Only about 15 per cent of the population lived in towns and cities but the numbers were growing each year as peasants left the land in search of jobs in the new factories. Conditions for the industrial workers were poor and they were often forced to live several families to a room. Many houses had no running water or sewage system. Workers were employed for long hours yet wages were low. Trade unions were banned. Strikes were illegal but became more common after 1900 as workers protested over bad conditions.

Religion played an important part in everyday life and the Russian Orthodox Church was a major landowner. Holy men or *startsy* were held in special regard and they taught respect for both authority and tradition. They claimed that it was a sin to oppose the tsar, who was portrayed as the 'little father' and their special protector.

The character of Tsar Nicholas II

Tsar Nicholas II was the head of the Romanov dynasty which had ruled Russia for over 300 years. He was the absolute ruler (autocrat) of Russia. The autocratic system needed a forceful and charismatic leader but Nicholas was weak. He was a family man, preferring to spend his time with his German wife, the Tsarina Alexandra, and their five children rather than dealing with matters of state. The couple's only son, Alexei, suffered from haemophilia (a rare blood disorder) and was not expected to reach adulthood.

Nicholas was deeply religious and believed that he had been chosen by God to rule. He thought that no one had the right to challenge him and that democracy would lead to the collapse of Russia. Supported in such beliefs by the tsarina, Nicholas fought to uphold the autocratic system. He knew little about the people he governed since he only ever mixed with the nobility.

OPPOSITION TO THE TSAR

Until the Revolution of 1905 opposition of any sort was banned and this made it difficult for groups who opposed the tsar to voice their opinions openly, so consequently some of them resorted to terrorist activities. By 1905, however, it is possible to identify three different opposition groups:

1 **The Liberals**
These were the most moderate of Nicholas's opponents and they consisted of men from the middle classes, who wanted to bring about peaceful political change. They wanted a democratic system in which the tsar shared power with an elected parliament, or Duma.

Their programme offered little to attract support from the peasants or workers. In 1905, following the legalisation of opposition, the Liberals split into two groups. The Constitutional Democrats, or Kadets, wanted to push for further constitutional change, while another group, the Octobrists, were more moderate and were satisfied by the promises made by Tsar Nicholas in his October Manifesto (see page 69).

2 **The Social Revolutionary Party (the SRs)**
Formed in 1901 and led by Victor Chernov, this group aimed to seize power by revolution. They wanted all the land to be taken from the wealthy landowners and given to the peasants. However, they were divided in both their aims and their methods. Some believed in the use of violent action.

3 **The Social Democratic Party (SDS)**
Formed in 1898 this group followed the teachings of Karl Marx (see information box on page 67) and aimed to use a revolution to bring about a communist system of government (see information box on page 67). However, they disagreed over how the initial revolution was to take place and in 1903 the movement split into two opposing groups, the Mensheviks and the Bolsheviks. The Mensheviks, led by Yuly Martov, believed in a mass party in which power was spread among as many members as possible. The Bolsheviks, led by Vladimir Lenin, believed that the party should be run by a small elite core of dedicated revolutionaries. They would make all the major decisions and lead the revolution.

SOURCE C

The cover of the anti-tsarist political magazine *Raven* (1906). This edition shows government ministers being blown up. Such publications were banned before 1905.

From 1903 onwards there were three important revolutionary groups operating in Russia – the Bolsheviks, the Mensheviks and the Social Revolutionaries (SRs). They all had the same aim – to destroy the tsarist system of government – but they could not agree over how this was to be achieved.

Q Questions

1 What can you learn from Source A and the text you have read about the state of Russian society at the turn of the twentieth century?

2 What was the extent of opposition to the tsar's rule by 1905?

MARXISM AND LENIN'S PLANS FOR REVOLUTION

SOURCE D Karl Marx.

Karl Marx (1818–83)

Marx was a German Jew who spent the majority of his life in exile as a result of his political beliefs. In his most famous work, *The Communist Manifesto* (1848), he outlined his theory of social change. This theory came to be known as Marxism.

Marxism

Marx saw history as being a series of struggles between those in power and those without power – between different classes in society. In 1848, Marx described Europeans as living in capitalist societies where power belonged to factory owners and merchants. They were powerful because they owned the means of production in society, such as factories and shops. In contrast, those people without power were the workers. The workers had to sell themselves as human labour to the factory owners and merchants. Marx predicted that, in all capitalist societies, the workers would eventually rise up in revolution against the factory owners and merchants and take power for themselves.

Lenin's ideas for revolution

Lenin, inspired by Marx's ideas, believed in a worker's revolution for Russia. However, Russia was largely a peasant society in 1900 and was not the capitalist society that Marx said would experience revolution. Lenin therefore adapted Marxism to suit his plans for revolution in Russia.

- Lenin said that the revolution shouldn't wait for capitalism to develop and that peasants should join the workers in revolution.
- Because the Russian revolution would meet with resistance, and would not be led by the workers, a small core of party activists would carry out the revolution. The government needed for this would be a dictatorship.

CAUSES OF THE 1905 REVOLUTION

There are both long- and short-term causes of the revolution which hit Russia during 1905. For a number of years there had been growing discontent among the peasants who had been badly hit by poor harvests in 1900 and 1902. 1902 saw the beginning of an industrial slump which caused workers to be laid off and resulted in strikes and demonstrations in many cities. Middle-class liberals were anxious for a say in the way the country was run and were pushing for reform, while some of the SRs were continuing their policy of political murders. Yet it was defeat in the war with Japan and the massacre on Bloody Sunday which were the immediate causes of major unrest.

The Russo–Japanese War, 1904–5

In 1904 Russia went to war against Japan, believing that a quick victory would help to distract people from the growing domestic tensions. The war itself was fought over the control of Manchuria and Korea in the Far East. Russia had leased Port Arthur from China in order to acquire an ice-free port for its navy.

Japan felt humiliated by this event and attacked Russian forces, capturing Port Arthur in December 1904. The Russians sent out a relief force but the fleet did not reach the area until May 1905. It was attacked and destroyed. Defeat was humiliating for Russia who was now forced to conclude a peace settlement by which Russia lost land and influence in the Far East.

The war of 1904–5 only served to make conditions worse within Russia. The war disrupted food supplies, causing shortages and prices to rise. Factories were forced to lay off workers, which in turn caused more strikes. Far from distracting attention away from the problems, the war illustrated the unpopularity of the tsar's government.

The events of Bloody Sunday

On 22 January 1905 a priest, Father Gapon, led a crowd of 200,000 workers through the streets of St Petersburg to the tsar's Winter Palace. They intended to deliver a petition to the tsar, listing their grievances, although the tsar was not in the palace at the time. As the crowd approached, the troops panicked and opened fire. Official figures record 96 deaths and 333 wounded but the actual number of deaths is probably closer to 1000. As a result the event has become known as the massacre of Bloody Sunday.

The 1905 Revolution

The events of Bloody Sunday sparked a wave of protests across Russia. Strikes and riots spread across the country and by the end of January over 400,000 workers were on strike. In some cities workers elected soviets, or councils, to take over control of affairs. In February the tsar's uncle, Grand Duke Sergei Aleksandrovich, was assassinated in Moscow, while in June the crew of the battleship *Potemkin* mutinied in protest over their terrible working conditions. During June and July 1905 peasant uprisings became widespread as they seized land and murdered their landlords. The crisis reached a peak in October when a general strike paralysed the country. On 26 October the St Petersburg Soviet was formed in order to co-ordinate the strikes. It consisted of representatives of factory workers and its chairman was Leon Trotsky. It soon established itself as the real source of power in St Petersburg and its success caused soviets to be set up in other cities.

SOURCE E Soldiers fire on the crowd marching towards the Winter Palace – a still from the film made about the event in 1925.

The October Manifesto

During the 1905 Revolution, the tsar's Chief Minister, Sergei Witte, convinced the tsar that the only way to end the crisis was to grant concessions to the Liberals and to win back their support. On 30 October, Nicholas issued the October Manifesto which introduced constitutional changes granting political rights and setting up an elected Duma, or parliament. This action regained the support of the middle classes. The tsar could now play for time and take action against the working classes.

THE TERMS OF THE OCTOBER MANIFESTO

This promised:
- an elected Duma
- all Russian men to have the vote
- all laws to be approved by the Duma
- civil rights e.g. free speech, freedom to hold meetings
- the right to form political parties
- uncensored newspapers.

In November 1905 the Tsar attempted to win back the support of the peasants by announcing an end to redemption payments. These were very unpopular payments that peasants had to make for land they had received after they had been freed from serfdom. By December most of the troops had returned to Russia after the war with Japan and this provided the tsar with the necessary power to win back control. He used force to shut down the St Petersburg Soviet and arrested its leaders. An armed uprising by the Moscow Soviet was severely put down by the army at the cost of 1000 lives. By the end of the year the tsar was back in effective control of the Russian Empire.

Some historians argue that the 1905 revolution had not been an attempt to overthrow the tsar but an attempt to register a protest at bad working and living conditions. The revolts had not been organised or planned well, and were in reality a series of unconnected outbursts of protest among peasants and industrial workers.

Q Questions

1. How did the Russo–Japanese War contribute to the 1905 Revolution?
2. Describe the events of Bloody Sunday.
3. To what extent did the October Manifesto change the political situation in Russia?

STOLYPIN AND HIS POLICIES

The tsar quickly regretted granting the October Manifesto and in July 1906 he dismissed Witte as his Chief Minister. In his place he appointed Peter Stolypin, a hardline politician who believed in strict government. He promised he would establish a policy of 'repression and reform'.

Limiting the power of the Duma

Elections for Russia's first Duma were held in March 1906. The result was a left-wing majority which was critical of the tsar's regime. In May, the tsar responded by passing the Fundamental Laws which restored his autocratic powers. Consequently when the Duma demanded a greater say in government, the tsar sent in troops to dissolve it. Russia's first Duma had lasted just 75 days.

Elections for a second Duma were held in 1907 and the result was an even greater swing to the left, with the SRs and the Social Democrats securing their first seats. This Duma ran for just three months before it was dissolved. Prior to the third Duma, which met later in 1907, the tsar changed the voting system. The richest 1 per cent of Russians would elect two-thirds of the representatives. In practice this meant that the Duma would be made up of conservative politicians who generally supported the tsar. This Duma ran for its full five years. The fourth Duma elected in 1912 also met with the tsar's wishes.

SOURCE F A Russian cartoon of 1906 which shows a gagged member of the Duma, flanked by two officials of the tsar.

Stolypin's policy of repression

To reduce the threat of further unrest and clamp down on the acts of terrorism started by the SRs in 1906, Stolypin began a policy of severe repression. Special courts called Field Courts for Civilians were set up to provide rapid justice for those 'obviously guilty'. During 1906, 1008 people were arrested, tried and executed for their part in the revolution, while 21,000 were sent to special prison camps in Siberia. Between 1907 and 1911 a further 1800 were hanged, causing the hangman's noose to be nicknamed 'Stolypin's necktie'.

Stolypin's policies of reform

Stolypin introduced a series of agricultural reforms which he hoped would secure the loyalty of the peasants and lead to stability in the countryside. The tsar had already scrapped redemption payments and in 1906 and 1907 measures were introduced to allow peasants to buy land from the *mir*. The *mir* operated a system of strip farming where each family was given a share of the best and worst strips. The system was restrictive as each farmer had to grow the same crop, the strips were too small to encourage the use of modern machinery, and the strips given to each farmer were often spread over a wide area. If farmers were able to purchase several neighbouring strips then they could create a small farm and, in this way, create a new class of farmers known as kulaks.

A Peasants' Bank was created to help peasants become kulaks but only about 15 per cent of peasant farmers took this up, as the majority were too poor to do so. Ultimately, Russia's entry into the First World War in 1914 stopped these developments.

PETER STOLYPIN (1862-1911)

SOURCE G

Peter Stolypin.

Stolypin was the dominant politician in Russia following the 1905 revolution. Clever, determined and efficient, he was made Minister of the Interior in May 1906 and two months later was promoted to Chief Minister. In an effort to make Russia more secure and prosperous he followed a dual policy of repression and reform. He had terrorists rounded up and executed. At the same time he introduced a policy of reform (see pages 70–1). His policies and methods led to him being assassinated in September 1911.

Stolypin believed that a prosperous Russia was the best way to reduce support for radical opposition groups. Measures were introduced to improve education and to provide a social insurance scheme. Conditions in the armed services were improved in an effort to prevent future mutinies, and a naval building programme was started with the aim of making Russia the third largest naval power by 1931. On the industrial front encouragement was given towards the building of new and larger factories.

Stolypin had laid the foundations for growth but his assassination in 1911 ended attempts at reform as his successors were less committed to it.

THE IMPACT OF ECONOMIC CHANGE

Between 1906 and 1914 Russia experienced an industrial boom and production rose by over 100 per cent. New factories were built and the cities swelled with the migration of peasant farmers in search of work. However, while the factory owners made healthy profits little was done to improve the living and working conditions of the workers. Conditions were terrible and the number of strikes rose sharply in the period 1910–14 to over 8000. The situation was thus already very tense when the decision was taken for Russia to enter the First World War.

Questions

1. Describe the work of the Field Courts for Civilians.
2. Use the information in Source F and your own knowledge to explain how the power of the Duma was restricted by the tsar.
3. Explain how Stolypin attempted to win back the loyalty of the Russian peasants to the tsarist regime.

3 EXAM PRACTICE

These questions test Section B of the examination paper.

RUSSIA UNDER THE TSAR, 1905–14

Study the information below and then answer the questions which follow.

INFORMATION

In 1905 the tsar stood at the head of Russia, helped by the nobles. Beneath were the mass of Russian workers and peasants.

EQ Exam Questions

1	**a** Describe the lifestyle of a Russian noble.	[2]
	b Explain why revolution broke out in Russia in 1905.	[4]
	c How successful was the revolution of 1905? Explain your answer fully.	[5]
2	**a** Describe the work of the Okhrana.	[3]
	b Explain why strikes by industrial workers were common during this period.	[4]
3	Had life improved for Russian peasants by 1914? Explain your answer fully.	[7]

What factors led to the Bolshevik seizure of power in October 1917?

RUSSIA'S INVOLVEMENT IN THE FIRST WORLD WAR

The opening stages

On 1 August 1914 Russia went to war against Austria–Hungary and Germany. News of the declaration of war was received with enthusiasm and resulted in patriotic demonstrations across the Russian Empire. Only the Bolsheviks showed open opposition to what they called an 'imperialist war'. Hatred of things German became commonplace and so the tsar renamed the capital Petrograd instead of St Petersburg, which he considered too German.

This initial enthusiasm for war soon ended following two military defeats at the battles of Tannenberg and the Masurian Lakes in the autumn of 1914. Over 250,000 Russian troops were killed, wounded or taken prisoner. The Russian forces, while outnumbering the enemy, were badly led and had insufficient weapons. Nearly a million soldiers were without rifles and many had no boots. The Germans advanced 300 miles (480 km) into Russia during 1915, and while a major counter-attack was launched under General Brusilov in 1916, it achieved little and over 1 million Russians died in the campaign.

The war had a big impact upon conditions within Russia. Fifteen million men were drafted into the army which meant that there were not enough men left to run the factories or work the land. In 1915 up to 600 factories had to close.

The transport system was also unable to meet the demands made upon it. Russia had too few trains to keep the army and towns supplied with food and materials. As food supplies in the towns dried up so prices rose, but wages did not keep up. To pay for the war effort the government printed more and more money, which caused the rouble to lose its value and resulted in a 400 per cent rise in inflation between 1914 and 1917. As conditions grew worse, strikes and demonstrations became common in Moscow and Petrograd.

The Tsar takes charge

In August 1915 the Tsar took personal command of the Russian army. This was to be a fatal mistake as he was a weak and incompetent commander.

SOURCE A Russian peasants queue for bread in Petrograd, 1917.

He would now have to take the blame for Russia's military failures. The tsar left Petrograd for the front, leaving Tsarina Alexandra in charge of the government. This was also a grave error since she relied too heavily on Rasputin (see Source B) and her German nationality caused people to mistrust her. The work of the government was interrupted by a frequent change of ministers under the tsarina, which made it difficult to co-ordinate policy. This lack of leadership and direction only added to Russia's problems.

SOURCE B

Deary, I heard that that horrid Rodzianko [leader of the Duma] wants the Duma to be called together – oh please don't, it's not their business, they want to discuss things not concerning them and bring more discontent – they must be kept away ... Listen to our friend [Rasputin] ... it is not for nothing God sent him to us ... we must pay attention to what he says.

Part of a letter written in 1916 by the tsarina to Nicholas which highlights the mounting political tension in Petrograd.

The influence of Rasputin

The tsarina's heavy reliance upon Rasputin, particularly in the selection of ministers, gave rise to rumours of 'dark forces destroying the throne' from within. There were rumours that the pair were German agents seeking to undermine the war effort. After the murder of Prime Minister Stolypin in 1911, Rasputin's influence over the royal family increased. Both the tsar and tsarina, grateful of Rasputin's control for their son's haemophilia, refused to listen to the stories of his wild lifestyle. Such stories only served to weaken the reputation of both the tsar and tsarina, and their reliance upon Rasputin shocked the nobles. In December 1916 a small group, led by Prince Yusupov, assassinated Rasputin.

Q Questions

1. Explain how the war affected living conditions within Russia.
2. How useful is Source B to an historian studying the growing political problems within Russia during 1916–17? Explain your answer using the source and your own knowledge.

i RASPUTIN (1871–1916)

SOURCE C Rasputin.

The son of a Siberian peasant, the ambitious and charismatic Gregori Efimovich became a holy man or *staretz*. His wild behaviour, which involved heavy drinking and numerous affairs, earned him the nickname 'Rasputin', meaning 'immoral' or 'disreputable one'. From 1905 onwards he gained influence in the tsar's court due to his capacity to control the haemophilia which afflicted the Tsarevich Alexei. It is thought he did this through hypnosis. The tsarina became heavily reliant upon him after 1915 and nobles increasingly came to obtain posts in government because they knew how to please Rasputin. In December 1916 a group of nobles killed him.

THE EVENTS OF FEBRUARY TO OCTOBER 1917

The February Revolution

By February 1917 Russia was in chaos. Food and fuel shortages, together with severe temperatures of 35°c below freezing, led to growing discontent, especially in the cities. Strikes became common as workers demanded higher wages and better conditions. On 23 February, International Women's Day, a group of women marched through the streets of Petrograd to protest about the queues for food. They were soon joined by over 90,000 strikers and protestors, and over the following days the crisis deepened. By the 26 February over 250,000 workers were on strike. The President of the Duma, Michael Rodzianko, sent a telegram to the tsar informing him of the increasingly tense situation in Petrograd (see Source D). The tsar dismissed his comments and issued orders for the army to clear the protestors from the streets.

On 27 February soldiers in Petrograd mutinied and refused to fire on the protestors. This signalled a turning point for, up to this time, the army had remained loyal to the tsar. Instead the soldiers joined the protestors and marched to the Duma to demand that it take control of the government. The police took no action.

SOURCE D

The situation is serious. The capital is in a state of anarchy. The government is paralysed; the transport system is broken down; the food and fuel supplies are completely disorganised. Discontent is general and on the increase. There is wild shooting on the streets; troops are firing at each other. It is urgent that someone enjoying the confidence of the country be entrusted with the formation of a new government.

A telegram sent by the President of the Duma, Michael Rodzianko, to the tsar on 27 February 1917.

The Provisional Government and the soviets

On 27 February, in response to the demonstrations and against the wishes of the tsar, 12 members of the Duma met to form a committee to take over the government. They called themselves the Provisional Government, intending to rule until proper elections could be held for a new Duma. At the same time representatives of the workers and strikers met and re-formed the Petrograd Soviet which had first appeared in 1905.

i THE RUSSIAN CALENDAR

In this period, Russia followed the Julian calendar which was 13 days behind the Gregorian (modern) calendar used by the rest of Europe. The revolution which took place in Russia between 23 and 27 February, according to the Julian calendar, is referred to as the March Revolution if the Gregorian calendar is used. Likewise the Revolution which took place on the 24–25 October, according to the Julian calendar, occurred on the 6–7 November if using the modern calendar. The Bolsheviks adopted the Gregorian calendar in February 1918. This book uses the dates from the Julian calendar.

SOURCE E Demonstrators gather outside the Winter Palace in Petrograd, February 1917.

Similar soviets began to appear in cities across Russia over the coming weeks.

On receiving news of the revolution, the tsar attempted to get back to Petrograd. However, soldiers stopped the train he was travelling on. Realising that he had no supporters the tsar signed a decree of abdication. As Alexei was too ill to rule, the throne passed to his brother Grand Duke Michael, but he too abdicated 24 hours later. In this way, the Romanov dynasty that had ruled Russia for 304 years was brought to an end.

SOURCE F

The First World War played a crucial part in the fall of the Tsar. Russia's defeats, and the enormous loss of life among her soldiers, were blamed on the Tsar, who had made himself Commander-in-Chief in 1915. The Tsar lost the confidence and the support of the army. The middle classes were disgusted by the defeats and by the incompetence of the Tsarina. The behaviour and influence of Rasputin made things worse. The workers were tired of the shortages and angry at the enormous price rises that threatened them with starvation. With few supporters left, the Tsar was easily overthrown. In March 1917, the bread rioters in Petrograd were joined by strikers. Many soldiers joined the rioters while the police refused to intervene. The Tsar was forced to abdicate.

A modern historian, Philip Ingram, explains why the tsar fell from power.

Dual Power

The Provisional Government, headed by Prince Lvov, a liberal, did not intend to change everything but did introduce a number of popular measures:

- Political prisoners were released.
- Revolutionary exiles were allowed to return to Russia.
- Free speech was announced and newspapers were allowed to print what they liked.
- An 8-hour day was introduced for industrial workers.
- The tsar's secret police, the Okhrana, was abolished.
- Equality for all was announced, irrespective of religion, class or nationality.
- The new Russian parliament was to be elected by all.

In reality, however, it was the Petrograd Soviet, not the Provisional Government, which controlled Petrograd. Consisting of 3000 elected members, the Soviet was the real power base and the Provisional Government could not rule without its support. Alexander Kerensky, a Social Revolutionary (SR), was a member of both and so acted as a bridge between them.

One of the first actions of the Petrograd Soviet was to issue Order Number One, which gave it control over the Russian armed forces. It also announced that it would accept the rulings of the Provisional Government but only if it thought they were appropriate. This power sharing became known as the Dual Government, or Dual Power. To begin with both bodies were able to work together. However, the increasing influence of the Bolsheviks within the Soviet pushed them apart since the Bolsheviks opposed the decision to continue with the war.

Two pressing issues faced the new regime, the most urgent concerned Russia's involvement in the First World War. The Provisional Government wanted to support the Allies and continue to fight. There was also the fear of being defeated and humiliated by the Germans and, should they decide to withdraw, having a harsh settlement imposed on them. With the backing of the Soviet the decision was taken to continue the war. In June 1917 Russia launched a major offensive but the advance failed and over 60,000 Russian troops were killed. This was a key failure for Russia. The war continued to go badly for Russia and soldiers began to desert in ever-increasing numbers. Continuing food and fuel shortages meant many Russians desperately wanted the war to end.

The other major issue concerned ownership of the land. The peasants wanted to own their own land, taking it from the nobles and the Church. The Provisional Government was reluctant to grant this, believing that it should be left for a newly-elected government to decide such an important issue. However, many peasants ignored this and began to take land illegally.

i ALEXANDER KERENSKY (1881–1970)

SOURCE G Kerensky.

Kerensky became involved in revolutionary activities as a young man and attached himself to the Social Revolutionaries. In 1912 he was elected to the Duma. Under the Provisional Government he was made Minister of Justice but was also elected a member of the Petrograd Soviet. He became increasingly influential as 1917 progressed, becoming Minister of War and then prime minister in July. Kerensky's support for the continuation of the war and Russia's worsening economic situation helped bring about his overthrow by the Bolsheviks in October 1917. He fled to France in 1918 and finally the USA in 1940.

To make sure they got their share many thousands of soldiers deserted which only added to the problems at the front.

The return of Lenin and the 'July Days'

In April 1917 Lenin returned to Russia from exile in Switzerland. On his arrival in Petrograd Lenin delivered a major speech to the Bolsheviks, the main points of which became known as the April Theses.

- The Bolsheviks should not give their support to the Provisional Government.
- There must be an end to the war.
- All land must be given over to the peasants.
- All banks must be nationalised.
- The soviets should work together to form a new government and push out the Provisional Government.

Lenin was telling the Bolsheviks to prepare for a second revolution, an idea which came as a great shock to many since they did not think the time was yet right to launch a coup. However, Lenin's appeals for 'Peace, Bread and Land' and 'All power to the soviets' proved popular slogans with the Russian people.

The failure of the June military offensive provoked the 'July Days'. Many deserting soldiers and the Kronstadt sailors went to Petrograd where they joined up with the Bolsheviks to demand an end to the Provisional Government. Over 100,000 soldiers, sailors and Bolsheviks roamed the streets of Petrograd and after three days of rioting Kerensky, then Minister of War, sent in troops to break up the demonstrators. Over 400 were either killed or wounded and Lenin was forced to flee into exile in Finland. He stayed there for the next three months. Kerensky replaced Prince Lvov as prime minister.

The Kornilov Plot, September 1917

In September the Commander-in-Chief of the army, General Kornilov, attempted to overthrow the Provisional Government. He wanted to continue the war with Germany without government interference. Prime Minister Kerensky had no army with which to defend Petrograd and so was forced to arm the Bolsheviks. Trotsky, the temporary leader of the Bolsheviks in Lenin's absence, took charge of organising this new force, which became known as the Red Guards.

SOURCE H The July Days: troops loyal to the Provisional Government fire on anti-government protestors in 1917.

Desertions and a strike by railwaymen weakened Kornilov's army and his troops were prevented from entering Petrograd. In this way the Bolsheviks stopped Kornilov and saved the Provisional Government, but the Red Guards refused to hand back their guns. Then, in the elections for the Petrograd Soviet later that September, the Bolsheviks secured a majority and increased their representation in the Moscow Soviet and in the soviets in other cities. By October 1917 the Bolsheviks were a strong political force in Russia.

Q Questions

1. Describe the events of the February Revolution.
2. Use the information in Source F and your own knowledge to explain why the tsar fell from power in February 1917.
3. What did the Bolsheviks achieve during the 'July Days' of 1917?
4. Why did General Kornilov attempt to overthrow the Provisional Government in September 1917?
5. Why did the Kornilov Plot fail?

THE BOLSHEVIK SEIZURE OF POWER

Although relatively small in 1917, the Bolshevik Party was well organised and effectively led. The party used propaganda to win support and published their own newspaper *Pravda* (meaning 'truth') to attack the government. The Bolsheviks were also the only party to offer the majority of the Russian population what they wanted, promising to end the war and bring peace, an end to the shortages, food for all and to start a programme of land reform. The Bolsheviks also had a disciplined armed force, the Red Guards, to help back up their demands for change.

The storming of the Winter Palace

During the autumn violence in the countryside grew more intense as peasants tried to grab land. Kerensky responded by sending out 'punishment expeditions' but he had problems in finding enough loyal troops. Lenin returned from Finland in disguise to avoid arrest and attended a meeting of the Central Committee of the Bolshevik Party where he convinced them that the time was ripe to carry out a revolution.

Trotsky was made head of the Military Revolutionary Committee and drew up the plans of attack. On the night of 24–25 October 1917 Red Guards took control of key points in Petrograd, such as the railway station and telephone exchange. A cruiser, the *Aurora*, was sent up the River Neva and fired blank shells at the Winter Palace where the Provisional Government was meeting. Red Guards and revolutionary soldiers stormed the building which was defended by some military cadets and the Women's Battalion. They arrested members of the government as they sat around the cabinet table. There was no resistance and it resulted in a bloodless coup. Kerensky managed to escape.

The next day Lenin announced the creation of a new Bolshevik government but it took several days to win control over soviets in other cities. The other political parties were either too disorganised or were reluctant to act, and only Lenin appeared to offer decisive leadership.

Lenin's contribution to the October Revolution

Lenin's role in the events of February to October 1917 has been a subject of debate among historians. Soviet writers have portrayed him as the central figure who pushed for, directed and secured a Bolshevik victory. Non-Soviet writers, while not denying Lenin's important role, have tended to emphasise the importance of factors such as the unpopularity of the Provisional Government and its decision to continue with the war, and the importance of Trotsky and other Bolshevik leaders in running the party during Lenin's exile.

SOURCE I

In the actual organisation of the final stages of the Bolshevik Revolution, Lenin's role fell far short of Trotsky's ... Yet there is no doubt that without Lenin the Bolshevik coup would have been postponed and might have failed.

Taken from Leonard Schapiro, *The Russian Revolutions* (1984).

SOURCE K

Hardly off the train, Lenin asked the party comrades, 'Why didn't you seize power?' And at once he comes out with his April Theses ... He is called mad and delirious ... But suddenly it becomes apparent that he has the ear of the man in the street ... His whole genius consists in his ability to say what these people want to say, but do not know how to say.

The view of V. Serge, a Bolshevik supporter in 1917.

Without Lenin the Bolsheviks would not have pushed for a revolution for several years, believing that the time was not yet right. Lenin disagreed and argued strongly for action in his April Theses (see page 78) and again in October 1917. Whilst in exile he had written to the Bolshevik Central Committee urging them to 'take state power into their hands' but his proposal had been defeated. Following his return to Petrograd he persuaded the Committee to agree to his plans for a *coup d'état*. Only Zinoviev and Kamenev opposed his plans.

i VLADIMIR ILYICH ULYANOV – LENIN (1870–1924)

SOURCE J Lenin.

After leaving university, Vladimir Ulyanov (who later changed his name to Lenin) trained to become a lawyer. In 1887 his brother was executed for attempting to assassinate Tsar Alexander III. In 1894 Lenin formed a Marxist group and his activities led to his arrest and exile in Siberia between 1895 and 1900, during which time he married Nadezhda Krupskaya, a fellow revolutionary. Upon their release the couple travelled to London where Lenin wrote *What is to be Done?* in which he argued that a small core of party activitists should carry out the revolution, not the masses. This idea split the Social Democrats and resulted in the formation of the Bolsheviks in 1903. Lenin remained in exile organising the Bolshevik Party until the revolutions of 1917. From the overthrow of the Provisional Government in October 1917 until his death in 1924 he controlled Russia.

If Lenin had not forced the issue it is unlikely the Bolsheviks would have staged an armed uprising.

Lenin also provided intellectual leadership for the party as well as drive and determination. He published dozens of books and articles, adapting the theories of Marx to fit the Russian situation, resulting in the creation of Marxist–Leninism. He founded *Pravda*, the Bolshevik Party newspaper, to help spread the party message. He was a gifted public speaker and possessed the ability to tell people what they wanted to hear. Yet Lenin had to rely upon the co-operation of other members of the Bolshevik Party to put his ideas into practice. Central to this was Trotsky who, as president of the Petrograd Soviet and commander of the Red Guards, directed the troops who undertook the Bolshevik seizure of power in October 1917.

Q Questions

1 Describe the events surrounding the storming of the Winter Palace in October 1917.

2 How important was Trotsky in the success of the Bolshevik seizure of power? Explain your answer.

3 What was Lenin's contribution to the Bolshevik seizure of power?

3 EXAM PRACTICE

These questions test Section A of the examination paper.

THE REVOLUTIONS OF 1917

Study Sources A–D and then answer the questions which follow.

SOURCE A

A cartoon showing Rasputin with Tsar Nicholas and Tsarina Alexandra.

SOURCE B

Before the war we thought of our Tsar as a God on Earth. I remember that when he visited the Kursk region in 1913 we all went to see him. My mother said, 'That's him, there. Our Little Father. If there was no Tsar, there would be no Russia'. All that changed by 1917. We thought that the Tsar didn't care. He didn't care that our food was stolen from us. Some men came to the town and they called him 'the executioner with a crown'. I don't think we believed this but no one would even have dared to say it before 1917.

Natalya Fyodorovna speaking in 1964.

SOURCE C

I honestly believe that there was a movement before 1917 towards revolution which nothing could have broken or stopped. It was this movement which brought Lenin to power. The reason why the Bolsheviks came to power is, I believe, because at that moment they had the people behind them. It was the people, not Lenin, who made the Revolution.

Joseph Berger, a Comintern staff worker imprisoned under Stalin, writing in Italy in 1973.

SOURCE D

The Bolshevik Party was waging a determined struggle to win over the masses. The struggle was headed by Lenin, who led and guided the Party's Central Committee. He frequently addressed mass rallies and meetings. Lenin's speeches, noted for their intelligent content and brilliant delivery, inspired workers and soldiers. The Bolshevik Party's membership began to grow rapidly.

A view of the role of Lenin by a communist writer under communist rule (1981).

EQ Exam Questions

1 What information does Source A give about Rasputin's role in Russia? [3]

2 Use the information in Source B and your own knowledge to explain how attitudes towards the Tsar had changed by 1917. [4]

3 How useful is Source C to an historian studying the events leading to the Bolshevik seizure of power? Explain your answer using the source and your own knowledge. [5]

4 In Source D the author is suggesting that the Bolshevik Party would not have come to power without the leadership and direction of Lenin. Is this a valid interpretation?
In your answer you should use your own knowledge of the topic, refer to the other relevant sources in this question, and consider how the author came to his interpretation. [8]

Why were the Bolsheviks victorious in the Civil War and how did they establish a communist state in Russia?

IMMEDIATE PROBLEMS FACING LENIN FOLLOWING THE SEIZURE OF POWER

Having achieved power in Petrograd Lenin now faced the problem of spreading Bolshevik influence over the rest of the Russian Empire.

The Constituent Assembly

To manage the running of the state Lenin set up a temporary Council of People's Commissars known as the Sovnarkom. It was a group of 25 members made up of Mensheviks, Social Revolutionaries and 14 Bolsheviks. Lenin was the Chairman, Trotsky was Commissar for War and Stalin Commissar for Nationalities. The Provisional Government had arranged for elections to be held in November 1917 for a new parliament, the Constituent Assembly. In order to maintain political support Lenin allowed the elections to take place but the result was not what the Bolshevik Party wanted. The largest percentage of votes went to the Social Revolutionaries. When the Assembly met for the first time in early January 1918 Lenin sent in troops to dissolve it after just one day.

In reality the main source of power lay with the Sovnarkom and during November and December 1917 it passed a series of decrees (laws) which laid the foundations of the new Russia:

- Peace talks were opened with Germany and Austria–Hungary to end the war.

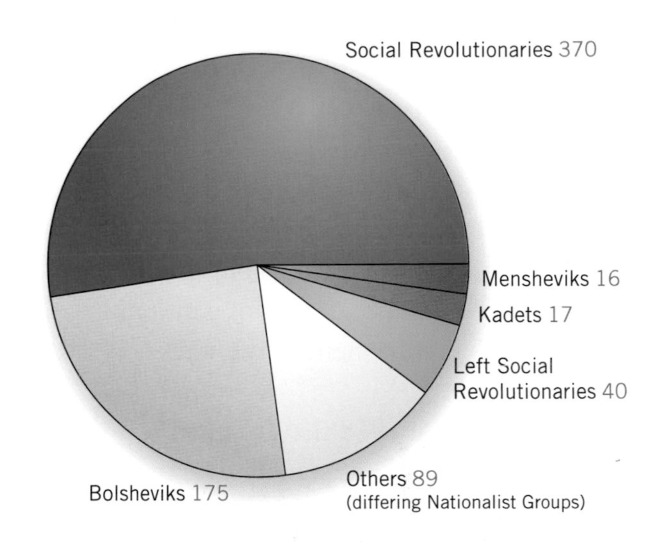

1917 election results for the Constituent Assembly (showing number of seats)

- Land which had belonged to the tsar, the Church and the nobility was re-distributed.
- All titles were abolished and replaced by 'citizen' and 'comrade'.
- Factory workers were to work a maximum 8-hour day and a 48-hour week.
- All non-Bolshevik newspapers were to close down.
- A secret police force, the Cheka, was set up.
- Marriage laws were relaxed to allow couples to have non-religious weddings and to make it easier to obtain a divorce.

In early 1918 Lenin renamed the Bolshevik Party the Communist Party and declared all political parties other than the Communist Party to be illegal. In doing so he helped to create a one-party state.

The Treaty of Brest–Litovsk, 1918

In order to stabilise conditions within Russia, to gain power and to avoid the mistakes of Kerensky, Lenin needed to withdraw his country from the First World War. In December 1917 representatives of the German, Austrian and Russian governments met at Brest-Litovsk to discuss peace terms and it soon became clear that Russia was going to have to pay a heavy price for peace. Trotsky was appalled by some of the demands but the Bolsheviks feared the consequences of continuing Russia's involvement in the war.

On 3 March 1918 the Treaty of Brest–Litovsk was signed. The terms demanded huge concessions:

- Russia lost 27 per cent of its farmland which included Finland, Estonia, Latvia, Lithuania, Poland, Georgia and the western Ukraine.
- Russia lost 26 per cent of its population (62 million people).
- Russia lost its most valuable industrial land which amounted to 74 per cent of its iron ore and coal.
- Russia lost 26 per cent of its railways.
- Russia had to pay a huge fine of 3 billion roubles as compensation to Germany and Austria–Hungary, which further damaged its economy.

SOURCE A

Our impulse is to refuse to sign this robber peace. Russia can offer no resistance because she is materially exhausted by three years of war. Wars are won today, not by enthusiasm alone, but by technical skill, railways and abundant supplies. Russia must sign the peace to obtain breathing space to recuperate for the struggle.

Lenin explains to fellow Bolsheviks in March 1918 why Russia had to conclude a peace.

Q Questions

1. Describe the role of the Sovnarkom.
2. Why do you think Lenin felt it necessary to dissolve the Constituent Assembly so soon after its election?
3. Explain why the Treaty of Brest–Litovsk was unpopular with many Russians.

THE RUSSIAN CIVIL WAR, 1918–20

Opposition to the Bolsheviks

As the communist dictatorship emerged, its enemies began to to organise resistance. During the summer of 1918 civil war broke out in Russia between the Reds (the Bolsheviks) and the Whites (those who opposed the Bolsheviks). The opposition was called the Whites because white was the traditional colour of the tsar but not all Whites were supporters of the tsar. The White armies included monarchists, those who wanted to see the return of the tsar as ruler, as well as Kerenskyists (which included the SRs and the Kadets) who wanted to see the return of the Constituent Assembly and parliamentary democracy. Landowners supported the Whites because they were angry that the peasants had seized their land, while foreign countries gave their support because they did not want to see Russia leave the First World War. They were also angry that the Bolsheviks were refusing to pay the tsar's debts to foreign countries, and they feared the spread of communism into neighbouring states.

Further support for the Whites came from a force of Czech soldiers who had fought on the Russian side against Austria during the First World War in the hope that if Austria–Hungary was defeated then a new state of Czechoslovakia would be created.

The strengths and weaknesses of the opposing forces

The Reds had a geographical advantage as they occupied the heart of the country and had control of the important cities of Petrograd and Moscow, the new capital. They also had control of the key industrial areas and a good railway network which enabled them to move their troops and supplies quickly. By the end of 1918 the Bolsheviks were threatened by invading White armies yet despite being outnumbered both in terms of men and equipment they had defeated their enemies by the end of 1920.

The Whites were not organised into a single fighting force but instead operated as a number of independent armies. They had little in common apart from a hatred of the Bolsheviks and did not co-ordinate their campaigns. Geographically their armies were spread over a wide area which made it difficult for them to keep their forces supplied and also to keep in contact with one another. This meant that the Red Army was able to pick off the White forces one at a time.

The White army was commanded by former generals of the tsar who included Deniken, Yudenich, Wrangel and Admiral Kolchak. They were helped with troops and supplies from over a dozen foreign countries, primarily Britain, the USA, France and Japan. In the spring of 1919 White forces under Admiral Kolchak invaded eastern Russia and advanced as far as Kazan, while British, French and US forces penetrated from the north, capturing Murmansk and Archangel. In the east the Japanese captured Vladivostok and held the port until November 1922.

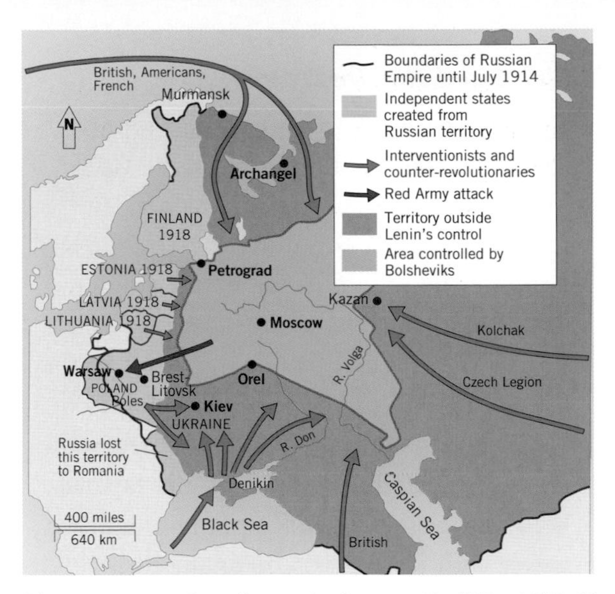

The main areas of conflict in the Russian Civil War, 1918–20.

SOURCE B

England, the USA and France are waging war against Russia. They are avenging themselves on the Soviet Union for having overthrown the landowners and capitalists ... and they are aiding and abetting the Russian landowners with money and military supplies.

A speech made by Lenin in 1919 attacking foreign intervention in the Russian Civil War.

During the late spring of 1919 General Deniken together with French support advanced with a White army from the Ukraine to within 200 miles (320 km) of Moscow. A counter-attack organised by Trotsky drove back Deniken's forces. In the Baltic region in the early summer of 1919 General Yudenich attacked, coming within 30 miles (48 km) of Petrograd, but he too was defeated. In June 1920, a White army led by General Wrangel attacked further south hoping to link up with an invading Polish army but had to withdraw his forces. The Bolsheviks also had to fight the armies of Latvia, Lithuania, Estonia and Finland, all of whom had been defeated by the end of 1920.

Poland and the Treaty of Riga

In 1920 the Poles, with French support, took advantage of the chaos of the Civil War to launch a surprise attack and captured Kiev. A counter-attack by the Red Army pushed them back but they then suffered a heavy defeat in the Battle of Warsaw in August. Under the terms of the Treaty of Riga signed in 1921 Russia was forced to sign away 130,000 kilometres of territory to Poland. Although the Japanese held out until 1922, the signing of a peace treaty with Poland is seen as the formal end of the Civil War.

The role of Trotsky and the Red Army

With the threat of Civil War the Bolsheviks knew that they needed an efficient, well-disciplined force to defeat the Whites. In March 1918 Trotsky was made Chairman of the Supreme War Council and he set about reorganising the Red Army. Conscription was introduced for all men aged 18 to 40. The ill-discipline which had characterised the old Russian army was stamped out and replaced with harsh regimented order. To make sure troops remained loyal, capital punishment was re-introduced for offences such as desertion or disloyalty. As many soldiers were new and inexperienced, Trotsky employed the best officers of the tsar's former army, and to ensure their loyalty their family members were sometimes taken hostage. Yet Trotsky was also prepared to promote new talent from outside the nobility and men like Zhukov emerged to become some of the Red Army's best generals.

Trotsky proved to be a brilliant leader and soon won the respect of his troops. He quickly realised the importance of the railways and saw trains as the modern cavalry. His visits to the front and his rallying speeches improved the morale of the Red Army. He turned it into an effective and united fighting force, quite unlike the White armies which suffered from low morale and mass desertions.

i LEON TROTSKY (1879-1940)

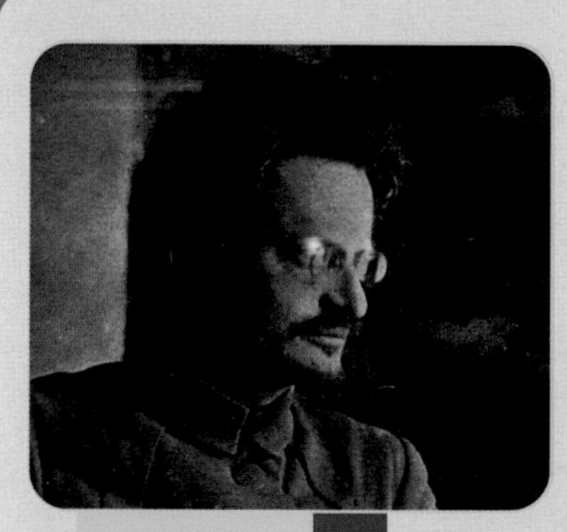

SOURCE C

Leon Trotsky.

Born in 1879, Lev Davidovitch Bronstein later changed his name to Leon Trotsky. He was educated at Odessa University where he became interested in the writings of Marx. Because he opposed tsarist rule he was forced to spend long periods in exile. Unlike Lenin and Stalin, Trotsky was at first a Menshevik and did not join the Bolsheviks until 1917. He played a leading part in the Bolshevik seizure of power in October 1917 and took charge of organising the Red Army during the Civil War of 1918–20.

In the struggle for power following Lenin's death in 1924 Stalin defeated Trotsky and Trotsky went into exile in 1929. He believed in permanent revolution (the idea that communism could survive only if it also spread to other countries) and he became increasingly critical of the Soviet regime. He was assassinated by Stalin's agents in Mexico in 1940, who used an ice pick to smash his head.

SOURCE D Trotsky gives encouragement to soldiers of the newly-formed Red Army in 1918.

Q Questions

1 Explain why Civil War broke out in Russia in 1918.

2 Use the information in Source B and your own knowledge to explain why foreign countries became involved in the Civil War.

3 How important was Trotsky in helping to ensure the success of the Red Army in the Civil War?

WAR COMMUNISM

To win the Civil War Lenin needed to keep the Red Army supplied with food and weapons, so he started the policy of War Communism. The state took over all aspects of the economy, nationalising major industry and controlling the production and distribution of all goods. War communism operated from 1918 to 1921. Normal economic life came to an end as the army's needs became the priority.

The situation in the towns

In June 1918 the Decree of Nationalisation brought all major industry under central government control. Factories were nationalised and a new body, the Vesenkha (the Supreme Council of National Economy) was set up to decide what each industry should produce. Lenin sent in his own managers to operate factories. Strict discipline was imposed on workers, trade unions were banned and the death penalty was introduced for strikers. The biggest problem was the shortage of labour and so people were prevented from leaving the cities. Prices rose and this inflation made the rouble lose its value. The rouble in 1920 was worth only 1 per cent of its 1917 value. Money ceased to be used and bartering became the norm. War Communism tightened the government's grip on industry but it did not lead to economic growth.

The situation in the countryside

War Communism forced peasants to produce more food but until the government was willing to pay what the peasants considered to be a fair price for grain there was little incentive for them to work harder. The government condemned the peasants' refusal to co-operate and Lenin ordered requisition squads headed by the Cheka to seize surplus food. Those found hoarding supplies were punished severely and between 1918 and 1921 requisition squads terrorised the countryside. The kulaks were particularly badly treated. Peasants did not want to hand over surplus crops so grew less – just enough to feed their families. The grain harvests of 1920 and 1921 produced half of that of 1913 and the result was famine on a massive scale.

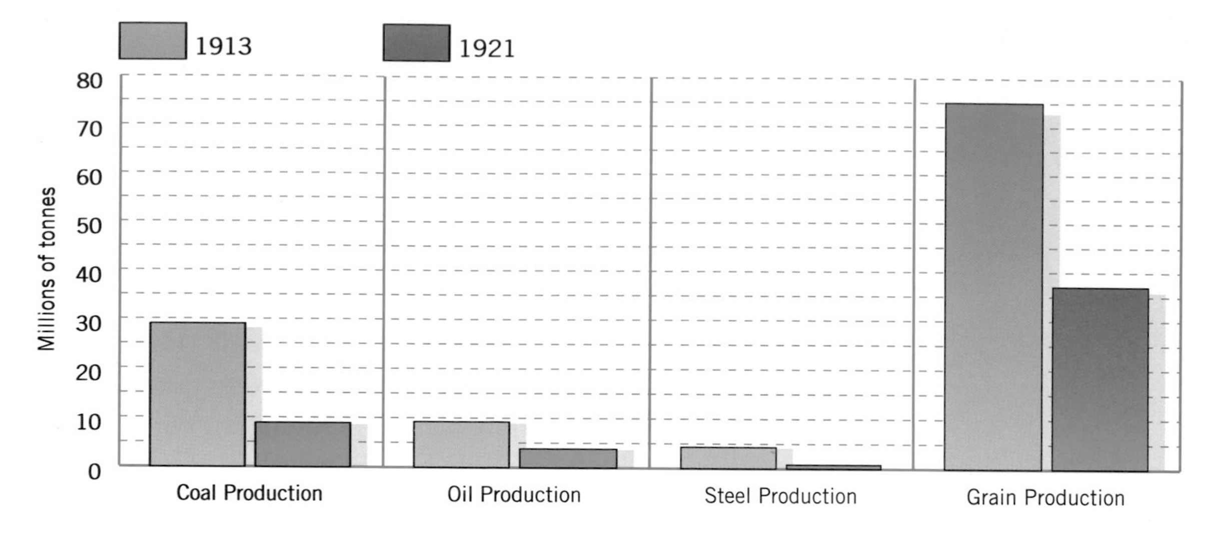

Production figures for 1913 and 1921.

The Cheka and the Red Terror

In December 1917 Lenin created the Extraordinary Commission for the Struggle Against Counter-Revolution, Sabotage and Speculation – the Bolshevik **secret police, better known as the Cheka.** It was headed by Felix Dzerzhinsky. It **arrested, tortured** and executed anyone who appeared disloyal to the Bolsheviks.

In August 1918 a Social Revolutionary called Fanya Kaplan shot Lenin three times at close range. The bullets entered his neck and lung but he survived. That same month the chairman of the Petrograd Cheka was assassinated. These events caused the Cheka to step up their terror campaign, the result being the Red Terror. Hundreds of Bolshevik opponents were executed.

Following their capture by the Reds the royal family had been held captive in Tobolsk in Siberia, but in April 1918 they were moved to Ekaterinburg in the Ural mountains. The tsar's continued existence posed a threat to the Bolsheviks since he was the focus of White plans to put him back in power. During July 1918 Kolchak's White Army was advancing towards Ekaterinburg and the Reds worried that the tsar might fall into White hands. On the night of 16–17 July 1918 the tsar, the tsarina, their children, together with some of their servants, were herded into the cellar of Ipatiev House and shot by Red soldiers (see Source E). Their bodies were cut up, and acid was poured over them to make the corpses unrecognisable before they were buried. They remained undiscovered until 1991 when DNA tests proved that bones found near Ekaterinburg were the remains of the Romanovs.

During the latter part of 1918 the Cheka became more and more brutal. Any person showing any sign of opposition was arrested and shot without trial or sent to work in labour camps. It has been estimated that between 1917 and 1924 the Cheka killed more than 250,000 people.

SOURCE E The celler of Ipatiev House where the murder of the Romanov royal family took place in July 1918.

Questions

1 What information does the table on page 88 give about industrial and agricultural production within Russia between 1913 and 1921?

2 Explain the policy of War Communism.

3 Describe what happened to the Romanov royal family in July 1918.

THE ESTABLISHMENT OF BOLSHEVIK RULE

The organisation of the CPSU

By 1921 Russia had been turned into a one-party state controlled by the communists. In 1918 the Bolsheviks had changed their name to the Communist Party of the Soviet Union (CPSU). In theory power lay with the Central Committee of the Communist Party (CCCP), but the real power lay with two smaller sub-committees who could make decisions faster. These were the Politburo and the Orgburo. The Politburo contained a small number of leading Bolsheviks such as Lenin, Trotsky and Stalin which met every week to make important decisions. The Orgburo (the Organisational Bureau) was responsible for carrying out those decisions and was led by the Secretariat, under Joseph Stalin.

The Comintern

At the Tenth Party Congress in March 1919 Lenin announced the creation of the Comintern or Third International, its purpose being to organise socialist revolutions across Europe and so spread communism beyond Russia. The existence of such a body alarmed Western countries and made them more willing to support the Whites during the Civil War. In 1920 the Red Army invaded Poland as part of a plan to achieve world revolution but its defeat convinced most communist leaders that plans for world revolution should wait. After Lenin's death in 1924 (see page 96) Trotsky continued to preach the idea of a 'permanent revolution' while his rival, Stalin, developed the approach of 'socialism in one country'.

Propaganda and censorship

In order to spread the communist message and to explain what the Party stood for it was vital to censor and gain control over the press. Newspapers, books and films were used for propaganda purposes and were only allowed if they carried the 'right' messages. In this way the Party influenced the way the Russian people thought and acted.

In a country where much of the population could not read or write, propaganda posters became very important.

During the Civil War the communists produced over 3000 posters which were designed to win loyalty to the Red cause. After the war the communists had the job of building loyalty to the new regime and spreading the Party message. To do this they sent out agitprop (agitation and propaganda) trains and boats which were designed to explain the ideas of communism to the people. They used a variety of methods including posters, pamphlets, films and theatre groups. Many Russians saw their first film on the travelling agitprop trains.

SOURCE F A propaganda poster designed to show 'Red Moscow at the heart of world revolution'.

Q Questions

1. Describe the organisation of the CPSU.
2. Explain why Lenin set up the Comintern.
3. How important was propaganda and censorship in helping to secure communist rule within Russia?

3 EXAM PRACTICE

These questions test Section A of the examination paper.

THE CIVIL WAR AND THE ESTABLISHMENT OF THE COMMUNIST STATE, 1918–21

Study Sources A–D and then answer the questions which follow.

SOURCE A

ПСЫ АНТАНТЫ.

ДЕНИКИН
КОЛЧАК
ЮДЕНИЧ

A Bolshevik Civil War poster from 1919. The 'dogs' represent the leaders of the White armies while Britain, France and the USA are shown in the background.

SOURCE B

People streamed out of the cities. Moscow lost half of its population, Petrograd almost two-thirds. Trade with other countries sank to zero. The allies imposed a total blockade. Nothing came into the country. Nothing went out. Railroad locomotives burned wood. The only commodity in ample supply was paper money. At the start of 1919 nearly 34 billion roubles were in circulation: a year later it was ten times worse.

Harrison Salisbury writing in *Russia in Revolution, 1900–30* (1978).

SOURCE C

I travelled across the war zone in my train, ordering the commanders to fight on and encouraging the men to victory. When they were aware of the train a few miles behind the firing line, even the most nervous units would summon up all their strength. Often a commander would beg me to stay for an extra half-hour so that news of my arrival might spread far and wide.

Trotsky writing in his autobiography, *My Life* (1930).

SOURCE D

The Communist Party, led by Lenin, sent the best of its members to join the Red Army. By the end of 1918 Lenin had sent over 1,700,000 men to fight the Whites. The Red Army was a formidable force. Even so, on every battlefront, Red Army units had to fight against an enemy who was better equipped, better trained and numerically superior. The Red Army was composed of workers and peasants who were utterly devoted to the cause of the revolution. That was what ensured their victory.

Written by an official Communist historian, Y. Kukushkin, in his *History of the USSR* (1981), when the Communist Party still ruled Russia.

EQ Exam Questions

1 What information does Source A give about support for the White armies during the Civil War? [3]

2 Use the information in Source B and your own knowledge to explain the condition of Russia in 1919. [4]

3 How useful is Source C as evidence to an historian studying the role of Trotsky during the Civil War? Explain your answer using the source and your own knowledge. [5]

4 In Source D the author is saying that the Red Army won the Civil War because of their commitment to the revolution. Is this a valid interpretation?
In your answer you should use your own knowledge of the topic, refer to the other relevant sources in this question, and consider how the author came to this interpretation. [8]

What were the major features of Lenin's final three years in power and the power struggle to succeed him?

ECONOMIC, SOCIAL AND POLITICAL CONDITIONS IN 1921

By 1921 Russia's economy was in ruins. Four years of rebellion and civil war had drained the country of its resources, while War Communism had added to the burdens faced by the workers and peasants. The situation was made worse by a drought in 1920 and 1921 which resulted in famine on a large scale when over 5 million people died from starvation. Some turned to cannibalism in a desperate attempt to survive (see Source B).

The situation was equally as bad in the cities where a shortage of labour and War Communism had resulted in a sharp decline in industrial production. Many workers had migrated to the countryside believing that they could find food and work there.

SOURCE A A starving peasant family during the famine of 1921.

SOURCE B

> Sometimes a starving family eats the body of one of its junior members ... Sometimes parents at night seize part of a body from a cemetery and feed it to their children.
>
> A contemporary account of the existence of cannibalism during the famine.

The Kronstadt rising and the abandonment of War Communism

Worsening economic conditions and the effects of War Communism caused opposition to Lenin's government to grow. Early in 1921 workers in Petrograd went on strike and by February they joined sailors and dockyard workers at the naval base at Kronstadt to demand better conditions for workers and the end of War Communism. Such demands came as a shock to Lenin since the Kronstadt sailors had proved to be some of his most loyal supporters.

The Kronstadt rising had to be put down and Trotsky ordered General Tukhachevsky to attack the naval base using 60,000 troops. During a three week struggle, over 10,000 men were killed or sent away to labour camps.

ECONOMIC CHANGE AND THE NEW ECONOMIC POLICY (NEP)

The Kronstadt rebellion convinced Lenin that War Communism had to be abandoned if the Communist Party was to continue to rule Russia. At the Tenth Party Conference in March 1921 he announced the introduction of a New Economic Policy (NEP) which would reduce central government control over aspects of the economy.

- The requisition squads were ended and elements of a free market economy were introduced.
- Peasants would pay a small fixed amount of grain as tax each year but any surplus grain could be sold on the open market.
- Small factories which employed less than 20 workers were returned to their former owners and allowed to make a profit.
- Traders could now buy, sell and make goods at a profit. This allowed 'Nepmen', or middlemen, to buy goods cheaply and sell them on at higher prices.
- Trade with foreign countries was encouraged. An Anglo–Soviet trade agreement in 1921 helped to boost the economy by opening up trading links with the West.

Lenin saw the NEP as only a temporary measure designed to allow the country to get back on its feet, but some within the Party saw it as a betrayal of communist ideals. They disliked the idea of allowing workers to make a profit. With its acceptance of private industry and private trade, many felt that the NEP represented a retreat back to capitalism.

How successful was the NEP?

The NEP was a success in helping to revive the Soviet economy and by Lenin's death there was evidence of a significant recovery. Food production had increased and a series of good harvests in 1922 and 1923 brought an end to the great famine. Industry also began to recover but at a slower pace. The switch away from war production meant that there was a greater variety of goods on sale in the shops. The introduction of a new rouble helped to control inflation and so reduce discontent among workers and peasants. The NEP lasted until 1928 by which time the Soviet Union was certainly better off.

However, the NEP was not a total success. The speed of agricultural recovery was not matched by industrial development. The increase in food production had resulted in a fall in the price of food.

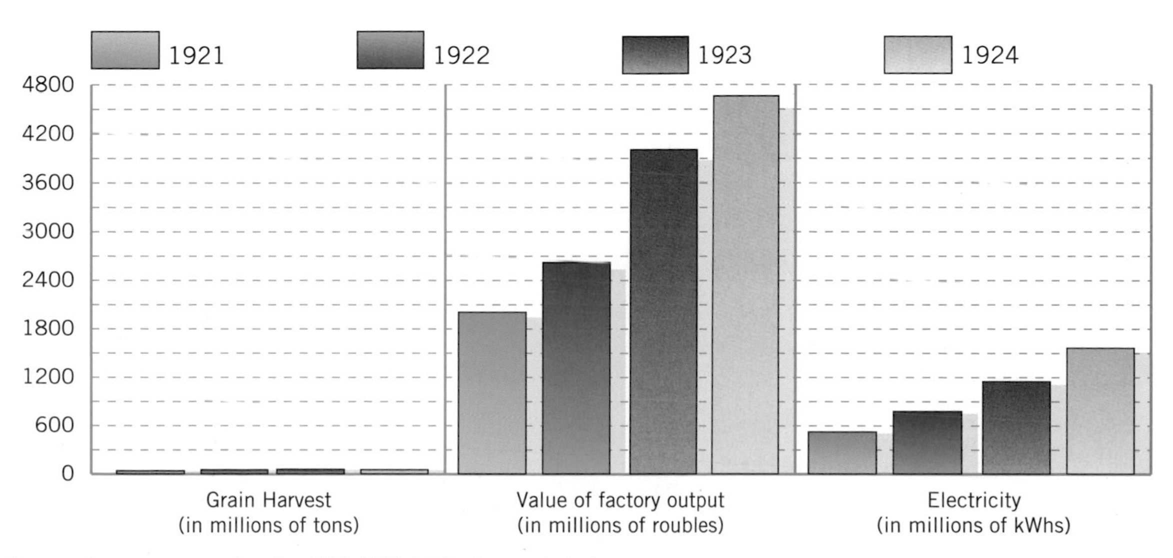

Economic recovery under the NEP (Official Soviet statistics).

However, on the industrial front the opposite was true as prices rose due to the scarcity of goods. By 1924 industry showed signs of recovering, so narrowing the gap. The Nepmen were criticised for being greedy capitalists, becoming rich upon the hard work of others, at a time when there was still high unemployment in urban areas.

Q Questions

1. Explain why Lenin took the decision to abandon War Communism.
2. How useful is the table of economic recovery to an historian studying the impact of the New Economic Policy? Explain your answer using the table and your own knowledge.

LIFE UNDER THE COMMUNISTS

Equality for women

Woman had led hard lives under the tsarist regime. They had been forced to work long hours in the fields and factories. They were paid only half the wages of men and were not allowed time off for pregnancy. One of the first actions of the Bolsheviks was to make women equal. Lenin later created a Women's Department of the Sovnarkom which was led by Alexandra Kollontai, the first female member of any European government.

A number of reforms were issued. In December 1917 the Marriage Law made it legal for men over 18 and women over 16 to marry. Divorce was made easier and in 1920 abortion on demand was made legal in all state hospitals. Women also gained more equality in the workplace. However, progress was slow as attitudes and traditional images of the family unit proved difficult to break down.

Suppression of religion

The majority of Russians were very religious, but Lenin saw the Orthodox Church as a possible centre of resistance to communism. He recognised that he would be unable to ban religion outright and so he adopted a middle way. He allowed people the freedom of belief and worship but at the same time he destroyed the power and wealth of the Church. All church property was seized and priests were made to pay high taxes. Land belonging to the Church was confiscated and many monasteries were closed down. A string of anti-religious laws was passed which banned priests from meeting without official permission, closed down all Sunday schools and banned the teaching of religion in schools.

Control of education

Lenin recognised the importance of controlling education and so the communists launched a massive literacy programme to help the party spread its ideas. Thousands of young activists were sent out to teach workers and peasants to read and a large number of new schools were built. The Young Communists' League (the Komsomol) was created to encourage the growth of communist ideas among the young.

Cultural life

Under the communists, the arts adopted a more modern, more progressive pattern, rejecting the old traditional forms. The new emphasis was art for the people and this was

SOURCE C A scene by Brodski, painted in 1929, which shows Lenin addressing the workers of the Putilov factory in May 1917. It gives the impression of mass support for the Bolsheviks.

reflected in the designs of buildings, streets, fabrics, clothes and furniture.

Cultural activities reflected the new feeling of equality. Artists were encouraged to work in teams and orchestras did away with conductors. The Russian film industry developed into one of the most innovative in the world and new communist films helped to spread party propaganda. Sergei Eisenstein's films *October* and *Battleship Potemkin* portrayed the power of the people as being the decisive factor in the Bolshevik seizure of power. Russian art dramatised the events of 1917 and Lenin was portrayed as the hero of the revolution.

Q Questions

1 Describe the attitude of Lenin's government towards women.

2 Explain why Lenin was so keen to suppress religion in the Soviet Union.

3 How useful is Source C to an historian studying how the communists used art to tell the story of the events of 1917? Explain your answer using the source and your own knowledge.

RELATIONS WITH OTHER POWERS: SOVIET FOREIGN POLICY

Lenin's government was not popular with Western powers. Russia's former allies felt betrayed and abandoned, and this was one reason why Britain and France supported the Whites during the Civil War.

Communist ideology was also viewed with suspicion by Western governments since it taught that state barriers were not important and stressed the importance of the workers uniting to bring about world revolution. The creation of the Comintern in 1919 and the Russian attack on Poland in 1920 sent alarm bells ringing across Europe. Many Western governments refused to recognise Lenin's regime.

Relations did improve slowly in the early-1920s as countries began to recognise the communist government and to trade with Russia. In April 1922 Russia signed the Treaty of Rapallo with Germany which established more friendly relations between the two countries and introduced measures to secure greater economic co-operation. Trade agreements were also signed with Britain and France.

LENIN'S ILLNESS AND THE LEADERSHIP POWER STRUGGLE

From 1922 onwards Lenin's health began to fail. In the spring of 1922 he suffered a stroke. He suffered further strokes in December 1922 and March 1923. He died from a brain haemorrhage on 21 January 1924 at the age of 53.

In December 1922 Lenin had dictated his *Testament*, detailing the strengths and weaknesses of the men who might succeed him. He came to the conclusion that no one person should take his place. Instead he wanted a collective leadership possibly by the Politburo, the chief members of which were Trotsky, Stalin, Kamenev and Zinoviev. Lenin felt that Trotsky was by far the most able, being a gifted writer and leader, but that he was too arrogant and self-assured to take on the top job. Another serious contender was Stalin but Lenin made it clear that he considered Stalin to be an unsuitable leader. As General Secretary of the Communist Party Stalin had used his position to appoint his own supporters to positions of importance within the Party. He had also been very rude to Lenin's wife and as a consequence Lenin had recommended in his *Testament* that Stalin be removed from his posts.

The power struggle after Lenin's death

Following Lenin's death the members of the Politburo began a power struggle to become leader. Stalin joined with Kamenev and Zinoviev to discredit Trotsky and block his chances of success. When Lenin called for Stalin's removal Kamenev and Zinoviev supported Stalin, claiming that Lenin was mistaken in his views. They also blocked all appeals by Lenin's widow to have his *Testament* published by the Party Central Committee. When Lenin died Trotsky was in southern Russia and he claimed that Stalin had lied about the date of the funeral. Trotsky's failure to appear at the funeral lost him support as it made him look disrespectful. Stalin, on the other hand, played a leading part in the proceedings and was seen as the chief mourner.

By 1929 Stalin had outmanoeuvred and expelled the other members of the Politburo to make himself supreme leader. Trotsky was forced to give up his post as Commissar for War in 1925 and in 1926 was expelled from the Politburo and the following year from the Communist Party itself. Trotsky and Stalin had clashed over their political views, with different ideas for the future of Russia. Also, Stalin no longer needed the support of Kamenev and Zinoviev, both of whom wanted to end the NEP. Stalin supported it and so used their objections to have them removed from the Politburo. By replacing the other members of the Politburo with his own supporters, Stalin was now firmly in control.

LENIN'S LEGACY

Lenin left behind a country which had gone through a tremendous change in a relatively short period. He had managed to secure the Bolshevik takeover of power, and restore some political, economic and social stability to the country by 1924. In 1924 Russia changed its name to the Union of Soviet Socialist Republics (USSR), or Soviet Union, recognising the important role the soviets had played in governing Russia.

i JOSEPH STALIN (1879–1953)

SOURCE D Stalin.

Born Josef Djugashvili, Josef was one of the few Bolshevik leaders to come from a working-class background. While at college he joined the Social Democratic Party and devoted himself to revolutionary activities. He supported Lenin and the Bolsheviks in the 1903 split and spent much of the period 1905–17 either in exile or on the run from the authorities. In 1913 he adopted the name Stalin, meaning 'man of steel'. He returned to Petrograd from Siberia in February 1917 and became the editor of *Pravda*. In 1922 he was made General Secretary of the Communist Party which enabled him to build up a strong challenge for the leadership after Lenin's death.

Lenin had played the central role in directing affairs after the Bolshevik seizure of power. He had made unpopular decisions, such as the introduction of War Communism, but he had done so in order to secure the victory of the Reds and the establishment of a communist state. His decision to abandon war communism in favour of the NEP was criticised by Party radicals but in reality it helped to save the Soviet Union from collapse.

However, Lenin's legacy was not all positive. Some historians see the harsh nature of Stalin's regime with its purges as the next logical step in the system created by Lenin after 1917. For instance, by the time of Lenin's death the Soviet Union already operated as a one-party state, it had a secret police force and had banned any form of opposition.

It was also unclear who should succeed Lenin after his death. He had suggested that a collective leadership might be adopted but had left no clear instructions about how this was to be achieved. Neither had he trained a successor. The result was a power struggle after 1924 which continued until the late-1920s, during which time the main leaders concentrated on securing their own positions rather than looking after the affairs of state. The future direction of the Communist Party was also unclear. It was only solved after a long struggle between Trotsky and Stalin.

Q Questions

1. Explain why Lenin thought that neither Trotsky nor Stalin should succeed him as leader.
2. How successful was Stalin in outmanoeuvring his rivals in the power struggle to succeed Lenin?
3. What improvements had Lenin made to the Soviet Union by 1924?

3 EXAM PRACTICE

These questions test Section B of the examination paper.

LENIN'S LATER YEARS, 1921–4

Study the information below and then answer the questions which follow

INFORMATION Lenin in his later years, c.1922

EQ Exam Questions

1 **a** Describe the events at Kronstadt in 1921. [2]
b Explain why there was such serious famine in Russia in 1921. [4]
c How successful was the New Economic Policy? [5]

2 **a** Describe how Lenin dealt with the Russian Orthodox Church. [3]
b Explain why Stalin was able to win the leadership power struggle. [4]

3 Did Lenin fail in all he tried to do during his final years? Explain your answer fully. [7]

4 THE UNITED STATES OF AMERICA, 1910–29

By 1910 the USA was emerging as the world's strongest and richest industrial nation. It was the land of opportunity which welcomed immigrants. Yet while it provided opportunity, personal freedom and great wealth for some, others experienced persecution, social exclusion and poverty. Following the experiences of the First World War the Open Door policy on immigration was restricted, and racial tension reached a new peak. In the 1920s, the USA made alcohol illegal (prohibition) and this gave rise to organised crime.

US banks and businesses grew rich on supplying goods to Europe during the First World War and this laid the foundations for a prosperous economy during the 1920s. Yet not all Americans experienced the economic boom: for groups like farmers, black people and Native Americans, times were hard. By the end of the decade the bubble of prosperity had burst.

Dramatic developments took place in US culture and society in this period. Silent films attracted vast audiences and led to the development of movie stars. Jazz music became popular. Women broke free from the secluded lifestyle of the pre-war era and enjoyed new fashions, more daring social activities and a more liberal environment.

At the start of this period the USA followed a policy of isolation and was reluctant to enter into European conflicts. It successfully kept out of the First World War until 1917, but the experiences of the war had a profound effect upon the nation. It once again returned to its policy of isolation yet its economic strength and status meant it was unable to become totally isolationist.

TIMELINE OF EVENTS

1909 NAACP formed to campaign against racial segregation

1913 Henry Ford pioneers assembly line production

1915 Sinking of *The Lusitania*

1917 The USA enters the First World War

1918 Wilson issues his Fourteen Points

1919 Paris Peace Conference

1920 Eighteenth Amendment introduces the era of prohibition
Nineteenth Amendment gives women the vote
Congress votes against joining the League of Nations

1921 Emergency Quota Act ends the Open Door policy of immigration

1922 Fordney–McCumber Tariff Act

1924 Native Americans granted US citizenship
The Dawes Plan

1925 Peak membership of the Ku Klux Klan

1928 The Kellogg–Briand Pact

1929 Wall Street Crash

What were the main problems and challenges facing the American people during this period?

THE USA: A NATION OF IMMIGRANTS

The Open Door policy

The US population today is a multicultural and multiracial society. This is the result of successive waves of immigrants who mainly came from Europe. Over 40 million people had arrived by 1919. The result was a melting pot of different races, cultures, religions and languages. During the late-nineteenth century this mass migration was encouraged by the US government, which was keen to populate the continent. The Open Door policy was designed to make entry into the country as easy as possible.

SOURCE A Immigrants from eastern Europe arriving at Ellis Island, New York, c.1914.

Why did people want to come?

A combination of push and pull factors caused people to migrate. The push factors were those that made people want to leave their homeland while the pull factors were those that attracted them to the USA. These factors included:

- an attempt to get away from the poverty of their home country
- a desire to escape from political and economic persecution
- the promise of religious toleration and chance to practise their faith safely
- the lure of plentiful land and the prospect of owning property
- the hope of building a better life for themselves and their families
- a sense of adventure in the land of opportunity.

SOURCE B

We'd have meat about once a year. We had goats and we had a cow, but most of the time we were brought up on goat's milk. And once in a while, mother would buy one of those short *bolognas* (a sausage) and everybody would get a little piece. I used to think, 'If I could get enough of that to fill my stomach!' Well, when we came to America, for a few cents we ate like kings. Oh, it was really heaven!

Memories of Charles Bartunek, who left Austria–Hungary as a child in 1914.

Immigrants arrive on Ellis Island near New York

Most immigrants arrived by sea, and more than 70 per cent landed at Ellis Island near

New York. During peak periods at Ellis Island as many as 5000 people a day would pass through immigration control. For the vast majority the processing, which involved medical and legal examinations, took between three and five hours. For others, a longer stay meant more testing and, for the unlucky ones who were refused entry, a return trip home.

Restriction of entry

As the numbers of immigrants continued to rise, some Americans began to resent the government's Open Door policy. Traditionally immigrants had tended to come from northern and western Europe – Britain, Ireland and Germany. Between 1900 and 1914, 13 million arrived, mainly from southern and eastern Europe – Italy, Austria–Hungary, Russia, Poland and Greece. Resentment against these 'new' immigrants quickly built up because:

- they were often poor
- many were illiterate and could not speak English
- many were Catholics or Jews and their cultural and religious background was different
- the traumas of the First World War and the fear of communism during the Red Scare of 1919 (see page 106) frightened many Americans.

As a result the US Congress passed three Acts to limit immigration, each Act being stricter than the previous one.

1. The Literacy Test, 1917

Immigrants had to pass a series of tests to prove that they could read and write. Many of the poorer immigrants, especially those from eastern Europe, had received no education and so were unable to pass this test and were denied entry.

2. The Emergency Quota Act, 1921

This Act set a limit of 357,000 a year on immigrants, as well as quotas: only 3 per cent of the total population of any foreign group already in the USA in 1910 would be allowed in after 1921.

3. The National Origins Act, 1924

This Act reduced the limit of immigrants to 150,000 a year, and cut the quota to 2 per cent, based on the population of the USA in 1890. It was deliberately designed to penalise immigrants from southern and eastern Europe who had not started to come to the USA in large numbers until after 1890. The Act also banned Asian immigration, which offended existing Chinese and Japanese communities in the USA.

This clamp down on immigration was a massive shift in policy. The once Open Door had now become a 'Closed Door' to many. The 'new' immigrants were no longer seen as enriching US life and culture. The result was a growing fear of immigrants and an increase in racial persecution.

Q Questions

1. Describe the Open Door policy on immigration.
2. Explain why the US government introduced restrictions on immigrants in the period after the First World War.
3. How useful is Source B to an historian studying the reasons why some people fled Europe for the USA? Explain your answer using the source and your own knowledge.

RACIAL PROBLEMS

The early-twentieth century saw a growth of racial prejudice and hostility towards those not seen as being 'true' Americans.

Inequality and poverty of the black population

In 1900, 12 million black people lived in the USA, 75 per cent of whom lived in the south. They were discriminated against in housing, jobs, education and few of them had the right to vote. The laws that imposed segregation (keeping black and white people separate) in the south were known as the Jim Crow Laws. These laws prevented black people from having access to the same facilities as white people. They established separate housing, hospitals and schools and, in some states, banned mixed marriages.

The majority of black Americans did not benefit from the booming economy of the 1920s (see page 110). This was especially true in the southern states where the economy was based mainly on agriculture, which suffered from the fall in prices throughout the 1920s and early-1930s. Black people were always worse off than white people, with the worst jobs and the lowest wages. Limited education meant they lacked the skills to challenge this situation.

Migration to the north and west

Life was hard for black people in the south, and in contrast the north seemed like a place free of segregation. Industrial expansion during the First World War helped to create a demand for manufactured goods and generated jobs in the growing industrial cities of the north. As a result black people from the south began to migrate north and west in search of better jobs and conditions. They flocked to cities like New York, Philadelphia, Chicago and Detroit. Between 1910 and 1930 Detroit's black population increased by 2400 per cent. The influx of black people caused race relations to deteriorate in the northern cities where black neighbourhoods, known as ghettos, sprang up, such as Harlem in New York. This was one factor that stimulated the growth in membership of the Ku Klux Klan (KKK).

SOURCE C

> The Great Migration was a revolt ... an idea – the idea of freedom – moved the people, sending them in ever-increasing numbers to Chicago, New York, Detroit. In the big cities of the north blacks freed themselves, casting off the garments of slavery and the feudal south.
>
> A modern black American's view of the Great Migration.

The revival of the Ku Klux Klan

The 1920s saw the revival of the Ku Klux Klan (KKK), which had developed in the deep south at the end of the American Civil War in 1865. It was a terrorist group founded by people who believed in white supremacy, and who wanted black people to stay as slaves. The movement was revived in 1915 by William J. Simmons. Membership grew quickly and by 1921 it had over 100,000 members. By the mid-1920s this had peaked at 5 million and had spread to big cities such as Detroit, Denver and Dallas.

The KKK discriminated against and attacked black people, Catholics, Jews and Mexicans. Only WASPS (White Anglo-Saxon Protestants) could join the Klan. The movement supported prohibition (see page 104) and was against dancing, divorce and extra-marital affairs.

SOURCE D A Ku Klux Klan lynching. These two men, Abram Smith and Thomas Shipp, had been accused of murdering a white man and dragged from jail by a lynch mob.

Klan members carried out lynchings (killing by hanging) of black people and often took the law into their own hands. Whipping, branding and castration were also used as punishments, as was stripping some of their victims and covering their naked bodies with tar and feathers. In many instances the local police failed to protect the victim and sometimes even played a part in killings. Those responsible were rarely brought to justice and Klan members knew that their friends in the courts would not convict them.

A burning cross became the symbol of their night-time meetings. Members wore white masks and cloaks, carried the US flag and took part in elaborate ceremonies. From 1922 their leader was Hiram Wesley Evans, who adopted the title 'Imperial Wizard'. They felt that the USA was fast becoming a 'garbage can' of different races and religions and so action was needed to purify it.

Why did the government find it difficult to act against the KKK?

Klan members often had friends in high places. Intimidation and fear of Klan activities were often enough to win support. The Federal Government in Washington found it difficult to change long-held views of white supremacy in the south and so tended to avoid getting involved for fear of losing white votes.

Decline of the KKK in the late-1920s

The Klan had a violent reputation and its actions often attracted media attention. However, it was a scandal at the heart of the movement itself that caused most damage to its status. In 1925 David Stephenson, the 'Grand Dragon' of the Indiana Klan, was found guilty of the rape and mutilation of a woman on a Chicago train. The scandal destroyed Stephenson's reputation. Klan membership declined sharply and by 1928 there were just a few hundred thousand members.

The black population fights back

By 1900 the black cause was being fought by a former slave, Booker T. Washington. He set up the Tuskegee Institute in Alabama to give black people education and training, believing that they could make no political progress until they had made economic progress. His views were not shared by the leaders of two organisations that attempted to draw attention to the unfair treatment of black Americans: the National Association for the Advancement of Colored People (NAACP), founded in 1909 by William Du Bois, and the Universal Negro Improvement Association (UNIA), founded in 1914 by Marcus Garvey.

Du Bois and Garvey both worked to improve conditions for black people, but their methods were so different that they became bitter enemies.

The NAACP concentrated on opposing racism and segregation through legal action and non-violent activities, such as marches and demonstrations. Du Bois campaigned for non-discrimination and the integration of people of all races into a USA which would have equal opportunities for all.

Members of the UNIA were more militant. Garvey encouraged black people to set up their own businesses employing only black workers. He wanted black people to return to Africa, their homeland; his most famous slogan was 'Black is beautiful'. The authorities were determined to stamp out the UNIA. In 1923 Garvey was convicted of misusing money given to the UNIA, jailed for five years and then deported to his homeland of Jamaica in 1927.

The treatment of Native Americans

During the late nineteenth century the US government introduced laws to force Native Americans to live like the white settlers. They were forced to live on reservations set aside for them, but the land was often of poor quality and lacked enough game for them to hunt. Rations and makeshift housing were provided but this was insufficient and many Native Americans lived a hard life. Their children were sent to boarding schools where they were taught the lifestyle of the white people. To stifle Native American customs and traditions men were made to cut their hair and women were forbidden to paint their faces. Missionaries tried to convert them to Christianity.

In 1924 Native Americans were granted US citizenship. They could now vote and be protected by the US legal system. Many saw this as a reward for the many Native American men who had fought in the US army during the First World War. However, citizenship did not change the fact that many Native Americans still had to live on the reservations and, like the black community, experienced racial intolerance.

Q Questions

1. Describe what is meant by the term segregation.
2. What information does Source D give about the activities of the Ku Klux Klan?
3. How successful was the government in dealing with the racist activity of the Ku Klux Klan in the southern states?

THE ERA OF PROHIBITION

On 16 January 1920 the Eighteenth Amendment to the constitution came into force, which made it illegal to sell alcohol anywhere in the USA. The Volstead Act of 1919 was designed to put the amendment into practice, and set down penalties for breaking the new law.

Reasons for the introduction of prohibition

Pressure was put on the government by organisations such as the Anti-Saloon League, the Women's Christian Temperance Union and some religious groups such as Methodists and Baptists, to ban the production and sale of alcohol. They claimed that alcohol was evil and against Christian teaching.

The failure of prohibition

The Volstead Act proved difficult to police. As gangsters took over the sale of alcohol, there was a large increase in organised criminal activity. People who sold alcohol were called bootleggers. Rum-runners smuggled liquor into the USA from Canada and Mexico. Moonshiners distilled their own home brews. Illegal drinking bars known as speakeasies sprang up and by 1925 there were over 100,000 in New York alone.

SOURCE E Poster issued by the Anti-Saloon League to highlight the evils of drink.

Corruption increased as gangsters bribed police officers, judges and politicians to ignore their illegal activities. High-ranking police accepted bribes from criminals such as Al Capone and John Torrio. It soon became evident that the legal system was unable to cope. The government attempted to tackle the problem by appointing a prohibition commissioner, John F. Kramer, in 1921 and he quickly established a force of 3000 agents. In 1924 the Bureau of Investigation (later the FBI) was set up under J. Edgar Hoover. His men used tougher methods.

The enforcement of the prohibition law was a failure. There were too few enforcement agents, they were poorly paid and open to bribery. It was impossible to persuade drinkers to change the habit of a lifetime.

Q Questions

1 Explain why prohibition was introduced across the USA in 1920.

2 What information does Source E give to help explain why some Americans supported the idea of prohibition?

3 Explain why the government found it so difficult to enforce prohibition.

i AL 'SCARFACE' CAPONE

Alfonso Capone was the most notorious gangster of the 1920s. Under the guidance of the Chicago mobster John Torrio he developed the skill of making money from the illegal sale of alcohol. When Torrio retired from the business Capone took over his empire and quickly established a reputation as a ruthless operator. He used extortion, intimidation and murder to control all forms of vice, including gambling, brothels and speakeasies. The problem for the authorities was lack of evidence to prosecute him: witnesses to his crimes would not speak out in court for fear of the consequences. However, he was eventually tried and imprisoned for tax evasion.

SOURCE F Al Capone in 1934 after being convicted for income tax evasion.

THE RULE OF THE GANGSTERS

Every city had its gangsters and during the 1920s rival gangs fought to gain control of particular districts. New York was dominated by Dutch Schultz, Detroit by Chester La Mare. In Chicago, Dion O'Banion controlled the bootleg business in the south of the city, John Torrio in the north. The Thompson sub-machine gun became their favourite weapon.

The St Valentine's Day massacre of 1929 was the climax of the gangster wars. Bugs Moran, who had taken over O'Banion's gang, killed one of Capone's friends. In retaliation seven members of Moran's gang were killed by Capone's men disguised as police officers.

The abolition of the prohibition law in 1933 took away the lucrative trade in illegal alcohol and this, together with a growing distaste for their violent crimes, helped to end the era of the gangsters.

SOURCE G The bloody aftermath of the St Valentine's Day massacre, 1929.

THE RED SCARE

The growing fear of communism

Many Americans were alarmed by the events of the revolution of 1917 in Russia. The growth of the socialist and communist parties within the USA together with the flood of immigrants from eastern Europe convinced many Americans that a communist-led revolution was possible.

This fear of communism, or the Red Scare as it became known, was strengthened by industrial unrest across the USA in 1919–20. In September 1920 a bomb exploded on Wall Street killing 38 people; another bomb destroyed the front of the Attorney-General's house. Such actions fuelled fears that communists and anarchists threatened the USA.

The Palmer raids

The Attorney-General, A. Mitchell-Palmer, organised a series of raids against left-wing groups in which over 6000 suspects were arrested, most of them immigrants. They were held in prison without charge and hundreds were deported. The Palmer raids were a reaction to a largely imaginary threat. Most immigrants were peaceable people who had come to the USA for a chance to make a fortune not to destroy the country. The detained suspects were eventually released and the Red Scare subsided.

The Sacco and Vanzetti case

The treatment of two Italian immigrants, Nicola Sacco and Bartolomeo Vanzetti, was typical of the Red Scare hysteria of the time. On 5 May 1920 they were arrested and charged with carrying out a robbery at a shoe factory in which two people died.

SOURCE H

Palmer went on a witch hunt. The witches were communists and anarchists. He took the law in his hands and, in two days of raids in major cities in 1920, agents invaded homes, clubs, union halls, pool halls and coffee shops, rounding up nearly 6000 people, who were held in jail, not allowed to call anyone, and treated terribly. Most weren't guilty of anything.

From an American school textbook, published in 1999.

From the outset their immigrant background and political beliefs meant that public opinion was against them.

The trial opened in May 1921. The evidence against them was not strong. Both men had guns when arrested and the bullets in Sacco's gun were said by the police to be the same size as the ones that killed the guard. Although 61 eyewitnesses identified the two men, the defence had a further 107 witnesses who swore that they had seen them somewhere else at the time of the crime. The jury found Sacco and Vanzetti guilty and they were sentenced to death. Even though a confessed murderer, Celestino Madeiros, later admitted to the crime, Sacco and Vanzetti lost their appeals and were executed on 23 August 1927.

Q Questions

1 Describe what is meant by the 'Red Scare'.

2 Explain why the Palmer raids took place in 1920.

3 What information does Source G give about gangsters in the 1920s?

4 EXAM PRACTICE

These questions test Section A of the examination paper.

PROBLEMS AND CHALLENGES

Study Sources A–D and then answer the questions which follow.

SOURCE A An American cartoon of 1924.

SOURCE B

There are three great racial ideas which must be used to build up a great America: loyalty to the white race, to the traditions of America and to the spirit of Protestantism. The pioneer stock must be kept pure. The white race must be supreme not only in America but in the whole world. The Klan believes the negroes are a special problem. Protestants must be supreme. The Roman Catholic Church is un-American and usually anti-American.

Hiram Wesley Evans, Imperial Wizard of the Ku Klux Klan, speaking in 1924.

SOURCE C

Prohibition, introduced in 1920, proved impossible to enforce and led to a major increase in organised crime. The sale of illegal alcohol was very profitable. Gangsters like Al Capone made $60,000,000 from beer and liquor in one year. With so much more money to be made, rivalry between the different gangs increased. Gangland shootings became increasingly common on the streets of American cities.

Information downloaded from a BBC educational history internet site.

SOURCE D

By the mid-1920s narrow-minded views and the emotional excitement of the Red Scare had been replaced by more tolerant attitudes which gradually restored America's reputation for freedom and justice.

Adapted from Harriet Ward, *The USA from Wilson to Nixon* (1998), a history textbook.

EQ Exam Questions

1 What information does Source A give about immigration into the USA in 1924? [3]

2 Use the information in Source B, and your own knowledge to explain the aims of the Ku Klux Klan. [4]

3 How useful is Source C as evidence to an historian studying the problems caused by prohibition? Explain your answer using the source and your own knowledge. [5]

4 In Source D the author is suggesting that by the mid-1920s US society had become more tolerant in its attitude towards such problems as immigration, racial issues and law and order. Is this a valid interpretation?
In your answer you should use your own knowledge of the topic, refer to the other relevant sources in this question, and consider how the author came to this interpretation. [8]

How did the American economy change during this period and why did the increasing prosperity come to a sudden end in 1929?

THE US ECONOMY IN 1910

By 1910 the US economy was developing into one of the world's strongest. The industrial potential of the country was beginning to bring economic benefits, while the development of rich farmland on the Great Plains ensured an efficient and advanced agricultural system. All social classes were beginning to benefit from improved productivity and efficiency. Increased orders and a greater demand for food meant regular employment and steady incomes. The economy was on the upturn but not all Americans were looking forward to a bright future, for example:

- the poor, illiterate immigrants seeking work in cities like New York
- black people living with segregation laws in the south
- Native Americans living in poor conditions on the reservations.

IMPACT AND CONSEQUENCES OF THE FIRST WORLD WAR

Because of its policy of isolationism (see page 124) the USA had been reluctant to enter the war that had affected Europe in 1914 and did not join until 1917. This decision benefited US industry and agriculture because they had to supply a war-torn Europe with food, munitions, raw materials and manufactured goods.

- US firms were able to take the lead in technological advances such as the use of new materials like Bakelite (plastic).
- Increased mechanisation and the development of mass production techniques helped to speed up production and lower manufacturing costs, making US goods attractive and affordable in Europe.
- US farmers sold their surplus produce across the Atlantic in Europe.
- Wealthy US banks lent huge sums of money to European countries to help finance their war effort.
- Businessmen and bankers invested large amounts in western European firms in the hope of making handsome profits once the war ended.

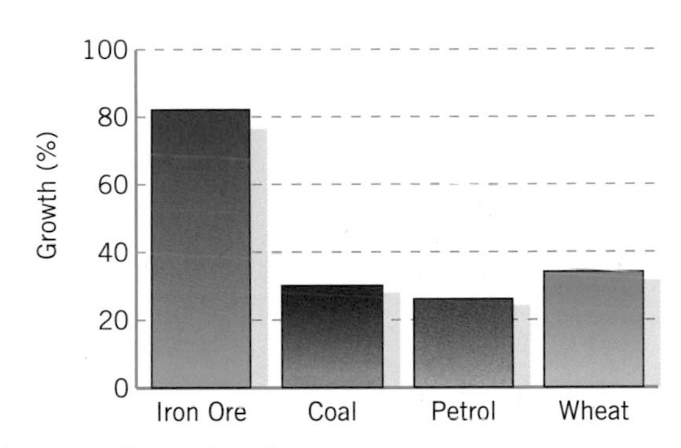

Increase in production.

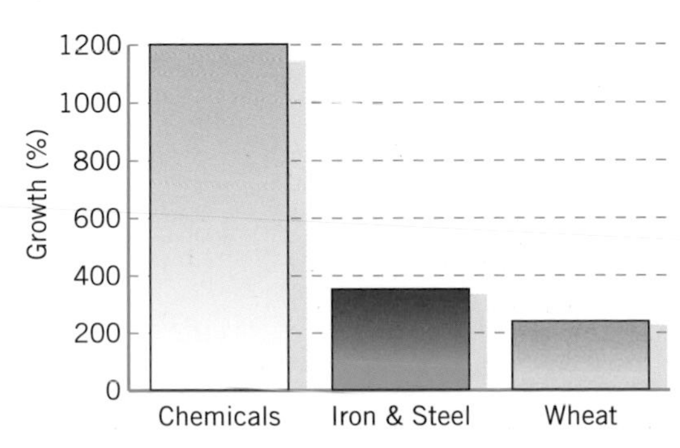

Increase in exports.

Increase in US production and the growth of exports between 1914 and 1917.

President Wilson's eventual decision to send troops to Europe did have an effect upon the US economy. In the months immediately following the German defeat in November 1918 many of the 1 million US soldiers who had been sent to fight in Europe returned home. At the same time, US factories, which had been expanding to cope with the demands of war production, began to shed workers as their order books shrank. This led to a rise in unemployment. Employers also began to refuse demands for wage increases, despite a substantial rise in living costs since 1914, because they knew that they could easily replace workers at a time of high unemployment. As a result, worker discontent also increased.

1919 saw a wave of strikes across the country, particularly in the textile, steel and coal industries. As the pressure of immigration increased so did the fear of communism. Racial tensions also erupted with race riots breaking out in many northern cities. 1920 was the beginning of an economic recession; by the following year over 5 million people were unemployed. Yet this slowdown did not last long and by 1922 the economy was displaying signs of recovery.

Q Questions

1 Use the information in the bar charts on page 109 to describe the condition of the US economy in 1917.

2 Explain why the US economy experienced a recession in the period 1920–2.

3 Why can 1919 be labelled 'the year of discontent'?

CAUSES OF THE ECONOMIC BOOM OF THE 1920S

From 1922 onwards the US economy experienced an unprecedented boom. Once started, this boom created a cycle of prosperity: mass production (see page 111) led to cheaper prices, which in turn led to higher sales. Firms took on more employees who in turn pumped money back into the economy. This confidence, and the period of sustained economic growth it generated, gave this time the label the 'Roaring Twenties'. There were many causes of this boom and they were often interrelated.

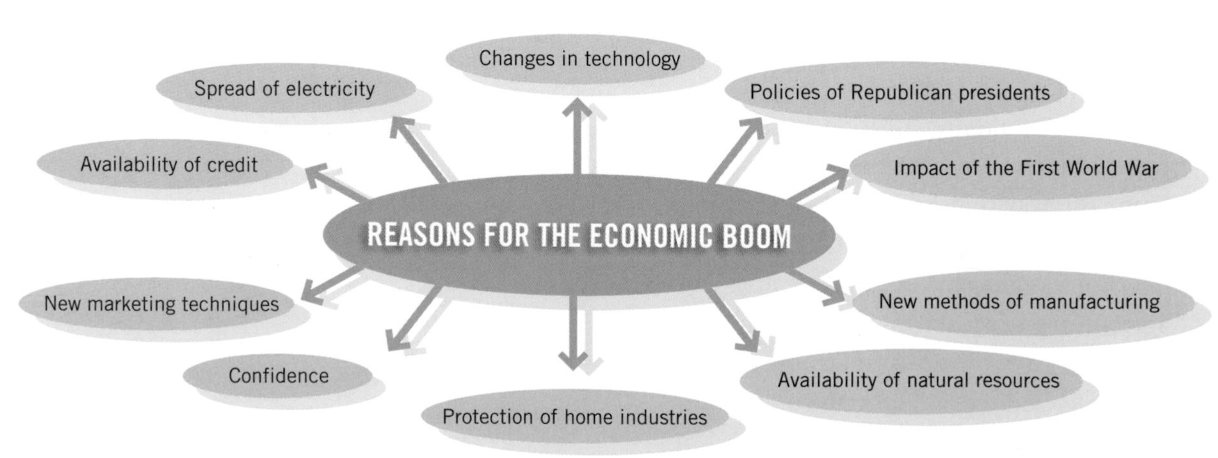

Reasons for the economic boom.

The policies of the Republican presidents

The presidents of the 1920s were all Republicans. They followed the policy of limited government intervention in the running of the economy, also known as *laissez-faire*. This allowed big businesses freedom to expand and prosper without the limits of government regulation.

When Warren Harding took office in 1921, he attempted to bring about a 'return to Normalcy'. Following a policy of non-intervention, he aimed to restore prosperity. He cut taxes to provide firms with more money to invest in development and growth, and to give ordinary Americans money in their pockets. To protect the country from foreign competition he introduced the Fordney–McCumber Tariff Act in 1922. This placed a tax on imported goods which made them more expensive than US goods.

When Harding died in 1923 he was succeeded by his vice-president, Calvin Coolidge. Known as 'Silent Cal' he continued his predecessor's policy of limited intervention in the economy, keeping taxes low and tariffs high. 'The business of America is business', he commented. During his time as president the economy flourished as never before. Despite his lack of action most Americans thought Coolidge a good president and he was very popular.

SOURCE A

Perhaps one of the most important accomplishments of my administration has been minding my own business.

Coolidge commenting on his time as president.

Herbert Hoover followed Coolidge as president in 1929. He was elected by a huge majority and promised to put 'a chicken in every pot and a car in every garage'. Like Coolidge, Hoover believed in *laissez-faire*, but also in the harsher policy of 'rugged individualism'. This was the belief that people should not expect help from the government, but should overcome their own difficulties through hard work. This attitude lost Hoover the presidency in the 1932 election.

New methods of production

The USA's industrial expansion almost doubled during the 1920s. It was most noticeable in new industries such as chemicals, electricity, electrical products and car manufacturing. Such advances were only made possible through the invention of faster manufacturing techniques, particularly that of mass production, which meant that a product could be manufactured in large quantities using a standardised mechanical process.

Cars	**1913 =** 1 million	**1929 =** 26 million
Telephones	**1915 =** 10 million	**1929 =** 20 million
Radios	**1920 =** 60,000	**1929 =** 10 million

Growth in sales of consumer goods, 1913–29.

The development of electrical power to drive factory machinery enabled mass production techniques to be used in many industries, for example the new range of household electrical appliances such as vacuum cleaners, refrigerators, washing machines and radios.

Henry Ford and the development of the car industry

Henry Ford cherished the simple dream of producing a cheap car which could be afforded by ordinary Americans. Up to this time cars had been made in small workshops, by groups of men who assembled the whole car, piece by piece. By 1913 Ford had pioneered the use of the electric conveyor belt which carried the partly assembled car past gangs of workers who performed just one task. The time taken to assemble a Model T was reduced from 13 hours to just 1 hour 33 minutes with the introduction of the assembly line. As production speeded up so prices fell. In 1908 the Model T cost $850; by 1925 it cost just $290, a price affordable to many Americans. Over 15 million of these cars were manufactured and sold, making it the most successful car of all time.

To offset the boredom of repetitive work on the assembly line, Ford doubled the wages of his workers to the previously unheard of sum of $5 a day. This increased demand in general because workers spent a sizeable proportion of their increased earnings on new consumer goods, many of which had been manufactured using mass production methods.

The growth of advertising and credit

The mass production of a range of consumer goods meant that firms now had to advertise their goods across a wider market. The amount of money spent on advertising rose sharply during the 1920s, with a growth in advertising on radio and cinema.

Chain stores made their first appearance in the 1920s; one of the largest chains was J. P. Penney, which had more than 1000 stores by 1929. Mail order became fashionable in the 1920s as did buying from catalogues, the advantage being that people could buy goods on credit using hire purchase. This became a very popular method of buying goods.

SOURCE B A 1920s advertisement from the Western Electric Company aimed at persuading women to buy the latest household appliance.

Developments in transport and construction

The increase in the number of cars, trucks and buses stimulated a boom in road construction and make it easier to distribute and sell goods. By 1929 the miles of surfaced road had doubled, while the number of trucks had tripled to 3.5 million. Aircraft made their first appearance for civil flights, making 162,000 flights a year by 1929.

Industrial growth created a demand for new buildings such as factories, offices and shops. The expansion in towns created the demand for public buildings such as hospitals and schools. The 1920s were the era of the skyscraper and corporations competed with one another for larger and grander headquarters.

Questions

1. Explain why advertising and credit played an important part in stimulating economic growth.
2. How important was Henry Ford to developments in the motor car industry?

DID ALL AMERICANS EXPERIENCE THE BOOM ?

Not all Americans shared the wealth and prosperous lifestyle associated with the economic boom of the 1920s. Over 60 per cent of the population lived close to the poverty line.

The farmers

A decline in European markets for American produce in the 1920s caused prices to fall and brought many farmers to the brink of economic ruin. As farmers struggled to find markets for their produce, they were forced to borrow money and fell deeper into debt. Those who lost their farms ended up as hoboes (tramps), touring the countryside looking for work.

SOURCE C A migrant black family during the 1920s.

Black people

Black people suffered economic hardship, particularly in the states of the Deep South where segregation existed (see page 102). Many were labourers or sharecroppers who lived in slum conditions and worked long hours for low pay. Conditions were little better for those who had migrated to the big cities in the north, where they were forced to live in ghettos.

Immigrants

Immigrants were seen as a source of cheap labour because they were willing to take whatever work was offered. They received low wages and suffered from increasing prejudice and discrimination.

Older traditional industries

The newer industries that adapted to mass-production techniques made healthy profits and could afford to pay decent wages, unlike the older, more traditional industries. Overproduction in the coal industry caused prices to fall and miners to lose their jobs. The shipbuilding industry also went into decline.

Questions

1. Use Source C and your own knowledge to describe the living conditions of black families residing in the industrial cities.
2. Explain why farmers did not prosper during the 1920s.
3. How accurate is it to say that the majority of Americans benefited from the economic boom?

WHY DID THE BOOM PERIOD COME TO A DRAMATIC END IN 1929?

Historians have identified a wide range of causes to explain the collapse of the US economy in 1929. These can be divided into long- and short-term factors.

Long-term factors

- **Overproduction in industry**
  By the late 1920s the US market had become saturated with unsold consumer goods. The supply of goods began to outstrip demand, but manufacturers did not cut back on production and continued to flood the market.
- **Overproduction in agriculture**
  Improvements in farming techniques had resulted in increased production and by the end of the 1920s farmers were producing too much food. The European markets had now recovered from the war, which meant that US farmers were exporting less. The US market did not expand to take up this excess and this resulted in overproduction. Prices were cut and the increased competition put many farmers out of business.
- **Trade**
  By the late 1920s the USA was struggling to sell its surplus goods to European countries who had by this time introduced their own tariffs on imported goods. This reduced trade and, because these countries were already short of money, they found it increasingly difficult to repay their debts to US banks.
- **Boom in property prices**
  House prices rose sharply during the early 1920s, most noticeable was the boom in Florida land values. After 1926 property prices collapsed and this left many Americans with 'negative equity'. This meant that they owned houses worth less than they had paid for them.
- **Falling demand**
  The wealth generated in the 1920s was not distributed evenly in US society and a large percentage of the population remained poor. While many had bought the new consumer goods they had done so by using the credit facilities on offer. As a consequence, many people were in debt, a problem they could overcome only if they remained in work.
- **Too many small banks**
  There was only limited regulation of the financial sector. There were too many small banks, which did not have the financial means to deal with the rush to withdraw their money during the Wall Street Crash of October 1929 (see page 115). As a result, many banks collapsed, leaving their customers with no money.

Short-term factors

- **The rise of the stock market and speculation**
  Share prices had risen to unrealistic levels and the prospect of being able to make money quickly appealed to many people. Investing in stocks and shares had become a popular pastime: the number of shareholders had risen from 4 million in 1920 to 20 million in 1929.

  The ready availability of credit meant that many bought 'on the margin'. This was borrowing money to buy shares in a particular company, believing that the share price would continue to rise. The hope was that the share price would rise so that they could pay off the loan and still be left with a profit. As prices continued to rise many gambled (speculated) with ever bigger sums, taking out even greater loans.

→ Loss of confidence and the sudden fall in prices: the Wall Street Crash

During the autumn of 1929 several financial experts warned of a dramatic readjustment in market prices as the growth in American businesses began to slow down. In September some large investors, worried about the slow down in the economy, began to sell huge quantities of shares. This created an atmosphere of uncertainty and caused small investors to panic and rush to sell their shares. On 24 October 1929, known as Black Thursday, 12.8 million shares were traded. A group of bankers attempted to halt the sale of shares by investing $30 million in the stock market. However, their efforts could not stop the collapse in the stock market and many investors watched their fortunes drain away. The heaviest day of trading was on 29 October, known as Black Tuesday, when 16 million shares changed hands at very low prices. The stock market had crashed.

SOURCE D

Sooner or later a crash is coming, and it may be terrific. Factories will shut down, men will be thrown out of work, the vicious circle will get in full swing and the result will be a serious business depression.

Speaking on 5 September 1929, business analyst Roger Babson warned of a major market readjustment.

THE IMMEDIATE CONSEQUENCES OF THE WALL STREET CRASH

The collapse in share prices brought the Roaring Twenties to a dramatic end. Many investors had lost money in the fall and were now unable to settle their debts. As a result many banks went out of business causing investors to lose their savings. There was a loss of confidence in the financial system. In the growing despair people stopped buying consumer goods like clothes and cars. Firms were forced to cut production, lay off workers and cut wages. Unemployment rose sharply over the coming months, marking the start of the Great Depression.

Q Questions

1. Describe what is meant by buying shares 'on the margin'.
2. How useful is the table of statistics (below) in helping to understand the seriousness of the economic collapse?
3. Was 'over-speculation' the most important factor in causing the crash? Explain your answer.

Company	3 September 1929	13 November 1929
American Can	189	86
General Electric	396	168
General Motors	182	36
Radio Corporation of America	505	28
Woolworth	251	52

Official statistics issued by the New York Stock Exchange, showing the dramatic fall in share prices (in cents).

4 EXAM PRACTICE

These questions test Section B of the examination paper.

THE AMERICAN ECONOMY

Study the information below and then answer the questions which follow.

INFORMATION

The early 1920s were boom years in the USA and this is reflected in the growth of the motor car industry.

EQ Exam Questions

1 a Describe what is meant by a *laissez-faire* policy. [2]
  b Explain why the Fordney–McCumber Tariff Act was introduced. [4]
  c How successful were the economic policies of the US presidents by 1929? [5]

2 a Describe how the US economy was affected by advertising and credit during this period. [3]
  b Explain why the US economy benefited from the First World War. [4]

3 Were all Americans prosperous during this period? Explain your answer fully. [7]

What were the main features of American culture and society during this period?

RELIGIOUS FUNDAMENTALISM AND THE 'MONKEY TRIAL'

The period 1910–29 saw a growing divide between the more conservative-minded rural areas and the modern city culture of urban America. In the rural areas church attendance remained strong, particularly in the south and midwest, an area which came to be called the Bible Belt. Here, laws were passed to keep out the evils of city life, such as the banning of indecent bathing costumes and gambling on a Sunday. Christian fundamentalists (those who believed in the Bible, word for word) were critical of the lively and decadent lifestyle of the cities, especially the jazz culture and the ways in which some women behaved.

In 1925 six states, including Tennessee, banned the teaching in schools of Darwin's theory of evolution. State authorities rejected Darwin's theory that humans, monkeys and apes had evolved from common ancestors over millions of years. Biology teacher Johnny Scopes deliberately ignored the new law and as a result he was arrested and put on trail. The case was heard in July 1925 and became known as the 'Monkey Trial'. It received national media attention and was broadcast over the radio. Scopes was defended by the famous criminal lawyer, Clarence Darrow; the anti-evolution case was put by the fundamentalist lawyer William Jennings Bryan. The trial concentrated upon the arguments for and against the theory of evolution and, while Darrow was successful in damaging the fundamentalist case, Scopes was found guilty of breaking the anti-evolution law and fined $100. The trial did much to ridicule the ideas of the fundamentalists.

SOURCE A

The people have the right to regulate what is taught in their schools. Right or wrong, there is a deep, widespread belief that something is shaking the fundamentals of the country, both in religion and morals. It is my own belief that the [anti-evolution] law is a popular protest against an irreligious tendency to exalt so-called science, and deny the Bible in some schools.

An interview with Austin Peay, Governor of Tennessee, reported in the *Nashville Banner* in March 1925.

Q Questions

1. Describe what is meant by the term Christian fundamentalism.
2. What opposition did Johnny Scopes face in his campaign to teach Darwin's theory?

DEVELOPMENT OF THE SILENT CINEMA

The cinema became popular after the First World War; by the end of the 1920s it had developed into the main form of entertainment. Every small town had its picture house and many Americans visited it several times a week as prices were cheap. Until 1927 all films were silent, the only sound came from a piano accompaniment.

i THE IMPACT OF THE MOVIE STARS

Clara Bow (1905–65)

SOURCE **B** Clara Bow.

Clara Bow became one of the most famous female movie stars of the silent era. Her most successful film was the 1927 hit *It* in which she was portrayed as a glamorous flapper. Her life off stage also attracted much attention, and stories of her wild parties and love affairs eventually damaged her reputation.

Rudolph Valentino (1895–1926)

He appeared in 14 major films and emerged as Hollywood's hottest male movie star. He established a reputation as a romantic lover who displayed great sex appeal. His popularity was such that his sudden death almost provoked riots and some fans committed suicide.

Charlie Chaplin (1889–1977)

His trademark was his tramp-like image, with a cropped moustache, bowler hat, ill-fitting suit and twirling cane. He appeared in dozens of silent films and made a successful transition to the talkies. His left-wing political views caused him to leave the USA for Switzerland in 1952.

Hollywood developed as the centre of the film industry and began producing westerns, crime stories, romantic tales and slapstick comedies. Emerging companies such as Paramount, Warner Brothers and MGM set up studios there, and through mass marketing and advertising they built up the reputations of their movie stars. Everyone wanted to read about them in magazines and they came to symbolise the new fashions and lifestyle of the Roaring Twenties.

Not everyone welcomed this, however, and critics argued that the films were too shocking and were lowering moral standards. Scandals in the private lives of some of the film stars gave added weight to these arguments. To stamp out criticism Hollywood attempted to regulate itself by setting strict rules about what could be shown on screen.

The release of *The Jazz Singer* starring Al Jolson in 1927 started the era of the talking film, or 'talkie', and added to the popularity of the cinema. The following year, Hollywood introduced its own academy award scheme in the form of the Oscars.

Q Question

1 How important was the cinema in the social and cultural life of the USA?

THE CHANGING STATUS OF WOMEN

Before the First World War few women had careers. Their lifestyle was restricted by social convention and middle- and upper-class ladies led secluded lives. Above all, women were not allowed to vote.

SOURCE C

There are few rules apart from those which would naturally govern the actions of any well-bred girl. While at college she is required to have a chaperone supervising her at any entertainment in Boston, or to a football game at Harvard, or to an afternoon tea, just as she would if she were at home with her own people.

An article in the *Wellesley College Magazine* describing the expected behaviour of girls attending the institution in Boston in the pre-war years.

The right to vote

The First World War gave women the opportunity to enter the workplace and do jobs that had previously been done by men. The contribution of women to the war effort made their demand for political equality hard to resist. As a result, the Nineteenth Amendment became law in 1920, granting women the right to vote.

SOURCE D Two flappers on their motorbikes during the 1920s. Such scenes generally shocked people.

Flappers

During the 1920s younger women in the middle and upper classes began to lead a more liberal lifestyle. Flappers were women who adopted the new fashion of short skirts and straight sleeveless dresses, wore make-up and perfume, went out alone with their boyfriends, drank bootleg liqour, smoked in public, and drove cars and motorbikes. They attended parties in the new dance halls and jazz clubs, enjoyed the new craze dances such as the Charleston, or went to the movies. With more leisure time and greater freedom many joined the growing feminist movement in the USA.

However, not all women enjoyed the flapper lifestyle. Poorer women could not afford the new fashions and did not have the time to attend social events. Flappers tended to be a city phenomenon: young women living in the more rural and conservative areas found it difficult to break away from traditional values and beliefs. Many of the older generation were outraged and some formed the Anti-Flirt League, but they were fighting against the spirit of the times.

Q Questions

1 Describe what is meant by the term 'flapper'.

2 What information does Source C give about the lifestyle of middle- and upper-class females before the First World War?

3 How important was the First World War in securing changes in the lifestyle of some American women?

THE JAZZ AGE

The development of jazz

Jazz developed from traditional forms of black music such as the blues and ragtime which originated in the southern states. By the early 1920s jazz was being played in the new clubs and speakeasies. The only black people allowed to many of these clubs were the musicians themselves. Bessie Smith became the greatest blues singer of the time and acquired the title 'Empress of the Blues'. She died tragically after a car accident, having been refused admission to an all-white hospital.

Clubs and dancing

The slow, formal dances of the pre-war years were replaced by more sexually suggestive jives, and rhythmic dances like the Charleston and Black Bottom. Many of the older generation were critical of the clubs and blamed jazz for causing a decline in moral standards.

The radio and gramophone

By the end of the 1920s the radio had developed into one of the most popular forms of entertainment, reaching over 50 million people. As a result, advertising grew in order to finance the radio programmes. There was a dramatic increase in political and social awareness among the population at large: people no longer had to be able to read to learn about the news. The popularity of jazz also meant that sales of records increased during this decade, resulting in an increased interest in the gramophone.

Fads, crazes and a passion for heroes

The 1920s saw a passion for short-lived fads and crazes. These ranged from the obscure – like a man called Shipwreck Kelly who balanced on top of a flagpole for 23 days and 7 hours – to the less dramatic craze for crossword puzzles. The new jazz dances swept the country and dance marathons were held. Beauty contests became popular and, for a short time, live goldfish-eating competitions!

i LOUIS ARMSTRONG (1900–71)

Loius Armstrong's childhood was spent in New Orleans, the birthplace of jazz. He displayed a unique talent on both the cornet and trumpet. In 1919 he got his first full-time job as musician, playing on the Mississippi riverboats, and went on to become a celebrated entertainer with his distinctive gravelly singing voice.

SOURCE E The Creole Jazz Band, Louis Armstrong kneeling.

SOURCE F The record-breaking pilot Charles Lindbergh and his plane *The Spirit of St Louis*.

The search for heroes symbolised the spirit of the times and celebrities emerged in sport and the cinema, achieving cult status and attracting loyal fans and supporters. Charles Lindbergh became the first pilot to fly non-stop from New York to Paris on 20–21 May 1927. The flight took 33 hours, 39 minutes: the single-engine monoplane *The Spirit of St Louis* had no radio and its pilot had no map and no parachute. It was a daring mission which captured the imagination of the American nation, and Lindbergh returned to New York a hero. A year later, Amelia Earhart, a female aviation pioneer, made a similar trans-Atlantic, non-stop flight.

The impact of the motor car

The motor car had a dramatic impact on the economic and social life of the USA. It stimulated growth in other industries such as steel, oil, plate glass and rubber, and it led to the building of new roads and provided jobs in service industries such as garages, motels and roadside restaurants. It improved travel and communication, and gave millions of Americans the freedom to engage in the new leisure activities such as the cinema, the sports stadium or the dancehall.

SOURCE G

The impact of the car on life in the USA cannot be exaggerated. It gave people great freedom to travel, whether to visit friends or take day trips to the cities. Many people moved out to live in the suburbs during the 1920s because they could drive into work. The car meant that young people could escape their parents and go off to cinemas or clubs. Not everybody was in favour of the car: some thought it was leading to a moral decline in young people; others blamed it for making crime easier.

A modern historian commenting on how the car helped to change US society during the 1920s.

Q Questions

1 Describe what made the new dances of the 1920s so popular.

2 Explain why the motor car had such a dramatic impact upon the lifestyle of ordinary Americans.

3 Did all Americans welcome and adopt the culture of the Jazz Age? Explain your answer.

DEVELOPMENTS IN SPORT

The growth in organised sport

In the years after the First World War people came to have more free time, as well as money, for leisure activities. This period witnessed the growth of organised sport, especially baseball, boxing, tennis and golf. The radio meant that events could be broadcast live across the USA. Sport became a profitable business attracting ever larger crowds.

SOURCE H

America fell in love with organised sports during the Roaring Twenties. Sports stars became American heroes. Working hours were changing, and more Americans had more leisure time. They could go to the ballparks or listen to games on radio. They could also play sports themselves. When the First World War ended there were very few tennis courts or golf courses in the nation. By the end of the '20s golf courses and tennis courts were popping up everywhere. Americans were hard at play.

From an American school textbook, published in 1999.

Sporting heroes

Matches and results were analysed and players' techniques discussed. The result was the cult of sporting heroes.

- The nation's most famous boxing star was Jack Dempsey, who became the world heavyweight champion in 1919. He lost the title to Gene Tunney in 1926 when over 120,000 people watched the fight in Philadelphia.
- In tennis Bill Tilden was ranked world number one throughout the 1920s, while in American football 'Red' Grange of the University of Illinois was the top player.
- Gertrude Ederle became the first woman to swim the English Channel. She broke the existing men's record in August 1926.

Questions

1. Use the information in Source H and your own knowledge to explain why sport became so popular during the Roaring Twenties.
2. To what extent did Americans develop a fascination for sporting heroes during the 1920s?

'BABE' RUTH (1895–1948)

Babe Ruth has been rated the greatest American baseball player of all time. He started playing in 1914 as a pitcher and went on to become the best hitter in the game, his best season being 1927 when he hit 60 home runs, a record not beaten until 1961. He established a lifetime record of 714 home runs, and his outstanding ability as a pitcher led the Yankees to win four world championships. He is credited with making baseball the dominant US sport of the inter-war period. He retired from the game in 1935 after becoming the most famous sports star in the USA.

SOURCE I

'Babe' Ruth in action.

4 EXAM PRACTICE

These questions test Section B of the examination paper.

AMERICAN CULTURE AND SOCIETY

Study the information below and then answer the questions which follow.

INFORMATION The period 1910–29 was a time of great change in the USA. Films and music reflected these changes, which included greater freedom for women.

EQ Exam Questions

1 **a** Describe the US movie business during this period. [2]
b Explain why Americans were able to enjoy popular culture during this period. [4]
c How successful were religious fundamentalists in attempting to keep hold of traditional US beliefs and values? [5]

2 **a** Describe how the lives of Americans were affected by the radio. [3]
b Explain why the new jazz culture was so popular among young Americans. [4]

3 Did the period 1910–29 see an improvement in the lives of all women in the USA? Explain your answer fully. [7]

Why did the United States enter the First World War and what were the main features of its foreign policy in the post-war years?

US FOREIGN POLICY IN 1910: 'ISOLATIONISM'

The presidents of the period after the civil war in the 1860s followed a foreign policy designed by President James Monroe in 1823. Known as the Monroe Doctrine it stated that the USA would not get involved in the affairs of other countries, and expected that such countries would not interfere in the USA's own domestic affairs. It resulted in the USA cutting itself off from world issues and adopting a policy of isolationism.

By 1910 the USA had emerged as one of the world's strongest industrial powers. Its economic wealth meant that it had to trade with other countries. For this reason it was impossible to remain completely isolationist and in 1887 it acquired Pearl Harbor in Hawaii to increase its naval strength in the Pacific. Yet, as far as was possible, the USA refused to get involved in 'entangling alliances' and ignored the quarrels between the European states.

THE USA AND THE FIRST WORLD WAR

When war broke out in Europe in 1914 the reaction within the USA was one of shock coupled with a strong urge to remain neutral, especially because the USA traded with many of the nations at war. President Woodrow Wilson stated that it was a conflict 'with which we have nothing to do, whose causes cannot touch us', and he attempted to negotiate peace between the warring sides but without success.

Yet, in 1917, the USA entered the war on the side of the Allied powers, Britain and France.

SOURCE A

The United States must be neutral in fact as well as in name during these days that are to try men's souls. We must be impartial in thought as well as in action.

The opinion of President Wilson in August 1914.

The abandonment of neutrality

Historians have identified several reasons to explain why the USA joined the war.

→ **German submarines sank US ships**
Early in the war Germany launched a submarine (U-boat) campaign to disrupt the USA's trade with Europe. Between 1915 and 1917 Germany's U-boats attacked shipping, a policy which gradually changed public opinion in the USA against its policy of neutrality. The worst incident occurred on 7 May 1915 when a passenger liner, *The Lusitania*, sailing from New York to Liverpool, was torpedoed off the coast of southern Ireland killing 1198 people, 128 of them Americans. Wilson protested to Germany and after this the German government curbed attacks, but in January 1917 it announced its intention of returning to a policy of unrestricted U-boat warfare. Several ships were sunk during February and March and Wilson responded by breaking off diplomatic relations with Germany. However, the US Congress was still not ready to declare war.

- **The Zimmerman telegram**
  In January 1917 British intelligence intercepted a coded telegram sent from the German foreign minister Alfred Zimmerman to the German ambassador in Mexico. It revealed that Germany was trying to encourage Mexico to create a diversion by fighting a war against the USA, in return for which it could reclaim territory in Texas, New Mexico and Arizona which it had lost to the USA in the 1840s. This was the final straw and on 6 April 1917 the US Congress voted to declare war on Germany.

SOURCE **B**

We intend to begin on the first of February unrestricted submarine warfare. We shall try to keep the United States of America neutral. In the event of this not succeeding, we make Mexico a proposal of alliance on the following basis: make war together, make peace together, generous financial support and an understanding on our part that Mexico is to reconquer its lost territory in Texas, New Mexico and Arizona … Signed: Zimmerman.

The Zimmerman telegram.

The USA at war: the home front

The US government grew more powerful during the war as it attempted to mobilise and organise the country:

- The War Industries Board was set up to regulate the production of supplies.
- A Food Administration Department was created to control food production. 'Wheatless Mondays' and 'meatless Tuesdays' were introduced on a voluntary basis to conserve these essential foodstuffs. People were encouraged to plant 'victory gardens'.

"All the News That's Fit to Print."

The New York Times.

LUSITANIA SUNK BY A SUBMARINE, PROBABLY 1,000 DEAD; TWICE TORPEDOED OFF IRISH COAST; SINKS IN 15 MINUTES; AMERICANS ABOARD INCLUDED VANDERBILT AND FROHMAN; WASHINGTON BELIEVES THAT A GRAVE CRISIS IS AT HAND

SOURCE **C** The sinking of *The Lusitania* as reported in *The New York Times*.

- The Selective Services Act of May 1917 introduced conscription and, as the men joined up, so women filled their places in the factories, mills, mines and farms.
- Taxes were increased to pay for the war and the public were asked to display their patriotism by buying Liberty Bonds.

Measures were introduced to ensure loyalty to the war effort:

- The Committee on Public Information, set up immediately after war was declared, used propaganda to whip up hatred of Germany and its Kaiser (emperor).
- Schools were banned from teaching German.
- The Espionage Act of June 1917 made it illegal to obstruct recruitment or to encourage disloyalty. The Sedition Act of May 1918 introduced heavy penalties for anyone criticising the government or the armed forces. Over 1500 people were imprisoned under these two Acts.

The USA at war: fighting in Europe

The USA entered the war in Europe at a crucial time for the Allies whose troops were nearing exhaustion and suffering from low morale. The overthrow of the tsar during the Bolshevik Revolution had resulted in Lenin withdrawing Russia from the war in March 1918, robbing the Allies of a second front to divert German forces. This allowed more than 1 million German troops to be moved from the Eastern Front to fight against the Allies in the west. That same month the Germans launched the Ludendorff Offensive along the Western Front, with the aim of taking Paris before US forces arrived.

SOURCE **D** A propaganda poster appealing for men to join the US army. As this failed to raise sufficient troops men had to be conscripted into the armed forces.

At first the Ludendorff Offensive was successful but the massive injection of US troops and weapons slowed down the Germans' progress and helped swing the war in favour of the Allies. At sea, US convoys helped protect shipping against U-boat attacks and so foiled Germany's gamble of starving Britain into defeat by cutting off vital supplies. By November 1918 over 1 million US soldiers had crossed the Atlantic. The combined Allied force was now sufficient to force the Germans to agree to an armistice on 11 November 1918, so ending the fighting on the Western Front.

Q Questions

1. Describe the Monroe Doctrine.
2. Use the information in Source B and your own knowledge to explain why the USA entered the war in 1917.
3. How important was the contribution of US troops in securing victory on the Western Front? Explain your answer.

WILSON AND THE SEARCH FOR A JUST PEACE

The First World War resulted in death and devastation on a scale that had not been seen before. Over 5 million Americans were mobilised by the US government: of these 53,513 were killed in action and 204,002 wounded. Wilson's views about how Germany should be treated now the war was over differed from those of the other Allied leaders. In both Britain and France there was a desire for revenge, particularly among the French who had suffered most. Wilson did not want to see Germany treated too harshly and he aimed to secure a 'just peace'.

WOODROW WILSON (1856–1924)

SOURCE E

Woodrow Wilson.

Wilson, a Democrat, was president between 1913 and 1921. He saw the USA's role as one of spreading the ideals of liberalism, democracy and capitalism. He managed to keep the USA out of the war until 1917 and played a leading part in the peace negotiations of 1919–20. His dreams of securing future peace were shattered when Congress rejected the USA's entry into the League of Nations. He suffered a stroke in 1919 and left office a broken man, having realised that the US people did not share his dream. He won the Nobel Peace Prize in 1919.

Wilson was an idealist and in December 1918 he hoped his Fourteen Points would form the basis of negotiations for the separate peace treaties to be imposed on the defeated countries of Germany, Austria–Hungary, Bulgaria and Turkey. Disagreement over the degree of punishment to be imposed meant that Wilson had to sacrifice many of his points, but he was successful in having his main idea of a League of Nations incorporated into the Treaty of Versailles.

OPPOSITION TO WILSON

When he returned to the USA, Wilson faced growing opposition to his attempt to have the Treaty of Versailles and entry into the League of Nations ratified (agreed) by Congress. The experience of the First World War had left many Americans wanting to withdraw from world affairs in favour of a return to the traditional policy of isolationism.

WILSON'S FOURTEEN POINTS

1. Replacement of secret treaties with open diplomacy
2. Freedom of the seas
3. Free trade between nations
4. Reductions in armaments
5. Colonies must have a say in their future
6. Germans must evacuate Russian territory
7. Belgium must be free and independent
8. Return of Alsace–Lorraine to France
9. Readjustment of Italian frontiers based on nationality
10. Self-determination for the people of Austria–Hungary
11. Romania, Serbia and Montenegro must be free and independent
12. Self-determination for the peoples of the Turkish Empire
13. Poland should be independent with access to the Baltic Sea
14. Establishment of a League of Nations to settle disputes between countries

Points 1 to 4 were designed to deal with the causes of the First World War; points 5 to 13 show Wilson's belief in self-determination (the right of people to decide their own future); point 14 was intended to ensure future peace through co-operation between countries.

SOURCE F US cartoon 1920. President Wilson conducts a script titled 'Everlasting Peace' for Japan, England, France, Italy, and Uncle Sam.

Senator Henry Cabot Lodge, the Republican chairman of the Senate Committee on Foreign Relations, led a campaign to reject membership of the League. He came up with 14 points of objection, called the Lodge Reservations. He argued that the decision to go to war should rest with Congress not with the League, and that membership would break up the traditional policy of neutrality. The USA could only join the League if Congress gave its approval and on 19 March 1920 it voted against signing the Treaty of Versailles and against becoming a member of the League.

After the 1920 presidential election the new president, the Republican Warren Harding, promised to return the nation to the policy of isolationism. In his first speech he confirmed this change in direction by commenting: 'We seek no part in directing the destinies of the world'.

Questions

1 Describe what is meant by self-determination.

2 Explain why the USA did not join the League of Nations.

DID THE USA RETREAT INTO TOTAL ISOLATION DURING THE 1920S?

While both Harding and his successor, Coolidge, believed the USA's role in the world was primarily economic, not political, many forces were pulling the USA into world affairs.

Reparations and war debts

As a consequence of the First World War, European countries owed debts totalling over $22 billion to the USA. US loans had helped European countries to cover the massive costs of the war, but with European economies further weakened by the war, ill feeling was beginning to develop over the USA's demands for repayment. Also, much of the ability of the Allies to repay the USA depended upon Germany's ability to pay its reparations (war debts) to the Allies. When Germany defaulted (failed to pay), the US organised a conference headed by Charles Dawes, a Chicago banker. The result was the Dawes Plan of 1924, which reduced Germany's annual payments, extended the repayment period and provided additional US loans to Germany. Five years later the Young Plan allowed Germany to make its repayments over an extended period of 59 years.

Disarmament and peace keeping

The idea of disarmament was popular among Republicans who saw it as a way of cutting military spending and taxation. President Harding was also concerned at the growth of Japanese naval strength in the Pacific, as well as Japanese advances into China. He therefore sponsored the Washington Disarmament Conference of 1921–2 at which three agreements were signed:

- **Five Powers Treaty, 1921**
  The USA, Britain, Japan, France, and Italy agreed to set limits on naval capacity.
- **Four Powers Treaty, 1921**
  The USA, Britain, Japan and France agreed to recognise the rights of others in the Far East and the Pacific.
- **Nine Powers Treaty, 1922**
  The Pacific powers agreed to respect the independence of China.

The Conference succeeded in slowing down the arms race, for a few years. In 1927 the USA attended the Geneva Conference on international relations. In 1928 the French Premier, Aristide Briand, and the US Secretary of State, Frank Kellogg, signed an agreement in which the great powers agreed not to go to war with each other. The Kellogg–Briand Pact was eventually signed by 62 nations who agreed not to use warfare to settle disputes, but it lacked any means to enforce this decision.

Q Questions

1. Explain the importance of the Dawes and Young Plans.
2. Explain why the USA was keen to set up the Washington Conference of 1921.
3. To what extent did the USA follow a foreign policy based on isolationism after the First World War?

4 EXAM PRACTICE

These questions test Section A of the examination paper.

FOREIGN POLICY: WAR AND ISOLATIONISM

Study Sources A–D and then answer the questions which follow.

A British cartoon on the problems created by war debts for the countries of Europe in the 1920s. The figure on the left with the stars and stripes is 'Uncle Sam', representing the USA.

SOURCE A

SOURCE B

I object in the strongest possible way to having the United States agree to be controlled by a League which may at any time be drawn into conflicts in other countries. No American soldiers can ever be sent to war except by the United States. This League is primarily a political organisation. I wish to limit strictly our interference in the affairs of Europe.

Senator Henry Cabot Lodge, the Chairman of the Senate Foreign Relations Committee, objecting to the Treaty of Versailles in the US Senate.

SOURCE D

After Harding became President in 1921, and under Coolidge in 1923 and Hoover in 1929, the United States was involved in the affairs of other countries. No country with the wealth of America, whose economy was so important to the prosperity of the whole world, could realistically cut herself off from all other countries.

John Vick, a modern historian, in a school textbook, *Modern America* (1985).

SOURCE C

Cartoon published in the British satirical magazine *Punch*, 10 December 1919. The figure leaning on the keystone marked 'USA' is Uncle Sam.

EQ Exam Questions

1. What information does Source A give about the USA and the war debts problem? [3]
2. Use the information in Source B and your own knowledge to explain why some Americans were against the Treaty of Versailles. [4]
3. How useful is Source C as evidence to an historian studying the USA's foreign policy? Explain your answer using the source and your own knowledge. [5]
4. In Source D the author is saying that the USA did not follow a policy of isolationism during the 1920s. Is this a valid interpretation?
   In your answer you should use your own knowledge of the topic, refer to the other relevant sources in this question, and consider how the author came to this interpretation. [8]

5 GERMANY, 1919-45

Germany emerged defeated from the First World War in 1918. The economy was in ruins, the Kaiser had abdicated, and there was turmoil as political groups fought for power. The Weimar government set up after the war, quickly ran into difficulties. The government was unpopular for accepting the harsh terms of the Treaty of Versailles. By 1923 Germany was unable to pay its reparations and faced financial disaster.

Under the leadership of Gustav Stresemann, the mid-1920s were a time of improved growth and confidence for the German people. Loans from the USA helped Germany to meet its war debts and the economy recovered. Relations with foreign countries improved. The Weimar period also saw a flourishing in art and culture. However, Germany's reliance on US loans meant that when the US stock market collapsed in October 1929, the Germany economy quickly fell back into depression.

The Nazi Party gained increasing support after the economy collapsed in 1929. By 1933 the Nazis were the largest political party in Germany with their leader, Adolf Hitler, as Chancellor. Hitler quickly turned Germany into a one-party state. Under Nazi rule, the German economy recovered, territories lost at Versailles were regained, and Germany's military strength was restored – but at a high price. Nazi beliefs were enforced on the German population at great costs to personal freedom. Those who opposed the Nazi regime were imprisoned and executed; those seen as racially inferior – Jews, Slavs and gypsies – were treated as sub-citizens and, after 1942, massacred during the Final Solution.

Hitler's aggressive plans to restore Germany to 'greatness' led Germany into the Second World War in 1939. By 1945 the country was once again suffering defeat, and was in financial and political ruin.

TIMELINE OF EVENTS

1918 Kaiser abdicates

1919 Treaty of Versailles

1923 French and Belgian troops enter the Ruhr
Munich *putsch*

1926 Germany joins the League of Nations

1929 Death of Stresemann and the Wall Street Crash

1933 January: Hitler appointed Chancellor
February: The Reichstag fire
March: The Enabling Law
July: Creation of a one-party state

1934 June: Night of the Long Knives
August: President Hindenburg dies; Hitler becomes Führer

1935 The Nuremburg laws take away German citizenship from Jews

1938 *Kristallnacht*

1939 Germany invades Poland

1941 Operation Barbarossa: Germany invades Russia

1942 Wannsee Conference discusses the Final Solution

1945 April: Hitler commits suicide
May: Defeat and surrender of the Third Reich

How successful was the Weimar Republic in dealing with its problems in the period 1919–29?

THE END OF THE FIRST WORLD WAR AND THE ESTABLISHMENT OF THE WEIMAR REPUBLIC

In 1917, following the withdrawal of the Russians from the war, Germany moved most of its forces to the west. The Ludendorff Offensive was designed to break through the Allied lines on the Western Front but it failed, and the arrival of US forces made defeat more likely. By 1918 the German people were suffering hardship and starvation. There were many strikes and demonstrations. On 3 November sailors and soldiers took over the naval base at Kiel and within a week workers councils had taken over the control of many cities, including Hamburg, Hanover and Berlin. Kaiser Wilhelm was losing control and he and the generals craftily shifted the responsibility for losing the war on to the government.

SOURCE A

Berlin, evening, 9 November 1918. And here we are right in the middle of the disturbance of a great revolution. Outside there is an excited mass of people constantly coming and going. Great military motor-lorries, packed with soldiers and sailors waving red flags and cheering and shouting energetically, force their way, the occupants trying to stir up the strikers to violence.

An eyewitness account of the violence on the streets of Berlin.

On 9 November 1918 the Kaiser abdicated and fled to the Netherlands. A provisional government was set up under Friedrich Ebert and a republic was declared. On 11 November the new government agreed to the signing of an armistice to end the First World War.

The Weimar constitution

The Weimar constitution was one of the most democratic in Europe. The new Reichstag (parliament) was elected by men and women over the age of 20. Political parties were awarded seats using proportional representation. This meant that seats were awarded in direct proportion to the number of people that voted for the party. The downside of this system was that it resulted in coalition governments because no one party ever achieved an overall majority in the Reichstag. During Weimar's fourteen-year history there were nine elections, two each in the years 1924 and 1932. The result was weak, and often unstable, government.

The republic was headed by a president who was elected for a seven-year term. The president held wide powers of responsibility. During times of crisis he could use Article 48 of the constitution to declare a 'state of emergency' and rule by Presidential Decree. This meant that the President could pass laws without the approval of the government. Article 48 was used by President Hindenburg after 1930.

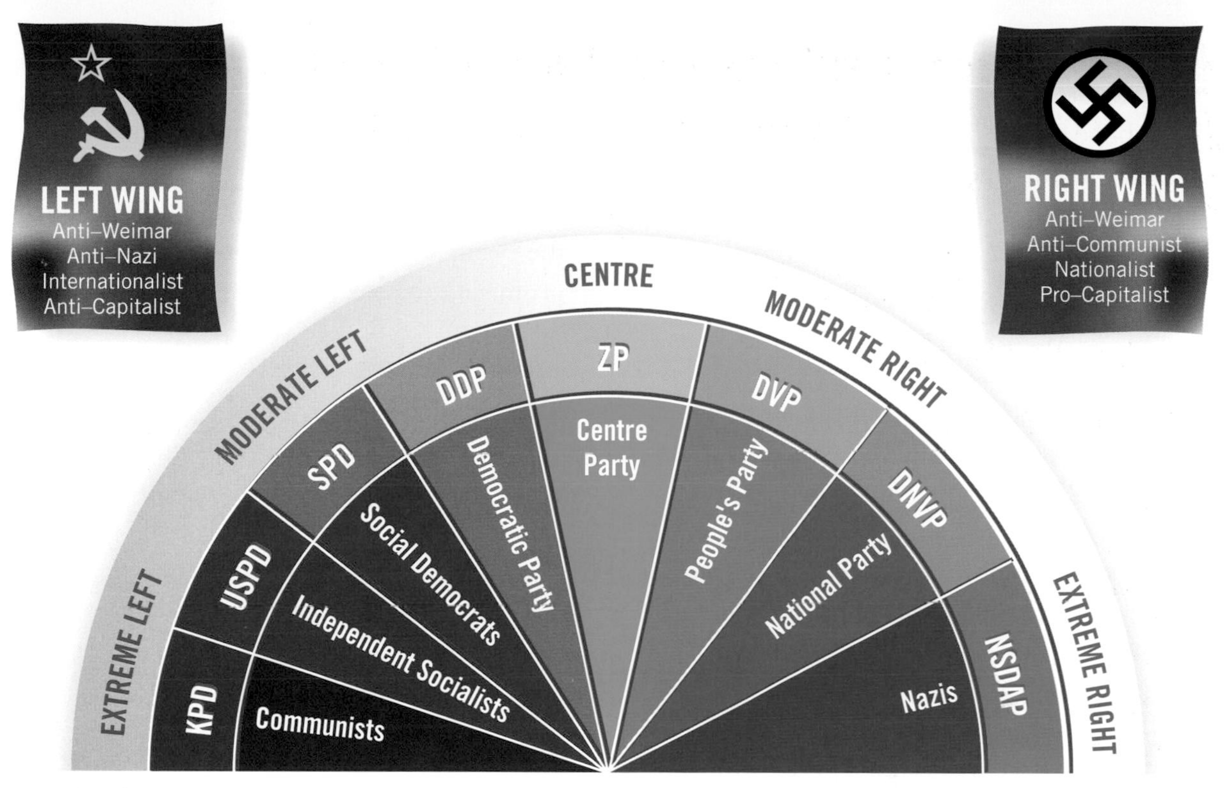

Political representation within the Weimar Republic.

The government was headed by a Chancellor appointed by the President. Until the appointment of Hitler, Weimar's chancellors mostly came from moderate parties, yet they ruled over Reichstags which included the extreme parties of both communists and Nazis. These extreme parties were anti-Weimar in their views and aimed to destroy the republic. During the early-1920s they won support but during the more stable years later they found it hard to pick up votes. Their chance came when Germany was plunged into chaos following the Wall Street Crash of 1929.

The Weimar Republic also faced resentment from conservative groups such as the army whose members preferred the Kaiser's rule. The civil service acted as a hindrance by slowing down government reforms, while the judiciary (legal system) showed bias towards right-wing groups.

Q Questions

1. What information does Source A give about conditions in Berlin in November 1918?
2. How successful were the Spartacists in their attempt to win power in January 1919?
3. Describe the strengths and weaknesses of the Weimar constitution.

INTERNATIONAL RELATIONS

Resentment against the Treaty of Versailles

German propaganda had not prepared its people for the surprise of defeat and surrender in November 1918. The politicians who agreed to the armistice were therefore referred to as the 'November criminals'.

The myth quickly spread that the undefeated German army had been 'stabbed in the back' by the civilian government when it could have gone on and won the war. Anger reached boiling point following the signing of the Treaty of Versailles on 28 June 1919.

The treaty contained 440 clauses and was greeted with horror when the terms became known. Particularly offensive was Clause 231, the war guilt clause, under which Germany had to accept full responsibility for having caused the war and agree to pay reparations of £6600 million for the damage caused. Harsh territorial losses (see below) robbed the country of 13 per cent of its land and the military restrictions robbed the country of its security. On top of this Germany was forbidden to join the League of Nations.

Such humiliating clauses only added to the problems facing the new Weimar government. The treaty gave ammunition to the opponents of Weimar. The bitterness against it later helped Hitler and the Nazis win political support by promising to seek revenge.

SOURCE B

The immediate effect of the signing [of the peace treaty] was a blaze of anger in the German press and depression among the people. In Berlin an atmosphere of profound gloom settled on the city … Serious mob violence was in evidence, especially in Berlin and Hamburg, throughout the week of the signing of the peace treaty.

A report from the *New York Times* in July 1919.

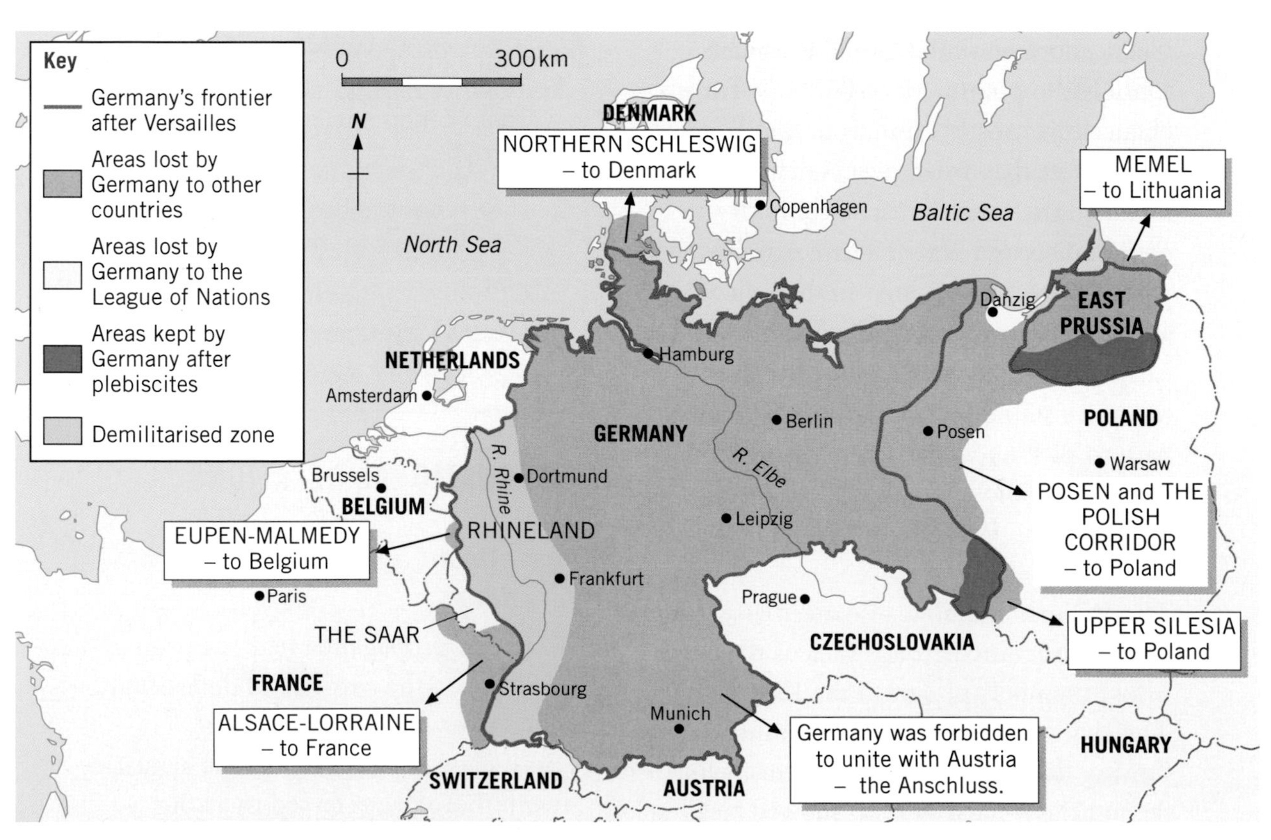

The treatment of Germany under the Versailles settlement.

INTERNAL PROBLEMS

The Spartacist rebellion

On 5 January 1919 the Spartacus League (communists) attempted an armed *putsch* (rebellion) in Berlin, their aim being to snatch power from President Ebert. They gained control of some newspaper offices but Ebert called upon the *Freikorps* (Fascist soldiers) to put down the revolt, which they did ruthlessly. By 13 January the Spartacist *putsch* had been stamped out and the two leaders, Rosa Luxemburg and Karl Liebknecht, had been murdered. The *putsch* demonstrated the political instability the new republic had to address.

Challenges from political extremists

In March 1920 right-wing extremists used the newly formed *Freikorps* to stage an armed rising in Berlin. The *putsch* was led by Dr Wolfgang Kapp and when Ebert called upon the army to crush the rising the soldiers refused to fire on the *Freikorps*. It was a general strike led by the workers of Berlin, in response to the government's call for support, that eventually caused the revolt to fizzle out after just four days. Kapp, with his accomplice General von Luttwitz, fled to Sweden.

The early years of the republic saw considerable political violence. Between 1919 and 1923 there were 354 political murders in Germany.

The Munich putsch

The effects of hyperinflation together with the Ruhr occupation aroused great anger among members of a small extreme right-wing party known as the Nazi Party. In November 1923 it attempted to seize power in the Bavarian state capital, Munich. The Nazi Party had been founded in January 1919 by Anton Drexler, who called it the German Workers Party. At the end of the war Adolf Hitler got a job as a government agent whose task was to check out the loyalty of the numerous parties that emerged in the post-war era. In September 1919 he attended a meeting of Drexler's party in a Munich beer cellar. He liked what he heard and he was invited to join. His organisational ability was quickly recognised and in 1920 he was put in charge of the party's propaganda machine.

By 1921 Hitler had replaced Drexler as leader. He changed the name of the party to the National Socialist German Workers Party (NSDAP) and he developed a new symbol, the swastika. He developed a squad of ex-army *Freikorps* and these men formed the core of the *Sturmabteilung* (SA). Also known as the 'stormtroopers' or 'brownshirts', they were led by Ernst Röhm. By the autumn of 1923 Hitler felt his party was strong enough to make a bid for power.

On 8 November 1923 Hitler, supported by 600 stormtroopers, burst into a public meeting held in the Burgerbrau beer hall in Munich, which was being addressed by Gustav von Kahr, the Bavarian chief minister. His aim was to hijack the meeting and persuade Kahr to join him in a forced takeover of the state government. With a gun pointing at his head Kahr could do little but agree to take part, but once Hitler had left he informed the police authorities of the plan. Ludendorff was arrested but Hitler managed to escape, only to be captured two days later. They were put on trial. Ludendorff was found not guilty while Hitler, found guilty of treason, was given a five-year prison term, of which he served only nine months.

Q Questions

1 How did the terms of the Treaty of Versailles create problems for the new Weimar government?

2 How successful were the Nazis in their attempt to seize power in Munich in November 1923?

ECONOMIC COLLAPSE AND RECOVERY

Economic collapse, 1923: reparations and hyperinflation

In 1921 Germany's reparations bill was finally fixed at £6600 million, to be repaid at a rate of £100 million per year. The government managed to make the first payment in 1921 but failed to pay the following year. The French were angry because they needed the money to help pay the USA for their war debts. By January 1923 they had lost patience. Believing that the Germans were deliberately avoiding making the payment, French and Belgian troops marched into the Ruhr to take the goods they needed in compensation. The Ruhr was Germany's main industrial centre and, in response, workers across Germany went on strike. Germans were united in their hatred of the French and Belgians and the government called for a policy of 'passive resistance' against the occupying forces. However, the government still had to pay the strikers so simply printed more money. This caused inflation to rise and by April 1923 the government was spending seven times more than it was receiving in revenue. The result was hyperinflation: the value of the mark, the German currency, fell rapidly until it became worthless.

Prices were rising so quickly that workers were paid twice a day. They took wheelbarrows or suitcases to work so they could carry home their wages. Shopkeepers used tea-chests to store the day's takings. The situation was particularly bad for those on a fixed income, such as pensioners. Life savings were wiped out in days. Some Germans began to look to the anti-Weimar parties for an answer.

1918	0.63 marks
1922	163 marks
January 1923	250 marks
July 1923	3,465 marks
September 1923	1,512,000 marks
November 1923	201,000,000 marks

The rising cost of a loaf of bread 1918–23.

Economic recovery under Stresemann

By the autumn of 1923 Germany's economy was in a desperate situation. Its recovery was largely thanks to Gustav Stresemann. One of Stresemann's first actions was to replace the existing inflated currency with a new one, the Rentenmark. He negotiated the Dawes Plan with the USA in 1924 which, while not reducing the total reparation bill, did reorganise repayments, making them dependent upon how much Germany could afford. To restart the economy the plan allowed for massive injections of US cash in the form of loans.

By 1930 the USA had pumped over $3000 million into Germany. Unemployment fell and coalmines, steel plants and factories began to prosper again. In 1925 Stresemann negotiated the final withdrawal of French and Belgian troops from the Ruhr.

Support for the extreme parties dwindled. In the election of May 1924 the Nazis won 32 seats but the number fell to 14 in the December election of 1924, while in 1928 they held on to just 12 seats. Support for the communists also diminished.

As the political situation stabilised, a cultural revival took place in Germany and Berlin developed as the pleasure capital of Europe. Writers, musicians and artists flocked to Berlin, while socialising in cafés and clubs became an important aspect of life in the city. There was little censorship and artists were free to express themselves, a freedom the Nazis later claimed created a culture that was 'degenerate' and 'un-German'.

How secure was the recovery made after 1924? The Wall Street Crash

Despite the apparent stability of the German economy in the mid-1920s, scholars have concluded that beneath the surface there were serious problems that threatened to destroy the Weimar Republic.

In the 1920s the German economy was heavily dependent on short-term high-interest US loans. During the winter of 1928–9 unemployment rose sharply to nearly 3 million. While big business benefited from US loans, small firms struggled. A worldwide slump in the demand for agricultural produce caused prices to fall and many farmers began to sink into debt. While the extreme parties found it difficult to win political support, the Nazi Party in particular had used these years to develop a network of local branches staffed with loyal party members who were waiting to gather new supporters when times became hard.

The Wall Street Crash in October 1929 caused the prices of stocks to plummet. Overnight people and banks lost millions of dollars. This is turn caused US banks to pull out their investments and demand the immediate repayment of their loans. This destroyed the basis of the economic recovery since 1924 and unemployment rocketed. The economic crisis led to a political crisis and by the early 1930s parliamentary democracy had ceased to exist in Germany.

i GUSTAV STRESEMANN (1878–1929)

SOURCE C

Gustav Stresemann.

During the 1920s Stresemann was the leader of the moderate right-wing German People's Party (DVP). He was Chancellor from August to November 1923 before going on to act as Foreign Minister between 1924 and 1929. Stresemann, more than any other politician, was responsible for achieving Germany's acceptance among the ranks of the Great Powers. Stresemann's major achievements lay in foreign policy. In 1926 he was awarded the Nobel Peace Prize for his diplomatic work. Stresemann also successfully tackled the economic crises of the 1920s, most notably conquering hyperinflation in 1923.

IMPROVED RELATIONS WITH FOREIGN POWERS

Stresemann's achievements were most noticeable in the field of foreign policy. His attempts to improve Germany's image abroad enabled it to reassert itself as one of the Great Powers. The Dawes Plan, together with the withdrawal of troops from the Ruhr, was followed in October 1925 with the signing of the Locarno Pact with Britain, France, Belgium and Italy. These powers collectively guaranteed the existing borders between Germany, France and Belgium. In September 1926 Germany was allowed to join the League of Nations and was given a permanent seat on the Security Council, a major achievement in light of the events of 1914–18.

In 1928 Germany was one of over 60 countries to sign the Kellogg–Briand Pact which stated that they would never go to war against each other. One of Stresemann's last achievements was the Young Plan of 1929, which significantly reduced Germany's reparation payments from £6600 million to £1850 million and extended the repayment period to cover the next 59 years.

Q Questions

1 Explain how the German economy was affected by hyperinflation.

2 Explain why the German economy was experiencing a downturn by late-1929.

3 How successful was Stresemann in restoring Germany's status abroad?

5 EXAM PRACTICE

These questions test Section A of the examination paper.

PROBLEMS OF THE WEIMAR REPUBLIC, 1919–29

Study Sources A–D and then answer the questions which follow.

Item	1919	Summer 1923	November 1923
1 kg loaf of bread	0.29	1,200	428,000 million
1 egg	0.08	5,000	80,000 million
1 kg of butter	2.70	26,000	6,000 billion
1 kg of beef	1.75	18,800	5,600 billion
1 pair of shoes	12.00	1 million	32,000 billion

SOURCE A Price of essential goods in German shops (in marks). From William Guttman and Patricia Meecham, *The Great Inflation: Germany, 1919–23* (1975).

SOURCE B

Today in the Hall of Mirrors the disgraceful treaty is being signed. Do not forget it. The German people will with unceasing [constant] labour press forward to reconquer the place among nations to which it is entitled. Then will come vengeance [revenge] for the shame of 1919.

An extract from the German newspaper *Deutsche Zeitung*, June 1919.

SOURCE C

The economic position is only flourishing on the surface. Germany is in fact dancing on a volcano. If the short-term loans are called in [by America], a large section of our economy would collapse.

Gustav Stresemann commenting on the state of the German economy shortly before his death in 1929.

SOURCE D

Gustav Stresemann contributed greatly to the stabilisation of the Weimar Republic. He was working for the speedy withdrawal of all foreign troops from German soil, for the removal of the shame of the war guilt clause and for Germany's entry into the League of Nations. By 1930, Germany was once again one of the world's great industrial nations. Her spectacular recovery was made possible by a huge amount of American investment.

William Carr, *The History of Germany, 1815–1945*, a general survey of German history, published in 1979.

EQ Exam Questions

1. What information does Source A give about the German economy in the early 1920s? [3]
2. Use the information in Source B and your own knowledge to explain the reaction of the German people to the signing of the Treaty of Versailles in 1919. [4]
3. How useful is Source C as evidence to an historian studying Germany's economic recovery after the crisis of 1923? Explain your answer using the source and your own knowledge. [5]
4. In Source D the author is saying that by 1930 Stresemann had successfully solved the problems which faced the Weimar Republic during the 1920s. Is this a valid interpretation?
   In your answer you should use your own knowledge of the topic, refer to the other relevant sources in this question, and consider how the author came to this interpretation. [8]

Why was Hitler appointed Chancellor in 1933 and how did the Nazis consolidate their power in the period 1933-4?

THE CRISIS YEARS, 1929–33

The onset of Depression

Much of the economic recovery of the late-1920s was heavily reliant upon US finance. As US banks recalled their loans so demand for consumer goods dried up and German factories began to lay off workers. The ripple effect in other countries closed overseas markets and unemployment figures began to rise, reaching a peak of just over 6 million by the early part of 1932. The result was social misery on a large scale, which affected people of all classes.

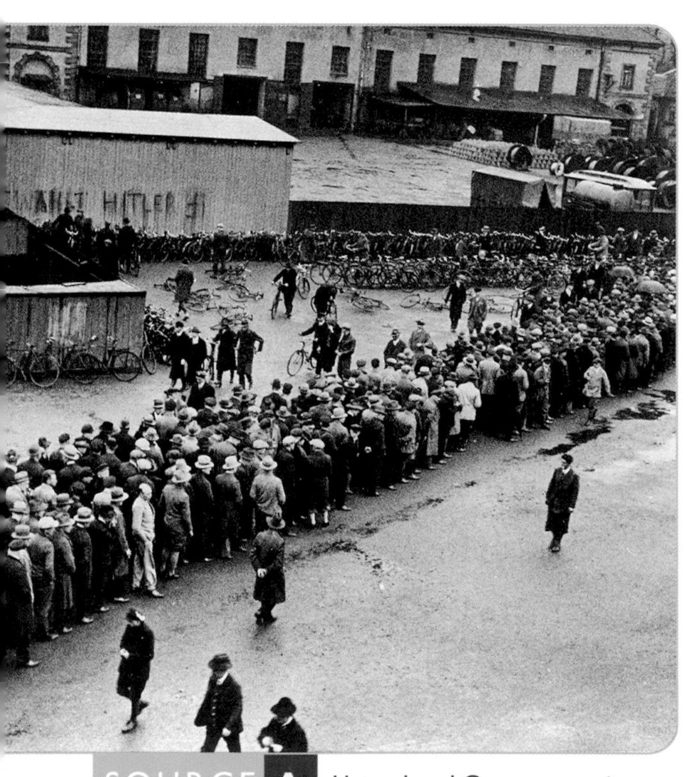

SOURCE A Unemployed Germans queuing in Hanover in 1930 to register for the dole. This scene was repeated across Germany in the early-1930s.

Homelessness became a huge problem. Strikes and demonstrations added to the misery of millions and the Weimar politicians seemed to offer no solutions to the problems. In desperation people increasingly began to turn to the extreme parties and support for both the communists and the Nazis rose sharply in the election of 1930.

The role of Hitler and his ideas

The failure of the Munich *putsch* and the trial that followed gave Hitler and the Nazi Party national publicity. Before 1923 the Nazis had been little known and few had heard of their leader, Adolf Hitler. While in prison Hitler realised that in order to win power the party, which had now been officially banned, would have to change its strategy (see Source B). Instead of an armed rising it would have to work towards achieving a majority and being elected into power in the regular way.

In 1925 Hitler and Drexler devised a Twenty-five Point Programme which concentrated upon nationalist themes such as race, the army and expansion, together with socialist themes such as control of life within the state and regulation of some sections of the economy. Hitler developed these ideas further and added others to them in a book called *Mein Kampf* (My Struggle) which he wrote in prison.

Hitler's success lay in finding scapegoats – people and groups who could be targeted and blamed for Germany's problems. Many of Hitler's ideas were not new but adaptations of existing and long-standing beliefs and prejudices. Anti-Semitism (hatred of the Jews) had been common in central Europe since the Middle Ages and it became a particular obsession with Hitler. He also believed in Social Darwinism, the idea that some races and individuals were superior to others. Hitler saw the Jews as the lowest of the 'inferior races' and referred to them as 'race polluters'. This developed into the master race theory, which stated that pure Germans, or Aryans, were the master race and should therefore control inferior races.

Other key ideas in Hitler's thinking were his fear of communism, and his hatred of democracy in general and the terms of the Treaty of Versailles in particular.

SOURCE **B**

Instead of working to achieve power by an armed rising, we will have to hold our noses and enter the Reichstag against Catholic and Marxist members. If outvoting them takes longer than outshooting them, at least the result will be guaranteed by their own constitution. Sooner or later we shall have a majority, and after that we shall have Germany!

In this letter written from Landsberg prison in 1924, Hitler spells out his change of strategy.

Elections and political scheming, 1929–33

The Great Depression resulted in a political as well as an economic crisis. The weak coalition governments proved unable to deal with the problems they faced and they soon collapsed, resulting in three general elections between 1930 and 1932. In March 1930 President Hindenburg appointed Heinrich Brüning as Chancellor.

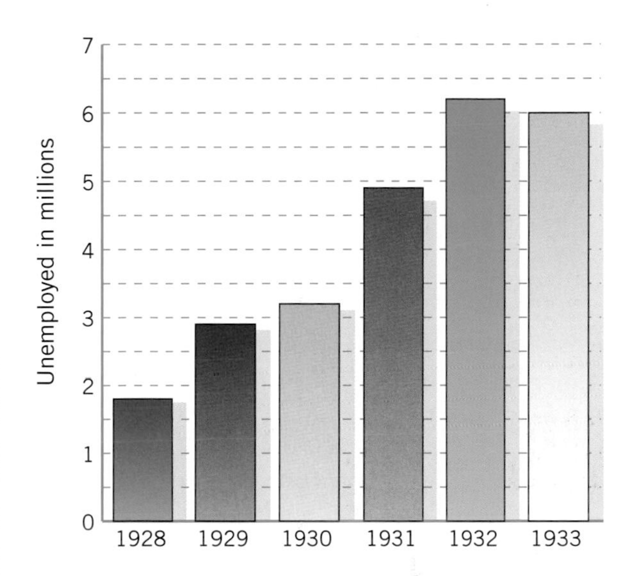

The rise in unemployment in Germany, 1928–33.

Elections to the Reichstag

Party	May 1924	December 1924	May 1928	September 1930	July 1932	November 1932	March 1933
Social Democrats	100	131	152	143	133	121	120
Centre Party	65	69	61	68	75	70	73
People's Party	44	51	45	30	7	11	2
Democrats	28	32	25	14	4	2	5
Communists	62	45	54	77	89	100	81
Nationalists	106	103	79	41	40	51	53
Nazis	32	14	12	107	230	196	288

Elections held, and seats won, 1924–33.

Brüning found it difficult to form a coalition and so Hindenburg used his powers under Article 48 to allow him to rule using Presidential Decrees. Without a majority in the Reichstag, Brüning's rule using the powers of Article 48 marked the end of parliamentary democracy in Germany.

As the Depression deepened Brüning's government became more unpopular and in May 1932 he resigned. In the election which followed in July the Nazis polled their highest ever vote, securing 230 seats (37 per cent), making them the largest party in the Reichstag. Hitler demanded the position of Chancellor but Hindenburg, who despised Hitler, appointed the Nationalist politician Franz von Papen instead. The crisis saw an increase in violence on the streets with battles and fights between the SA and the communists.

By this time Hitler had become a well-known figure in German politics: in March 1932 he had stood against Hindenburg in the presidential elections, securing an impressive 13.4 million votes against Hindenburg's 19.3 million. Unable to secure a majority von Papen was forced to call another election in November when the Nazi vote fell and they obtained just 196 seats. Yet the Nazis were still the largest party in the Reichstag and, ignored by Hindenburg, Hitler refused to co-operate with von Papen in his attempts to form a government. Eventually Von Papen agreed a deal with Hitler and persuaded Hindenburg to allow a Hitler–von Papen government to be formed. He claimed that Hitler could be controlled as Chancellor, and with only three of the eleven cabinet posts being given to Nazis and von Papen as Vice-Chancellor, Hitler would have little room to manoeuvre. Hindenburg finally agreed and on 30 January 1933 Hitler was appointed Chancellor of Germany after considerable political scheming.

SOURCE C

In 1930 the banks failed. No one had any money. Everything gone. Do you know what that means? I own nothing. No money, no work, no food. Seven marks a week as unemployed. Families with two children, ten children and more, seven marks. And then came 1932. My mother and father went and heard Adolf Hitler. The next morning they told us what he had for goals, for ideas, how he was on the side of the unemployed. My mother wept for joy. My parents prayed dear God give this man all the votes so that we could get out of need. There was no one else who promised what he did.

A German woman, Frau Mundt, recalls the hardship of the early-1930s.

Q Questions

1 Describe Hitler's ideas on race.

2 Compare the chart on page 141 showing the rise in unemployment in Germany with the table of Reichstag election results on page 141. What conclusions can you reach about support for the Nazi Party during the period 1924 to 1933?

3 How useful is Source C to an historian studying the reasons why many Germans voted for the Nazi Party in the elections of 1932? Explain your answer using the source and your own knowledge.

REASONS FOR THE NAZI ELECTORAL SUCCESS

The Depression created the political and economic circumstances that caused millions of Germans to switch their voting habits and support the Nazi Party in the elections of the early-1930s. People were worried about the worsening economic conditions and many feared a communist revolution.

Propaganda and Hitler's appeal

Central to the Nazi success was the use of propaganda. As head of the Nazi propaganda campaign, Dr Josef Goebbels used a variety of techniques to deliver the party message, including newspapers, posters, the radio and cinema newsreels. The Nazis promised to restore Germany's status and secure strong government and national unity. These were powerful messages to people who were desperate for answers.

Hitler established a reputation as a rousing public speaker who captivated his audiences. He toured the country delivering speeches to ever larger audiences in halls and sports stadia. He kept his message simple and found something to offer all sections of German society.

- **The middle classes (*Mittelstand*).** Hitler promised to protect them from the communists, to increase prosperity, and to restore law and order on the streets of the large cities.
- **The upper classes.** He promised to avenge the Versailles settlement, to provide strong government, and restore Germany's status.
- **Big industrialists.** By promising to stem the growth of powerful trade unions, Hitler won the backing of powerful business people, who in turn financed the Nazis' electoral campaigns.
- **The working classes.** Hitler promised to tackle unemployment and protect workers' rights.
- **The peasants.** He promised to reverse the decline in prices for agricultural produce.
- **Women.** The Nazis emphasised family life, children's welfare and moral values.

SOURCE D 'Our last hope: Hitler' – a Nazi propaganda poster, used in the 1932 general election, which targets the unemployed.

Q Questions

1 Describe Hitler's attraction as a public speaker.

2 Explain why middle-class Germans voted increasingly for the Nazi Party in the elections of the early-1930s.

THE NAZI CONSOLIDATION OF POWER, 1933–4

Between 1933 and 1934 Hitler turned Germany into a dictatorship. By the end of August 1934 Hitler had created a totalitarian regime under which the Nazi Party ruled Germany for the next 12 years, a period known as the Third Reich. How had Hitler achieved this?

SOURCE E The burning of the Reichstag, 27 February 1933.

The Reichstag fire, 27 February 1933

Despite being made Chancellor in January 1933, Hitler still had very limited powers and his first aim was therefore to increase the number of seats his party had, so that he could pass the laws he wanted. He persuaded Hindenburg to dissolve the Reichstag and call an election, which was planned for 5 March. The Nazi propaganda machine went into full swing and the SA took to the streets to harass left-wing groups.

On the night of 27 February, the Reichstag building went up in flames. A young Dutch communist, Van der Lubbe, was arrested and charged with starting the fire. Many historians believe that the Nazis started the fire and blamed the communists in order to discredit them before the election. Whatever the truth, Hitler used the event as evidence that the communists planned a revolution and persuaded Hindenburg to pass an emergency law giving him special powers to act to protect the country. The Decree for the Protection of the People and the State restricted free speech and the right of assembly, limited the freedom of the press and allowed imprisonment without trial. Hitler used this decree to arrest many communist and socialists.

The Enabling Law, 23 March 1933

The March election took place under an atmosphere of intimidation and propaganda. Political opponents were arrested and on the day of the election SA men watched each vote being cast. As a result the Nazis obtained their best ever result, although they failed to gain an overall majority.

Hitler now proposed to change the constitution and pass an Enabling Law, which would allow him to pass laws without consulting the Reichstag. To get the bill passed he would need a two-thirds majority in the Reichstag but the opposition was unlikely to vote in favour. He therefore banned the communists from attending and on the day of the vote the Kroll Opera House, the temporary home of the Reichstag, was encircled by SA men who prevented some representatives from entering and voting. As a result the bill was passed by 444 to 94 and became the foundation stone of the Third Reich.

Use of the Enabling Law.

April 1933	A law removes Jews and political opponents of the Nazis from their posts in the civil service.
May 1933	Trade unions banned and strikes made illegal.
July 1933	Law Against the Formation of Parties creates a one-party state.
October 1933	Reich Press Law imposes strict control and censorship of the press.

The Night of the Long Knives, 30 June 1934

Hitler relied heavily on the actions of the SA to put his policies into practice. By 1934 the SA was very powerful and its leader Ernst Röhm was emerging as a potential rival to Hitler. Röhm felt that Hitler was introducing change too slowly and rumours circulated that Röhm wanted the SA to take over the army. Hitler now had to make a choice between the SA and the army. He chose the latter and on the night of 30 June 1934 carried out a purge to eliminate the last challenges to his power. 400 'enemies of the state', including Röhm, were shot by the SS. The event became known as the Night of the Long Knives.

The death of Hindenburg: Hitler becomes Führer

On 2 August 1934 President Hindenburg died. Hitler now seized the opportunity to combine the two posts of president and chancellor and gave himself the new title of Führer (meaning 'leader'). He was now head of state and commander of the army. That same day the officers and men of the German army were made to swear an oath of loyalty to the Führer. Hitler was now absolute dictator of Germany and, to make his seizure of power appear legal, he asked the German people to vote on his actions. The Nazi propaganda machine made sure there was a 90 per cent vote in his favour.

Q Questions

1 Describe the events of the Reichstag fire.

2 Explain why Hitler took the decision to eliminate Röhm in June 1934.

3 How important was the Enabling Law in allowing Hitler to become dictator of Germany? Explain your answer.

i ERNST RÖHM (1887–1934)

SOURCE F

Ernst Röhm, leader of the SA.

Röhm joined the *Freikorps* and was quickly made leader of the SA. He took part in the Munich *putsch* and later helped Hitler in his rise to power by eliminating political opposition on the streets and protecting Nazi speakers. After Hitler was appointed Chancellor he felt he should have been rewarded with more power, especially control over the army. In this way Röhm became a threat to Hitler. He was shot in his cell by two SS officers on the Night of the Long Knives.

THE NATURE OF NAZI RULE

Control over central government

Hitler was the central source of all power within the Third Reich, and Germany came to be governed by 'the will of the Führer'. Orders issued by the Führer would be followed without question and he had the power to make laws without the consent of others.

Government policies were carried out by an elite core of Nazi leaders, including Hermann Göring, Josef Goebbels, Heinrich Himmler, Rudolph Hess, Martin Bormann, Joachim von Ribbentrop, Robert Ley and Albert Speer. The key to power and influence in Nazi Germany was securing access to and maintaining the support of the Führer.

Control over regional and local government

In January 1934 Hitler abolished all the individual states of Germany and brought them under central control. The country was divided into regions, or *Gau*, each headed by a Reich governor (*Gauleiter*). They were loyal party officials directly appointed by the Führer and given wide-ranging powers. At the local level Nazi officials were given the power to appoint and dismiss the town mayor and all local councillors. Through these means Hitler maintained a tight hold over what went on at the regional and local level.

The Nazi police state: the use of the SS and Gestapo

The Nazis used a combination of terror and intimidation to keep the German people in line. The two bodies responsible for internal security and ensuring Nazi ideas and policies were enforced were the SS and the Gestapo.

The SS (*Schutzstaffel*) were formed in 1925 as a bodyguard for Hitler and were part of the SA. Their distinguishing feature was their black uniform. In 1929 they came under the control of Heinrich Himmler. After the Night of the Long Knives the SS replaced the SA as the main security force in Germany. In 1936 the SS took control of the police force which included the Gestapo, the secret state police.

The Gestapo had been set up by Göring in 1933 but three years later was brought under the supervision of Himmler's deputy, Reinhard Heydrich. Its function was to search out enemies of the state, monitor their activities and then eliminate them. Most Germans conformed to Nazi directives from fear of execution or the concentration camp if they did not. The first such camp opened at Dachau in April 1933.

Between 1934 and 1939, 534 people were sentenced to death and executed for political opposition. In 1939 alone, there were over 160,000 people under arrest for political offences. The concentration camps were filled with all types of 'undesirables', including intellectuals, communists, homosexuals and Jews. Life in these camps was harsh; during the Second World War many were turned into extermination camps (see pages 160–1).

Q Questions

1. Describe what was meant by 'the will of the Führer'.
2. Explain why Hitler wanted to control regional and local government.
3. How did the SS and Gestapo help Hitler control the German people?

5 EXAM PRACTICE

These questions test Section B of the examination paper.

THE RISE OF THE NAZIS, 1929–31

Study the information below and then answer the questions which follow.

INFORMATION

Nazis celebrating in Berlin in January 1933 when Adolf Hitler was made Chancellor of Germany.

EQ Exam Questions

1 **a** Explain the main ideas of *Mein Kampf*. [2]
b Explain why the SA were so important to the Nazi Party. [4]
c How important was the Depression to the rise of the Nazi Party? [5]

2 **a** Describe what happened during the Night of the Long Knives. [3]
b Explain the importance of the Enabling Law. [4]

3 Did Hitler have total control of Germany by the end of 1934? Explain your answer fully. [7]

How did the Nazis affect the lives of the German people?

ECONOMIC POLICY

Control of the economy

By the time Hitler was appointed chancellor in January 1933 the German economy was showing the first signs of recovery since the Depression. Hitler set himself three targets:

- to reduce unemployment;
- to undertake rearmament to create jobs, avenge the Treaty of Versailles and prepare for the expansion of Germany;
- to bring about economic self-sufficiency so that Germany was not reliant on importing goods.

Hitler appointed Hjalmar Schacht, a financial expert who was President of the Reichsbank, to carry out his ideas but soon became impatient with Schacht's cautious approach. In 1936 Hitler replaced Schacht with Hermann Göring who introduced the Four-Year Plan (1936–40). This was designed to speed up rearmament and prepare the country for war. It led to a push for autarky, a policy designed to make Germany self-sufficient.

Control of the workforce

Hitler saw trade unions as the breeding grounds for socialism and communism and banned them in May 1933. Their funds were confiscated and their leaders arrested. Their place was taken by the German Labour Front (DAF) which had complete control over the discipline of workers, regulating levels of pay and hours of work. Under the new system, working hours increased, wages were frozen and it became impossible to complain about working conditions.

Alongside the DAF was the National Labour Service (RAD), directly under the control of the Nazi Party. Vast sums of public money were pumped into the RAD which put men to work on public works schemes, such as the building of *Autobahns* (motorways), tree planting and the construction of houses and schools. A law of July 1935 made it compulsory for all German men aged 18–25 to do six months training in the RAD. They had to wear military uniform and live in camps.

Unemployment fell dramatically and by 1939 the figure stood at less than 350,000. However, these figures hid the true picture because women and other groups such as the Jews were no longer counted in the official statistics as being unemployed, and conscription had been introduced.

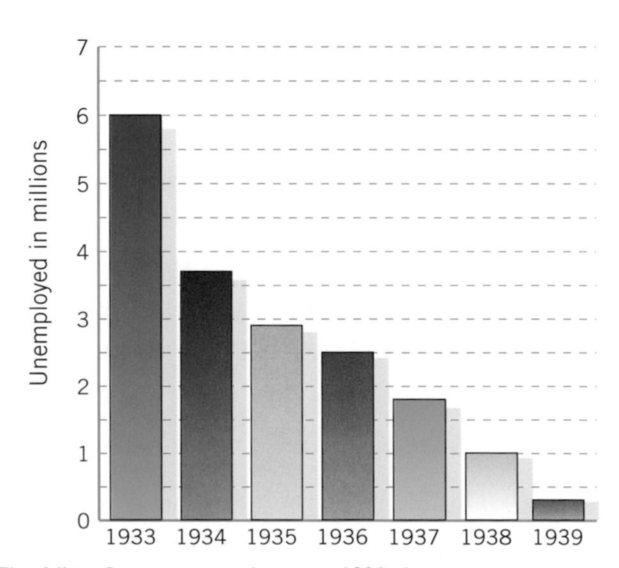

The fall in German unemployment, 1933–9. (Official government statistics.)

i HERMAN GÖRING (1893–1946)

SOURCE A

Hermann Göring in 1935.

Göring became one of the most powerful Nazi ministers after Hitler. In 1933 he became President of the Reichstag and was later appointed Air Minister, setting up the *Luftwaffe* (air force). He also set up the Gestapo and opened Germany's first concentration camp. Despite having little financial expertise he took over the direction of the economy from Schacht in 1936. He was captured by Allied forces in 1945. Sentenced to death at the Nuremberg trials, he cheated the hangman by taking cyanide.

Rearmament and drive for autarky

Hitler's decision to rearm transformed German industry and created hundreds of new jobs in armaments production and in the supply of essential raw materials. Billions were spent on manufacturing military equipment such as tanks, ships and aircraft.

SOURCE B

'We are not building roads [*Autobahns*] just for aeroplanes to look at,' one man said. 'Of course they can rush military supplies and troops to the frontiers in times of need.' It is easy to see why. They point arrow-wise towards the heart of Poland. Two roads lead into Holland, two into Belgium, two into Austria, and two into Poland.

Stephen Roberts, *The House that Hitler Built*, 1939.

Hitler also gave orders that Germany should try and achieve economic self-sufficiency (autarky) because he felt that Germany was too reliant upon foreign imports. Artificial substitutes were also sought to replace oil, rubber, textiles and food such as coffee. However, the policy did not prove successful. Agriculture suffered from a lack of machinery and manpower, and Germany continued to import large amounts of foodstuffs such as butter and vegetable oil. In 1939 Germany still imported 33 per cent of its raw materials.

Did Germans benefit from Nazi economic policies?

Most Germans were grateful for the creation of stable and relatively safe jobs. Industrial workers enjoyed regular work and while they had lost their trade union rights they had the benefit of stable wages and controlled prices. Big business did well, but many smaller businesses owned by the middle classes were squeezed out. Farmers obtained government help but were told what to grow and what the prices of their produce should be.

The price for such economic stability was high in terms of personal freedom. The German people now lived in a police state where every aspect of their lives was controlled and opposition was suppressed. Economic growth centred on rearmament and preparing the country for war.

Q Questions

1. Describe the activities of the RAD.
2. Why did German unemployment fall before 1939?
3. According to Source B, why did the Nazis build *Autobahns*?

SOCIAL POLICY

Nazi attitudes towards women

During the Weimar period women made considerable advances in German society. They had been given equal voting rights with men, had been encouraged to obtain a good education and by 1933 many had risen to high ranks within the professions. These advances were reversed during the Third Reich. The Nazis saw men as decision makers, while women were responsible for the home and bringing up children.

In 1921 the Nazis had banned women from holding office in the party or from standing as candidates in elections. No women were represented in the senior ranks of the party and this sexist attitude was adopted across German society after 1933. Shortly after 1933, Hitler banned women from professional jobs such as doctors, lawyers and senior civil servants.

Nazi propaganda glorified the mother image and emphasised the importance of the family unit. Women were expected to concentrate upon the Three Ks: Kinder, Kirche, Kuche (children, Church, kitchen) In 1938 the Motherhood Cross award was introduced: every year on 12 August, the birthday of Hitler's mother, medals were awarded to women who had large families. The German population did rise quite sharply between 1933 and 1939, as did the number of marriages. However, at the same time abortion was illegal and access to contraceptive advice was severely restricted.

Nazi attitudes towards women were linked to their theory of race. The aim was to breed a 'master race' and this meant avoiding intermarriage with people the Nazis saw as racially impure.

In 1936 special maternity homes were set up for unmarried mothers. They were designed to act as breeding centres. Aryan women were matched with 'racially pure' SS officers for the production of pure Aryan children.

Many women welcomed the security the state now offered German families. Other women resented their loss of freedom and personal choice, and protested. Some joined opposition groups such as the communists. Others criticised the Nazi's policies on women while otherwise remaining loyal to the party. Women who protested were usually disciplined.

SOURCE C A Nazi poster of 1937 which stereotyped the role of a German woman as that of housewife and mother.

Nazi treatment of the Church

Hitler viewed the Church and the Christian faith as a powerful threat to Nazi policies. Roughly one-third of Germany's population was Catholic and two-thirds Protestant, and to begin with both Churches co-operated with the Nazis. Many viewed the Nazis as a protection against communism and as upholders of traditional family values and morals (see Source D).

SOURCE D

> We all know that if the Third Reich were to collapse today, communism would come in its place. Therefore we must show loyalty to our Führer, who has saved us from communism and given us a better future.
>
> A Protestant pastor, speaking in 1937, justifies his support for the Nazis.

Hitler gave the impression that he would protect the Church and in July 1933 he signed a Concordat with the Pope. This allowed the Catholic Church full religious freedom to operate without state interference; in return the Pope promised to keep the Church out of politics.

In 1936 the National Reich Church was set up to 'nazify' the Christian church structure. The Bible, cross and other religious objects were removed from the altar and replaced with a copy of *Mein Kampf* and a sword. Catholic youth clubs, which were viewed as competition for the Hitler Youth, were closed down and Catholic schools were taken out of church control. Such measures provoked demonstrations and in 1937 Pope Pius XI protested against the abuse of human rights. However, up to 400 Catholic priests were arrested and sent to Dachau concentration camp.

Nazi actions also provoked opposition among the Protestants. In April 1934 Martin Niemoller formed the Confessional Church which openly attacked the Nazi regime. In 1937 he was arrested and sent to Dachau and Sachsenhausen concentration camps where he remained until 1945. Another leader, Dietrich Bonhoeffer, tried to organise resistance against the Nazis. In 1943 he was imprisoned and later executed by the Gestapo. The Jehovah's Witnesses also refused to give in to the Nazis and during 1934–5 many were also arrested and sent to concentration camps.

The Nazis never succeeded in destroying the Church in Germany. Priests and pastors had to make the choice of staying quiet and giving the appearance of conformity or being arrested by the Gestapo. Most chose to support Hitler.

The control of young people

Hitler realised the importance of indoctrinating young people in Nazi beliefs, hoping to turn them into loyal and enthusiastic supporters of the Third Reich. To achieve this he controlled out-of-school activities and encouraged membership of the Hitler Youth organisation which had existed since 1925. This offered a variety of leisure activities.

The Hitler Youth Law of 1936 granted the movement equal status with home and school and made it difficult to avoid joining, blocking the promotion of parents who refused to allow their children to join. The second Hitler Youth Law of 1939 made membership compulsory. The movement grew rapidly, from 108,000 members in 1932 to 8 million in 1939.

Boys were instructed in military skills such as shooting, map reading and drill. They also followed academic studies because they were being trained as future administrators or members of the armed forces.

Girls received physical training in preparation for their role as mothers and were not allowed to study academic courses. Some youths refused to join the Hitler Youth and became members of opposition groups, such as the Swing Kids.

Age	Boys	Girls
6–10	**Pimpfen** (Little Fellows)	
10–14	**The Jungvolk** (Young Folk)	**Jungmädel** (Young Girls)
14–18	**Hitlerjugend** (Hitler Youth)	**The Bund Deutsche Mädchen** (German Girls League)

The organisation of the Hitler Youth.

Control of leisure time

The Strength through Joy (*Kraft durch Freude* – KdF) organisation was set up with responsibility for controlling the leisure activities of German workers. The KdF sponsored a wide range of leisure and cultural activities, such as concerts, sporting events and adult education classes. Two ocean liners were built to take workers on cruises at bargain prices, although places were reserved for loyal and hardworking Party members. Critics of the regime claimed that it was yet another example of the Nazi state exercising total power over the individual by making everyone conform, even on holiday.

Q Questions

1. What information does Source C give about Nazi attitudes towards women?
2. Explain why the Nazis felt it necessary to control the activities of young Germans.

POLITICAL CONTROL

The use of propaganda and censorship

In addition to controlling the German people through fear and intimidation, the Nazis also used indoctrination. Its purpose was to brainwash people into accepting and believing Nazi beliefs, values and ideas. The messages of racial purity, national greatness and the cult of the leadership of the Führer were constantly reinforced. Hitler's public speeches attracted vast crowds as did the annual Nuremberg party rally, which was a masterpiece of propaganda. Their ideas were kept simple and repeated time and time again.

SOURCE E

5 September 1934.
The hall was a sea of brightly coloured flags. Even Hitler's arrival was made dramatic … Hitler appeared in the back of the auditorium and, followed by his aides, Göring, Goebbels, Hess, Himmler and the others, he strode slowly down the long centre aisle while 30,000 hands were raised in salute … In such an atmosphere no wonder, then, that every word dropped by Hitler seemed like an inspired Word from on high … and every lie pronounced is accepted as high truth itself.

William L. Shirer, a US journalist, was present at the 1934 Nuremberg rally and recorded what he saw in his diary, *Berlin Diary* (1941).

In March 1933 the Ministry for Popular Enlightenment and Propaganda was set up under Josef Goebbels. What was printed in newspapers quickly became censored and journalists were told what to print. Books written by 'unreliable' authors were destroyed. Over 2500 writers were banned and their works were publicly burnt.

SOURCE F The public burning of banned literature by SA squads, May 1933.

Goebbels viewed the radio as a vital tool to help spread Nazi ideas and he organised the mass production of cheap radio sets, resulting in 70 per cent of German homes possessing a radio. Hitler regularly made broadcasts, as did Goebbels. What was broadcast was subject to control and the music played was heavily censored. Cinema-going was popular and audience figures rose sharply during the Third Reich. Before each film an official newsreel was shown, glorifying Nazi achievements and Hitler's leadership. As a result of such censorship Germany lost many gifted authors, musicians, artists and film-makers: many, like Thomas Mann and Bertolt Brecht, fled abroad to escape persecution and imprisonment.

Education

Education was viewed as another means of indoctrinating young people. The Nazis laid down strict rules about what was taught in all schools across Germany. All subjects had to be delivered according to the Nazi point of view: textbooks were rewritten to reflect these ideals. History came under close control with a heavy emphasis on German military glory. The Jews and communists were blamed for problems such as the Depression. Biology lessons were used to study racial theory and the importance of the 'master race'. The teaching profession was purged of Jews, socialists and 'undesirables'. All teachers had to belong to the Nazi Teachers League, and students were encoraged to inform upon any teacher who did not deliver the new curriculum.

Control of the legal system

The Nazis aimed to control the courts and the legal system. Courts had to adopt the new ideals of National Socialism, and judges who refused to were replaced.

i DR JOSEF GOEBBELS (1897–1945)

SOURCE G Josef Goebbels.

Goebbels had a talent for public speaking and in 1929 he was made responsible for running the Party's propaganda machine. This task of selling the Nazi message became increasingly important during the war years when it was vital to keep the population loyal and keep up morale. Goebbels remained loyal to Hitler to the end and committed suicide in the bunker in Berlin in 1945, after killing his wife and children.

Alongside this system the People's Court was set up in 1934 to try enemies of the state: by 1939 it had sentenced over 500 people to death and sent others to camps. The number of crimes punishable by death rose from three in 1933 to 46 in 1943, and included such offences as listening to a foreign radio station and publishing anti-government leaflets.

The law did nothing to protect individuals from the SS and Gestapo and many judges were appointed for their loyalty to the Nazi Party rather than their legal knowledge. Judges and lawyers had to belong to the National Socialist League for the Maintenance of Law and Order, which forced them to accept Nazi policy, and in October 1933 10,000 lawyers swore an oath of loyalty to the Führer.

The treatment of Jews in Germany before the Second World War

Hitler put his ideas on race in his book *Mein Kampf*, in which he argued that Aryans were the superior race. Aryans were characterised by being tall, with fair hair and blue eyes. Hitler argued that, over time, Aryans had interbred with non-Aryans and so it was necessary to purify the race. This meant stopping certain groups from having children and, in extreme cases, eliminating them. Homosexuals, black people and gypsies came under attack and once in power the Nazis began to sterilise people from these groups. Then they began to sterilise mentally ill and physically disabled people and, after 1939, to kill them.

i MEASURES TAKEN AGAINST JEWS LIVING IN GERMANY

1933

April Nationwide boycott of Jewish shops and businesses.

April Jews banned from working in the civil service and in occupations such as teachers, doctors, dentists and judges.

September Jews banned from participating in all cultural activities.

October Jews banned from working as journalists.

1935

July Jews banned from entering the armed forces.

September The Nuremberg Laws take away from Jews the rights of German citizenship and make it illegal for them to marry or have sexual relations with Aryans.

1936

November Jews banned from using the German greeting 'Heil Hitler'.

1938

July Jews issued with separate identity cards.

August Jews forced to adopt the Jewish forenames of 'Israel' for a man and 'Sarah' for a woman.

October Jewish passports to be stamped with a large red 'J'.

November The events of *Kristallnacht* (the Night of Broken Glass).

December Forced sale of Jewish businesses.

1939

February Jews made to hand over precious metals and jewellery.

April Jews evicted from their homes and forced into ghettos.

German Jews experienced more widespread persecution. Anti-Semitic attacks (attacks against Jews) were commonplace in Europe in the early twentieth century, particularly in Russia, and many Jews had fled Europe in search of a new life in the USA. The Nazis played upon existing hatred and stirred up racial tension to win political support. Once in power persecution was stepped up (see page 154). In 1933 there were 550,000 Jews in Germany: by 1939, 280,000 of them had emigrated, including Einstein who had left for the USA in 1933.

SOURCE H

My grandmother was 90 years old. She went to a shop to buy some butter. In the door of the shop was a Stormtrooper with a gun. He said, 'You don't want to buy from a Jew'. My grandmother shook her stick and said, 'I will buy my butter where I buy it every day'. But she was the only customer that day. No one else dared. They were too scared of the man with the gun.

A Berlin woman recalls the actions of her grandmother during the boycott of Jewish shops in April 1933.

The Nuremberg Laws of September 1935 made life increasingly difficult for Jews. The loss of German citizenship meant they were no longer protected by law. They could be attacked on the street and their property destroyed without any legal right of protection. Signs began to appear stating that Jews were not welcome in public places such as restaurants and cinemas.

A more active period of persecution began in 1938 following the murder in Paris of a Nazi official by a young Polish Jew. In response Goebbels organised a *pogrom*, a nationwide attack on Jewish property by members of the SA. The events of 9–10 November became known as *Kristallnacht* (the Night of Broken Glass) because of the number of windows that were smashed. Over 7500 Jewish shops were destroyed, 400 synagogues burnt down and many Jews killed. More than 30,000 Jews were arrested and taken to concentration camps. Following the outbreak of war the Nazi attitude towards the Jews became more radical and they were forced to in live designated areas called ghettos, before being transported to the death camps in eastern Europe.

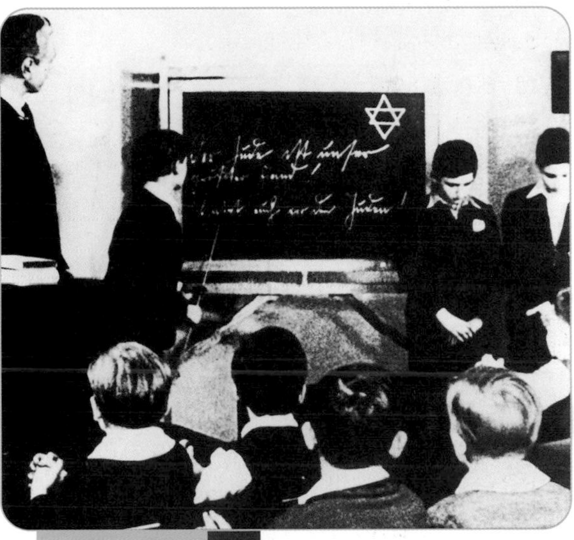

SOURCE I

Two Jewish boys are humiliated in front of their class in 1935. The writing on the board reads 'The Jews are our greatest enemy! Beware of the Jews!'

Q Questions

1. Explain how the Nazis controlled education.
2. Why did life become increasingly difficult for Jews in Germany between 1933 and 1939?

5 EXAM PRACTICE

These questions test Section B of the examination paper.

CHANGING LIFE IN GERMANY, 1933–9

Study the information below and then answer the questions which follow.

INFORMATION Enthusiastic crowds cheer their Führer during a visit to Nuremberg in 1936.

EQ Exam Questions

1 **a** Describe the aims of the Four-Year Plan. [2]

b Explain how the Germans reduced unemployment between 1933 and 1939. [4]

c How important were propaganda and censorship in persuading people to accept Nazi ideas and policies? [5]

2 **a** Describe Nazi attitudes towards the role of women. [3]

b Explain why young Germans were expected to join the Hitler Youth Movement. [4]

3 Did life improve for all people living in Germany between 1933 and 1939? [7]

What impact did the Second World War have on the lives of the German people?

GERMANY AT WAR: AN OVERVIEW

A study of Germany at war can be divided into two phases. The first covered the years up to 1942 – a time of military success when the demands of war had limited impact upon the civilian population. The second period followed a number of key defeats in 1942 and led to military disaster, economic hardship and misery on the home front.

The outbreak of war in September 1939, which followed the invasion of Poland by Hitler's forces, was not greeted with widespread enthusiasm across Germany. The memories of the horrors of the First World War were still fresh in people's minds. Yet the rapid successes resulting from *Blitzkrieg* (lightning war) tactics served to boost morale. German armies met with little resistance and swept through western Poland in 1939 and Holland, Belgium, Luxembourg, Denmark, Norway and France in 1940.

However, the Germans were defeated from 1942 onwards as they struggled to win a war fought against too many enemies. On the home front, bombing raids on German cities resulted in civilian deaths on a scale never known before. The country was put under severe pressure as it was forced to adjust to the demands of total war and by 1945 it was approaching economic ruin.

LIFE IN GERMANY, 1939–41

Rearmament

In 1934 Hitler ordered a massive expansion of Germany's armed forces, an action which went directly against the terms of the Treaty of Versailles.

SOURCE A Civilians and soldiers socialise at a café on the Unter den Linden in Berlin. Such scenes were common in the early years of the war.

Compulsory military service was introduced the following year and by 1938 Germany had 900,000 men in the *Wehrmacht* (army). The *Luftwaffe* (airforce) was created and expansion took place in the *Kriegsmarine* (navy). By 1939 Germany possessed the most modern and technologically advanced fighting machines in the world.

The economy

The rearmament programme helped to revive the German economy. Göring introduced the Four-Year Plan in 1936 to oversee this growth (see page 148). The aim was autarky – to make Germany self-sufficient in food and raw materials. During the early part of the war the Nazis were able to take resources from the conquered territories. Food and luxury goods were sent back to Germany from occupied Poland, Denmark, Norway, Holland, Belgium and France. Foreign labour was used in German factories.

Rationing

From the start of the war rationing was introduced in Germany. Ration cards were distributed to ensure a balanced diet. Artificial substitutes were found for some everyday items, such as ersatz coffee, which was made from barley seeds and acorns. Clothes were rationed from November 1939. To save fuel, hot water was permitted for only two days per week and soap was rationed. Toilet paper became impossible to obtain. Despite rationing there was a flourishing black market and people turned to bartering to obtain items in short supply.

Evacuation

To avoid the danger from the expected bombing raids, arrangements were made to evacuate children from Berlin in September 1940, but many stayed behind. It was not until 1943 that the mass evacuation of children occurred, with Austria and Bavaria being the main destinations.

Q Questions

1. What information does Source A give about conditions on the German home front during the early years of the war?
2. Explain how life on the home front was affected by the introduction of rationing.

LIFE IN GERMANY, 1942–5

Total war

By the end of 1942 it was clear that the war was no longer going in Germany's favour so the Nazis introduced the policy of total war, which in practice meant gearing up all sections of the economy and society towards the war effort.

Labour shortages

Labour shortages in the factories forced the Nazis to reverse their policy towards women and work. Measures were introduced to encourage women to enter the workplace but were not successful. In 1943 the Nazis tried to mobilise all women, and 3 million women aged 17–45 were called to work. Many tried to evade the call up and only 1 million took jobs. The fact that women were not employed on a large scale was a factor that contributed to Germany's defeat in 1945. Instead, large numbers of foreign workers were drafted into factories, and by 1944 they amounted to 21 per cent of the workforce. Inmates from concentration camps were also used as slave labour, and by 1944 the number of inmates working in industry had risen from 30,000 to over 300,000.

The Volkssturm

As the combined Allied forces began to push towards Germany's borders during 1944, the *Volkssturm*, a people's home guard, was formed. It proved little more than a propaganda stunt to boost morale. Its members lacked experience and were poorly trained. It consisted of men who were too old or too young to join the Wehrmacht, and the wounded or sick.

SOURCE B A propaganda poster depicting the *Volkssturm* defending the Fatherland.

The propaganda war

Military defeat on all war fronts meant that conditions on the home front grew harsher. Shortages of food and fuel began to hit civilians. To keep up morale Goebbels launched an intensive propaganda campaign. Posters played on the fear of communism and offered the German people the stark choice of 'Victory or Bolshevism'; others instructed them to save fuel and essential commodities. The propaganda appeared to work. The Germans fought for Hitler to the bitter end and any resistance that did develop was crushed.

SOURCE C

The British claim that the German nation has lost its faith in victory. I ask you: Do you believe, with the Führer and with us, in the final, total victory of the German people? I ask you: Are you resolved to follow the Führer through thick and thin in the pursuit of victory, even if this should mean the heaviest of contributions on your part?

'Do you want total war?' A speech delivered by Goebbels on 18 February 1943.

The impact of Allied bombing

The RAF had bombed military and industrial targets in Germany since 1939. A change came in May 1943 with the start of a heavy bombing programme against German cities. The aim was to destroy morale and force an end to the war. Berlin, Cologne, Hamburg and Dresden were all severely bombed. As a port and an industrial city, Hamburg was an obvious target. One raid caused a fire storm which wiped out large sections of the city. Raids on Dresden in February 1945 destroyed 70 per cent of the buildings in the city and more than 150,000 civilians were killed in just two night attacks.

SOURCE D The effects of the Allied bombing upon Dresden. The photograph was taken in 1944.

By 1944 the continuous bombing was beginning to damage manufacturing output. However, the bombing also made the people even more determined to resist. Allied bombing did not have a high accuracy rate: up to 50 per cent of bombs fell on residential areas and only 12 per cent on factories and war industries. One estimate has placed the number of civilians killed during the Allied bombing campaign at 800,000.

Q Questions

1 Describe the policy of total war.

2 Explain how the Nazis dealt with the shortage of labour during the war years.

3 How successful was the Allied bombing campaign against Germany between 1943 and 1945?

THE FINAL SOLUTION

Following the outbreak of war in 1939, the Nazi persecution of the Jews intensified. The result was the Holocaust, which involved the mass murder, or genocide, of the Jewish people. The Nazi invasion of Poland in 1939 brought 3 million Jews under Nazi control. To begin with, as in Germany, Jews were herded into ghettos. They were forced to live under harsh conditions and virtually imprisoned, since no one was allowed to leave or enter without a special permit. The ghettos were overcrowded: over 500,000 people died from starvation or disease because of the severe conditions in the ghettos.

In June 1941 the Nazis invaded the Soviet Union. This brought even more Jews under their control. Special units known as *Einsatzgruppen* (killing squads) began to round up and shoot Jews, burying them in mass graves. But the Nazis considered this method too slow to deal with such large numbers. In July 1941 Göring ordered Heydrich to draw up a plan for 'the Final Solution of the Jewish question'. The result was the building of concentration camps and the mass transportation of Jews into these camps.

On 20 January 1942 a special conference of leading Nazis was held at Wannsee in Berlin to consider the 'Final Solution to the Jewish problem'. Himmler was given the task of expanding the concentration camps and developing more efficient killing methods using gas. Special gas chambers were built at camps such as Sobibor, Treblinka, Maidanek and Auschwitz in

The main concentration camps in Germany and Nazi-controlled Eastern Europe.

Poland. On arrival at the camps, the Jews were divided into two groups. Those fit for work became forced labour; those labelled unfit were taken to 'showers'. Up to 2000 people could be crammed into a single gas chamber, which was fitted with fake shower heads, in Auschwitz. Historians have estimated that up to 6 million Jews were murdered during the Holocaust.

SOURCE E

When I set up the extermination building at Auschwitz, I used Zyklon B, which we dropped into the death chamber from a small opening. It took from three to fifteen minutes to kill the people in the chamber ... We knew when the people were dead because their screaming stopped ...

Rudolf Hoess, the commandant of Auschwitz 1940–3, describes how the gas chambers operated.

i REINHARD HEYDRICH (1904–42)

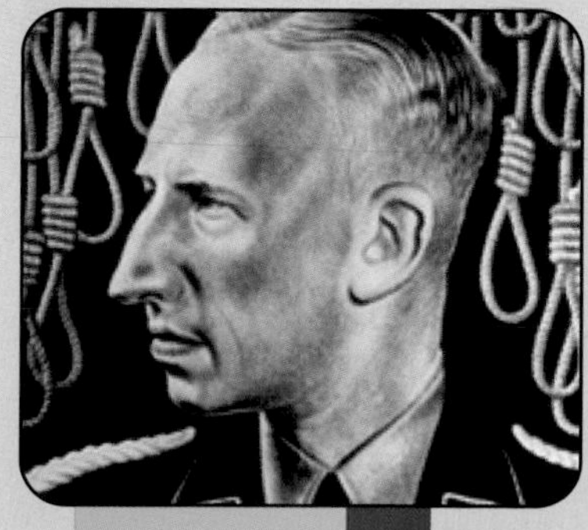

SOURCE F Reinhard Heydrich.

Known as the 'Blond Beast', Heydrich had typical Aryan features. The son of a musician who may have been Jewish, a suggestion he tried to keep secret, Heydrich played a key role in the extermination of the Jews. After the Night of the Long Knives, he was made Deputy Head of the SS and then Head of the Gestapo in 1936. He was assassinated in Prague in May 1942 by Czech freedom fighters.

HEINRICH HIMMLER (1900–45)

SOURCE G Heinrich Himmler.

Himmler became one of the most feared men in the Third Reich. By 1936 he was Chief of German Police and Reich Leader SS and controlled the machinery of terror. Following the outbreak of war he was given responsibility for organising the concentration camps in the conquered territories in the east. Captured by British forces at the end of the war, he committed suicide on 23 May 1945.

Questions

1. Describe what is meant by the term 'Holocaust'.
2. Explain why Hitler wanted a 'Final Solution' to the Jewish question in 1942.

RESISTANCE AND OPPOSITION TO NAZI RULE

Some Germans had opposed the Nazi regime but the efficiency of the SS and Gestapo limited their impact. As the war turned against Germany resistance and opposition to the regime became more common, particularly among certain sectors.

Opposition from young people

→ **The Edelweiss Pirates** were youngsters who objected to the way the Nazis attempted to control all aspects of the lives of young people. Barthel Schink, the 16-year-old leader of the Cologne Pirates, was hanged in November 1944.

SOURCE H The execution of twelve Edelweiss Pirates in Cologne in 1944. They were found guilty of anti-Nazi activities.

- **The Swing Youth** tended to be middle class and were inspired by British and US music, especially jazz. Swing clubs sprang up in various German cities, and here young people would dance the jitterbug and listen to banned music. They rejected the lifestyle imposed upon the young by the Nazi regime.

Opposition from students

Following the military defeats of 1942 students at the University of Munich, including Hans and Sophie Scholl, formed the White Rose group and called for a campaign of passive resistance against the Nazi regime. On 18 February 1943 they were arrested by the Gestapo for distributing anti-Nazi leaflets, tortured and hanged.

Opposition from Christian groups

Once the true nature of the Nazi regime became apparent, opposition developed from some people within the Church. Martin Niemoller set up the Confessional Church as an alternative to the Reich Church (see page 151). The Catholic Archbishop of Munster, von Galen, spoke out critically against the Nazi euthanasia policy by which mentally ill people were executed. Dietrich Bonhoeffer, a Protestant pastor, opposed Nazi policies towards racism and helped Jews to escape.

Opposition from the military

Opposition within military circles was led by General Ludwig Beck, who had resigned his post in the army in 1938 following the invasion of Austria, and Karl Goerdeler, a Nazi official. This group was prepared to use violent methods to rid Germany of Hitler, and it was responsible for two failed assassination attempts in March and November 1943, as well as the July Bomb Plot of 1944.

The July Bomb Plot, 1944

Codenamed Operation Valkyrie, the plot aimed to assassinate Hitler and seize control of Berlin using the army. On 20 July 1944 Colonel Claus von Stauffenberg, a senior army officer, left a bomb in a briefcase under the table in a conference room at Hitler's headquarters in east Prussia. Hitler had just arrived when Stauffenberg made an excuse to leave the room. Within minutes the bomb had exploded killing four people, but Hitler received only minor wounds. Those involved in the plot were quickly hunted down. Within months, over 5000 people suspected of being involved in the plot were executed, including 19 generals and 26 colonels.

Q Questions

1. What information does Source H give about how the Nazis dealt with opposition?
2. Describe the resistance and opposition to Nazi rule from young people.

THE DEFEAT OF GERMANY IN 1945

By 1945 it was clear that Germany had lost the war. During the closing months of the war Hitler refused to leave Berlin and directed the war effort from his bunker deep underneath the Reich Chancellery building. On 24 March 1945 the Allies crossed the Rhine from the west and on 22 April the Soviet Red Army entered Berlin from the east. Millions of German refugees were fleeing to escape the bombing of the cities, or to avoid the advancing Russian forces. Over 2 million refugees died from cold, hunger, disease and exhaustion.

SOURCE I

Winter 1945. When I reached the Gedachtnisplatz [in Berlin] I was surrounded by a frozen sea of shattered ruins ... In the Budapesterstrasse house after house was an empty shell, not one single building had survived ... The centre of Berlin – capital of Hitler's mighty empire which, he had boasted, would last for a thousand years, and I was alone in a silent ghost town.

An entry from the diary of Christabel Bielenberg, taken from her book *The Past is Myself*, 1968.

Not wanting to be captured by the Russians, Hitler committed suicide on 30 April 1945, after marrying his mistress Eva Braun. He left the control of the state to Admiral Karl Doenitz, who agreed Germany's unconditional surrender with the Allies on 7 May 1945. Hitler's thousand-year Reich had come to an end after just 12 years.

The trials of 21 top Nazi Party leaders took place at Nuremberg between 1945 and 1947. Ten were hanged; others like Speer were imprisoned for 'crimes against peace and humanity'; Göring committed suicide. Following the division of Germany into zones of occupation by the four Allied powers, a vigorous policy of denazification was put into action, to clear away evidence of the Third Reich.

5 EXAM PRACTICE

These questions test Section A of the examination paper.

GERMANY DURING THE SECOND WORLD WAR, 1939–45

Study Sources A–D and then answer the questions which follow.

SOURCE A A photograph showing the conference room where Hitler narrowly escaped death during the July Plot of 1944.

SOURCE B

People here are fed up with the war. On their faces one can read despair, can sense wretchedness and irritation wherever one happens to be. How different the atmosphere is from the first year of the war when red Nazi flags were flown and drums were beaten whenever the radio announced another victory. Since Stalingrad and the realisation of total war all is grey and still. Shop after shop has closed down. One tolerates discomfort, forgets that life was ever different.

Mathilde Wolff-Monckeberg, a German housewife in Hamburg, records her experiences of the Second World War in her diary in 1943.

SOURCE C

The day of reckoning has come. This is the day when German youth will get their revenge on Hitler. In the name of German youth we demand from Adolf Hitler the return of our personal freedom which he took from us. There can be but one word of action for us: Fight the Nazis. Each of us must join in the fight for our future. Students, the eyes of the German nation are upon us. The dead of Stalingrad beg us to act.

A pamphlet published by 15 members of the White Rose group at Munich University on 18 February 1943.

SOURCE D

For much of his rule Hitler was very popular, so for most people there was never any question of opposing the Führer or the Nazis. As all other political parties were banned it was difficult to organise opposition. The Gestapo dealt ruthlessly with any persons who did try to oppose Nazi rule.

Adapted from a school history textbook by Richard Radway, *Germany 1918–45* (1998).

EQ Exam Questions

1 What information does Source A give about opposition to Hitler in wartime Germany? [3]

2 Use the information in Source B and your own knowledge to explain the reactions of the German people to the war. [4]

3 How useful is Source C as evidence to an historian studying opposition to Hitler during the Second World War? Explain your answer using the source and your own knowledge. [5]

4 In Source D the author is saying that there was little resistance to Hitler and the Nazis from within Germany. Is this a valid interpretation?
In your answer you should use your own knowledge of the topic, refer to the other relevant sources in this question, and consider how the author came to this interpretation. [8]

6 SOUTH AFRICA, 1960–94

In the seventeenth century, the southern tip of Africa was colonised by Dutch settlers, known as Boers. After 1815, the Cape became a British colony and the Boers resettled to the north and east, fighting a series of wars against the local tribes to secure new land. The discovery of diamonds in the Boer colonies sparked an English invasion and the Boer War of 1899–1902. The British won this war and the Boer colonies became part of the British Empire. The Union of South Africa formally united these colonies in 1910.

Though united in name, the peoples of South Africa were deeply divided. In 1926, Britain granted self-government to South Africa. The period between the First and Second World Wars saw the further removal of political rights for both the black people of South Africa and Indian settlers. Afrikaans, the language spoken by Boers, became the official language.

In 1948, the National Party came to power under Daniel Malan. The new government immediately introduced a series of racist laws known as apartheid, designed to keep all political and economic power in the hands of the white minority. Race laws touched every aspect of life and created a brutal system of segregation and control. Opposition to apartheid from within South Africa was violently suppressed.

By the 1970s, resistance to apartheid from both within and outside South Africa created pressure for change. An international ban of economic and sporting links with South Africa began to damage the country's economy. The 1980s saw limited reform to the apartheid system. Sweeping changes came under President de Klerk following the release of Nelson Mandela in 1990. In 1994, the country's first democratic election signalled the end of the apartheid system in South Africa.

TIMELINE OF EVENTS

1912 African National Congress (ANC) founded

1948 Afrikaner National Party comes to power

1949-56 Apartheid laws passed

1961 South Africa becomes a republic; withdraws from Commonwealth

1962 UN votes to impose sanctions on South Africa

1964 Nelson Mandela sentenced to life imprisonment

1976 Rioting and killings in Soweto

1985 European Community imposes economic sanctions
'Petty apartheid' is abolished; Mixed Marriage Act is repealed

1986 Pass Laws are repealed

1989 F.W. de Klerk becomes President

1990 ANC and PAC are legalised
Nelson Mandela is released from prison

1991 Apartheid laws are repealed

1994 South Africa holds its first democratic elections
Nelson Mandela becomes President

What were the major features of the apartheid system and how did it affect the people of South Africa?

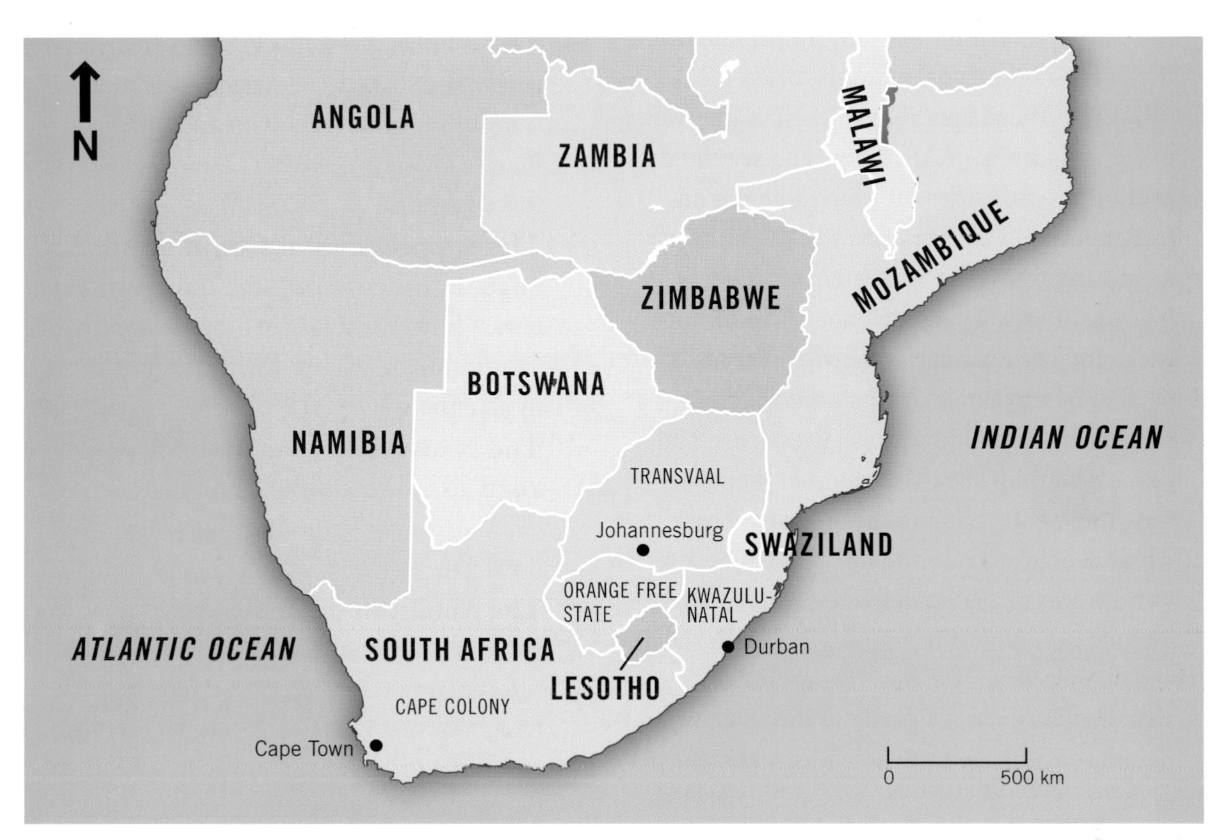

Map of southern and central Africa.

WHITE RULE IN SOUTH AFRICA

In 1652 the Dutch established a settlement in Cape Town and began colonising the region. The settlers developed their own language, Afrikaans, and were known as Boers (farmers). They were loyal to the Dutch Reformed Church, which taught that God had created the white man as superior to 'lesser races'. Slavery was adopted and the black labour force became the basis of Dutch prosperity.

Britain conquered the colony in 1814 because it was an important point on the trade route to India. When slavery was abolished in the British Empire in 1833, some 10,000 Boers left Cape Colony and created two independent republics – the Orange Free State and the Transvaal. The British and Dutch lived in relative peace until gold and diamonds were discovered in Boer territory. This discovery resulted in a struggle for control which led in turn to the Boer War of 1899–1902. The Boers were defeated by the British in 1902. In 1910 the four colonies of the Transvaal, the Orange Free State, Natal and Cape Colony were joined together as the Union of South Africa. The new union was allowed to establish its own government and in 1931 the Afrikaner-led colony was granted independence.

THE NATIONAL PARTY AND APARTHEID

In 1948 the Afrikaner-led National Party came to power under Dr Daniel Malan. The Afrikaners formed about 55 per cent of the white population but only 13 per cent of the entire population of South Africa. However, Malan appointed a cabinet that was made up entirely of Afrikaners and set about putting their theories on white domination into practice. The Afrikaans word apartheid means 'apartness' or 'separateness'. The National Party argued that apartheid meant 'separate development' – the idea that black people, white people and coloured (mixed race) people should live their lives apart, and that each group should develop in their own way. But 'apart' came to mean 'control by white people' and 'apartheid' came to be a set of measures to maintain white supremacy and exclude non-whites from every political, social and economic advantage. The system of apartheid was already partly in existence when the National Party took power in 1948. But, in the years after 1948, the system of apartheid was extended and ruthlessly enforced.

SOURCE A

It is a policy which sets itself the task of preserving and safeguarding the racial identity of the white population of the country; of also safeguarding the identity of indigenous peoples as separate racial groups with opportunities to develop into self-governing national units.

The National Party defined its policy in a pamphlet issued in 1947.

THE APARTHEID LAWS (TO 1960)

The apartheid system was introduced by a series of laws.

- **Prohibition of Mixed Marriages Act, 1949** banned marriage between black people and white people.
- **The Population Registration Act, 1950** categorised people into three groups – White, Natives (black Africans) and Coloureds (mixed race).
- **The Group Areas Act, 1950** restricted each group to its own residential and trading sections of towns and cities. People living in 'wrong' areas were forced to move.
- **The Suppression of Communism Act, 1950,** in order to enforce the apartheid laws, allowed the government to define 'communism' as any form of opposition to apartheid.
- **The Native Laws Amendment Act, 1952** aimed to control the movement of black Africans by giving the police the power to arrest at will.
- **The Abolition of Passes Act, 1952,** in spite of its name, actually introduced a reference book or *dompass* (accursed pass). All black Africans had to carry one and produce it on demand. It contained the person's photograph, address, job title and fingerprints.
- **The Reservation of Separate Amenities Act, 1953** identified separate facilities in public places, such as offices and parks, for black and white people.
- **The Bantu Education Act, 1953** stated that black people were to receive a more basic education, to prepare them for less-skilled work.
- **The Resettlement of Natives Act, 1954** led to the compulsory movement of 100,000 Africans.
- **The Senate Act, 1956** removed the right of black people to vote.

Q Questions

1. Explain the term 'apartheid'.
2. How did the National Party put its theories into practice?

CHANGES TO THE APARTHEID SYSTEM UNDER VERWOERD

In 1958 the premiership passed to Dr Hendrik Verwoerd. He set out to introduce a form of independence for the Bantu areas (black Africans were known as Bantus). A Bantustan was a homeland for black people which had self-government. Verwoerd believed that black Africans should be denied political rights because they were not really South African. He believed that different African 'nations' should be given political rights in their own self-governing homelands. Verwoerd described apartheid as a 'policy of good neighbours'.

SOURCE B Cartoon commenting on Verwoerd's 'policy of good neighbours', *Daily Mail*, 6 March 1961.

'Bantustans'

Seven areas – Bantustans – were set aside for black Africans to live in and farm. The first, Transkei, was set up in 1962. In theory, each was to be independent with its own government. In reality the Bantustans were controlled economically and politically by the white South African government, which could overrule any decision made by the Bantustans, and were little more than a further consolidation of apartheid. Though black Africans made up nearly 70 per cent of the population, the Bantustans consisted of only 13 per cent of the land.

Enforced movement of black Africans

The government underestimated the growth rate of the African population. When it realised that there would be 37 million Africans and not 21 million by the end of the twentieth century, it accelerated the process of moving 'surplus' blacks out of white areas. This process had already been set in motion by the Group Areas Act of 1950. Four categories of black Africans qualified for removal:

1. the elderly and unfit who did not qualify to live in towns
2. redundant labourers in white farms
3. inhabitants of 'black spots' on white areas
4. skilled workers who were needed in the homelands.

An estimated 3.5 million people were uprooted from their homes, often with a bulldozer close behind, in order to clear areas designated as 'white'. Sophiatown in Pretoria was bulldozed and rebuilt as a neat suburb called Triumph which, for many white people, it was.

SOURCE C

They came for us at half-past five in the morning. There were five white men rattling the gate and shouting 'maak julle oop' ('Open up'). My husband could only watch in horror as two lorries pulled up. We were ordered to take everything and throw it outside. My husband had built the house with his bare hands, it was our kingdom, and now we were put on lorries and moved to Meadowlands.

An enforced move described by Jane Dakile, a teacher at St Cyprian's Anglican School, Sophiatown, 10 November 1958.

Many black Africans were forced to live in townships on the edge of cities, such as Soweto – the South West Township – at Johannesburg.

Questions

1 How does Source B contradict Verwoerd's view of apartheid as a policy of good neighbours?

2 How independent were the homelands?

CULTURAL LIFE UNDER APARTHEID

Cultural apartheid was extended by the State-Aided Institutions Act of 1957. This enforced segregation in libraries and places of public entertainment if they were controlled by public authorities.

Literature, music and art

Much of the literature of South Africa reflects the nation's political and social tension. The black writer Ezekiel Mphahle, the coloured novelist Peter Abrahms and the white writer Alan Paton all describe how apartheid has affected the South African nation. In 1991 the white writer Nadine Gordimer received the Nobel Prize for Literature for her novels criticising racism.

The jive of New York mixed with traditional African dance steps produced the *tsabe-tsabe*, an energetic dance that inspired black musicians. In 1954, August Musururgwa's tune 'Skokiaan' topped the US hit parade as 'Happy Africa'. The Separate Amenities and Group Areas Acts of the early 1950's closed down many of the music and arts venues used by black Africans, stifling creativity and forcing many musicians to flee abroad. Pianist Dollar Brand (later Abdullah Ibrahim), the world renowned trumpeter Hugh Masekela and the singer Miriam Makeba all left South Africa. Black African music now became rooted in townships like Soweto.

The artist Gerard Sekoto's painting *Woman Ironing* (1941) was inspired by his stay in Sophiatown. The dark, murky atmosphere of the painting reveals his view of black life under white domination. The candle provides the only light and is symbolic of hope to black Africans.

SOURCE D *Woman Ironing* by Gerard Sekoto, 1941.

Questions

1 Describe the effects of government legislation on the arts in South Africa.

2 How did writers and artists express their opposition to apartheid?

LIFE AND WORK UNDER APARTHEID

Employment

Farms in the homelands were much smaller and less productive than farms owned by whites. The soil was often exhausted as so many people were forced to live in a relatively small area, and many people were forced to seek work in the cities. However, black people were only permitted to live in cities as temporary inhabitants if they had jobs with white employers. Discrimination was most evident in the wages paid to each sector of society (see chart below).

Unemployment among black Africans was high and, although they could join trade unions, they had limited powers to strike and workers in essential industries (including mining) were barred from striking. This meant that they had little opportunity for improving their situation.

Education

To members of the National Party, the black African was different from the white man and so had to be taught differently. Education aimed to teach Africans to 'know their place' and so they expected and received very little. Pupils between the ages of 7 and 16 of each racial group were required by law to attend separate public schools, but the law did not actually require black children to attend school until 1981.

Resources in black African schools were limited and facilities were poor. In 1972, £9.50 was spent on each black African schoolchild while £129 was spent on each white student. Black students were not taught English or Afrikaans (the languages most commonly used in business and politics) and received a very basic education. The Native Affairs Department controlled the training and appointment of teachers and, in Verwoerd's words, 'The Bantu teacher serves the Bantu community, and his salary must be fixed accordingly.'

SOURCE E

The native needs vocational guidance. His destiny is to become a miner, agricultural worker or a factory worker in his own reserves. A limited application of the three Rs [reading, writing and arithmetic] will do him more good than a ton of culture. Knowledge of writing may be used to forge passes.

Part of an article in the newspaper *White African*, August 1954.

Black political organisations like the African National Congress (see page 175) argued that education was the key to political and economic progress and many parents withdrew their children from schools in protest against government policy.

1966	Black African	Coloured	Asian	White
Population (in millions)	12.47	1.8	0.5	3.48
Annual income per head (in Rand)	87	109	147	952
Average salary:				
Mining	152	458	458	2562
Manufacturing	422	660	660	2058

Figures from UNESCO.

SOURCE F A township in South Africa: Sophiatown, Johannesburg's shanty town, in February 1955.

However, police raids and prosecutions forced most children back into Bantu education by the mid-1950s. Apartheid was introduced into university education by an act of 1959. 'Non-white' universities were set up and allowed to admit only members of specified Bantu groups. Both the courses offered and student life were strictly controlled.

SOURCE G

Soweto, a vast dormitory town for Johannesburg black workers, housed 600,000 people in its 100,000 'housing units'. In reality, the number of inhabitants was nearer 1.5 million with hundreds of thousands of desperate job-seekers crowding from six to 25 into three or four-bedroom boxes of houses. Some 86 per cent have no electricity and 97 per cent no running water. There is one hospital. Over half the population is under 20 and the majority of children suffer from malnutrition. The township was continuously racked by a high crime rate.

Extract from *How Long Will South Africa Survive?* by R.W. Johnson, 1982.

Housing

As most black people were prevented from living in the cities, black Africans were forced to live in townships on the edge of South African cities. The most famous was the South West Township of Johannesburg, known as Soweto (see Source G). Concentrating such large numbers of black people into such small areas made the townships difficult to control. They also became rich recruiting grounds for anti-apartheid groups such as the African National Congress (ANC) and Pan African Congress (PAC).

Q Questions

1 Describe how the apartheid system affected life for black Africans.

2 How useful and reliable is the table of figures from UNESCO (page 171) to someone studying discrimination in the workplace? Explain your answer.

3 What does Source E reveal about government policy in educating black Africans? Explain your answer using the source and your knowledge.

BANNINGS, DETENTIONS AND CENSORSHIP

The Suppression of Communism Act of 1950 outlawed the Communist Party along with any other organisation deemed unfit by the government, that is any anti-apartheid group. The Criminal Law Amendment Act of 1953 made it an offence to protest against any law and the Riotous Assemblies Act (amended 1956) made it unlawful to intimidate people during strike action. The legislation was aimed at the African National Congress (ANC), trade unions and, in particular, members of the Defiance Campaign, a militant movement within the ANC.

Banning and detention

On 26 June 1952, the Defiance Campaign was launched (see also page 176). The campaign was a non-violent protest against apartheid in which groups of protestors in black settlements throughout South Africa deliberately broke laws they saw as unjust. Hundreds of arrests followed in swift retribution. By October over 8000 black Africans had been arrested. During the same period membership of the ANC rose from 7000 to 100,000.

A meeting planned for 26 June 1955 to adopt a Freedom Charter (see page 176) drew a massive security presence. Everyone at the meeting was arrested on suspicion of treason and 'bannings' were served. 'Bannings' meant that suspects were prevented from writing, making broadcasts, attending meetings or even leaving home.

On the day that ANC president Albert Luthuli received news that he had won the Nobel Peace Prize, John Vorster, the Justice Minister, announced legislation to 'limit freedom of speech and the movement of agitators'. The Sabotage Act of 1962 made political opposition punishable by death and the No Trial Act of 1963 gave police the power to arrest anyone and hold them in prison for up to 90 days (increased to 180 days in 1965). South Africa had been transformed into a police state. On succeeding Verwoerd, Vorster tightened up state security by setting up the Bureau of State Security (BOSS) in 1969. This was a secret police force which provided support for the uniformed police and helped enforce apartheid laws.

Censorship

The South African Broadcasting Company was very pro-white and did not broadcast material which was against apartheid. The Sabotage Act required newspapers to deposit large sums of money which would be forfeited if the paper was subsequently banned by the government. In 1967 the editor of the *Rand Daily Mail* was put on trial for publishing an article about prison conditions. Wide powers were given to the Publications Control Board to ban the import of works and films deemed a threat to state security and in 1974 the government went so far as to ban a book written in Afrikaans – Andre Brink's *Kennis Van die Aand* (Knowing the Night).

Q Questions

1 Describe how South Africa had become a police state by the end of the 1960s.

2 Explain why the government censored newspapers and other publications.

6 EXAM PRACTICE

These questions test Section B of the examination paper.

THE FEATURES OF APARTHEID

Study the information below and then answer the questions which follow.

INFORMATION The picture shows a typical scene of black South Africans having their passes checked by the police.

EQ Exam Questions

1 a Describe the main features of separate development. [2]
b Explain why the Bantu Educational Act was passed. [4]
c How successful was the Group Areas Act? [5]

2 a Describe how the apartheid laws affected the coloured people of South Africa. [3]
b Explain why the government was keen to stop coloured people from voting. [4]

3 Was apartheid fully supported by all the white people of South Africa in the 1960s? Explain your answer fully. [7]

What were the main features of opposition to apartheid in South Africa?

BLACK RESISTANCE: THE CAMPAIGNS OF THE ANC AND PAC

When the National Party came to power in 1948, the African National Congress (ANC) became the leading voice for political and social change for black Africans. It had been set up in 1912 to campaign for the rights of black South Africans, but under the leadership of men such as Albert Luthuli, Nelson Mandela, Walter Sisulu and Oliver Tambo, it became more organised.

Its aims were to fight for freedom from white domination and to gain representation of black Africans in all official institutions. It aimed to achieve these ends by peaceful protest, but the need for a more militant, more violent approach led to the formation of the Pan African Congress (PAC) in 1959. Formed by Robert Sobukwe, the PAC rejected collaboration with Asian and coloured South Africans.

SOURCE A

We claim Africa for the Africans, the ANC claims Africa for all.

Robert Sobukwe of the Pan African Congress speaking in 1983.

NELSON MANDELA (born 1918)

SOURCE B

Nelson Mandela.

Born in Umtata, Eastern Cape province, Mandela was expelled from the University of Fort Hare in 1940 for planning a student demonstration. He completed his law degree by correspondence and then at the University of Witwatersrand. He became involved in the ANC, helping to set up its Youth League in 1944, before becoming its president in 1951.

In 1956 he was charged with treason but was acquitted after a trial lasting five years. After Sharpeville the ANC and PAC were banned and Mandela helped to establish the ANC's military branch, Umkhonto We Sizwe (Spear of the Nation), in 1961. He slipped abroad to Algeria where he trained in guerrilla warfare but was arrested back in South Africa in August 1962 for incitement and leaving the country illegally. He was sentenced to five years but this was increased to life at the Rivonia trials in 1964. Mandela became the symbol of resistance against apartheid while imprisoned at Robben Island. He was released from prison in 1990.

Day of Defiance and the Treason Trials

The Youth League of the ANC argued that petitions and deputations would not lead to change and advocated a programme of civil disobedience. On 26 June 1952 – the Day of Defiance – thousands of black Africans walked through 'forbidden areas' without their passes. Over 8000 people were arrested and nearly all were convicted. On 26 June 1955 a gathering of the Congress of the People met to approve a Freedom Charter which demanded the right to vote and equality before the law and in education and the workplace. Armed police arrested the delegates on charges of treason. In the following months hundreds more were indicted in the Treason Trials which were to drag on for two years.

Sharpeville

The newly-created PAC launched its first attack on apartheid by organising a nationwide protest against the pass laws. Sharpeville in the Transvaal was a 'model township' containing 21,000 people. Unemployment was high especially among the young, rents had risen sharply and those unable to pay had been sent back to the homelands. An expectant crowd of between three and five thousand (later to swell to 20,000) gathered in Sharpeville on 21 March 1960. Eyewitnesses later reported that the crowd was noisy but not hostile. However, when a fence surrounding the police station was trampled and an officer knocked down, the police opened fire with stun guns. When the shooting stopped, 69 Africans had been killed: over half of them had been shot in the back (trying to flee from the police bullets). A further 186 were wounded.

SOURCE C

Then the shooting started. We heard the chatter of a machine gun, then another, then another ... One woman was hit about ten yards from our car. Her companion thought she had stumbled but when he turned her over, he saw that her chest had been shot away.

Before the shooting, I heard no warning to the crowd to disperse. There was no warning volley. The shooting did not stop until there was no living thing in the huge compound in front of the police station.

An eyewitness account of the Sharpeville massacre in 1960.

Aftermath of Sharpeville

Following the massacre, a day of mourning was called by Albert Luthuli and many Africans stayed off work in protest. Gun shops in the Transvaal and Cape Province sold out as white people rushed to arm themselves.

A Commission of Enquiry was held but its findings were inconclusive. No actual order to shoot was given and no warning shots fired. Many of the officers on duty were inexperienced and undisciplined and had continued to shoot after the ceasefire was ordered.

Consequences of Sharpeville

The South African government was defiant: public gatherings were banned and the ANC and PAC were declared illegal. Some 18,000 people were detained and a state of emergency declared. Sobukwe was sentenced to three years' imprisonment but was held for a further six years.

Protest marches were staged in Durban and Cape Town where 30,000 people marched on the parliament, demanding the release of black African leaders. The government declared another state of emergency, and bannings, curfews and arrests were made.

The ANC and PAC, forced underground, came to realise that non-violent protest had achieved nothing. The ANC set up a military wing, Umkhonto We Sizwe (the Spear of the Nation, or MK), and the PAC set up Poqo (Pure) to carry out violence. The MK began a sabotage campaign against post offices, electricity and railway stations. Poqo began a more violent campaign and in 1962 eleven police officers and suspected informers were killed.

SOURCE D

We are starting again Africans ... we die once. Africa will be free on 1 January. The white people shall suffer, the black people will rule. Freedom comes after bloodshed. Poqo has started.

From a pamphlet distributed in the Cape Town township of Nyanga, December 1961.

The Rivonia trial

MK was broken up after the arrest in August 1962 of Nelson Mandela and others on charges of sabotage. The government held a show trial at Rivonia in an attempt to destroy the image of the ANC and the Communist Party. Those found guilty were sentenced to life imprisonment. After Rivonia, the political trial became a feature of government policy and until 1987 every year saw at least one major trial.

Q Questions

1 What were the aims of the ANC before 1960 and how did its members hope to achieve them?

2 Describe the events at Sharpeville.

3 Explain why Sharpeville was a turning point in the history of the ANC and PAC.

i BANTU STEVE BIKO (1946–77)

SOURCE E

Steve Biko.

Biko had been introduced to politics as a teenager by his brother, a Poqo activist. At the black medical section of Natal University he became drawn into the activities of the National Union of South African Students (NUSAS). He began to campaign for an all-black university movement and in 1969 the South African Students' Organisation (SASO) was established with Biko as president. He called for a freeing of the mind after years of black people being conditioned as underdogs. Black consciousness now became the rallying call for all Africans. The movement was seriously damaged in 1977 when Biko died after 26 days in police detention. The autopsy revealed the cause of death as a forceful blow (or blows) to the head.

THE GROWTH OF BLACK CONSCIOUSNESS

Soweto: 'a riot waiting to happen'

In 1976, as part of a programme of educational 'reform', the government ordered that up to half the teaching in black schools had to be delivered in Afrikaans, a language not understood and despised by black Africans. This came at a time when youth unemployment was high and when moves were being made to make the Transkei independent. For those living in the Transkei, this would result in their losing the rights of South African citizenship and access to the job market.

A protest march of students was planned for 16 June 1976 in Soweto. A senior pupil spoke to a crowd of several thousand and appealed for calm. Police surrounded the gathering and a teargas canister was thrown into the crowd. A single shot led to more shootings which killed two and wounded twelve. News of the shootings spread among the black population and barricades were erected. Hundreds of police reinforcements arrived and Soweto erupted in violence. A wave of raids and arrests followed, many of those arrested were children.

The official number of dead was given as 176 up to 25 June 1976 and the findings of a Commission of Enquiry added a further 575 in the aftermath of rioting. The list contained 104 children under the age of 17. The government banned all movements associated with black consciousness, including the SASO.

SOURCE F A fatally injured 13-year-old, Soweto, 1976.

Soweto was again the focus of attention in 1980 when a move to employ white national servicemen as teachers in black schools triggered a boycott and burning of buildings. The early-1980s also witnessed unrest in the workplace as membership of trade unions increased. Thousands of young Africans left the country to join the ANC in exile. Support for the ANC grew in the townships and the draping of its flag on the coffins of people killed in the troubles became a common sight. On 21 March 1985 (the twenty-fifth anniversary of Sharpeville), 20 Africans were shot dead by police during a funeral procession (see Source G). Protests spread and culminated in a bombing campaign in Durban and Port Elizabeth.

Q Questions

1. How important was Steve Biko to the black consciousness movement? Explain your answer.
2. Describe the riots at Soweto.

SOURCE G Black mourners carry the coffins of 20 people shot dead at Uitenhage, 21 March 1985.

OTHER OPPOSITION TO APARTHEID

White opposition groups

Supporters of apartheid were almost exclusively white but this did not mean that all white people in South Africa were in favour of apartheid.

- The **United Party** became the official party of opposition in 1948. However, while it rejected the apartheid system it still supported segregation and upheld the belief in white superiority.
- In 1959 a breakaway group of twelve United Party MPs formed the **Progressive Party** although in the election which followed only one, Helen Suzman, an outstanding campaigner against apartheid, retained her seat. The Progressive Party favoured the protection of human rights and parliamentary representation of all racial groups in South Africa.
- The **Liberal Party** spoke out against apartheid but dissolved itself in 1969 rather than submit to a law that prohibited all parties from allowing different races to organise into one body.
- The white **Congress Party** opposed the belief in white supremacy but, because many of its members came from the outlawed Communist Party, it was banned.
- **Black Sash** was a human rights organisation run by white women which campaigned against apartheid and took up legal cases on behalf of black people.

Inkatha ya KwaZulu and the UDF

The black opposition movement Inkatha ya KwaZulu was set up by Chief Buthelezi, prime minister of the homeland KwaZulu, in 1975. The party's aim was to establish independence from South Africa for the Zulu nation. This aim was in conflict with the ANC's desire for a united South Africa, a difference which the government tried to exploit by inciting, and possibly carrying out, massacres of ANC and Inkatha supporters.

The United Democratic Front (UDF) was formed in 1983. 565 separate groups, including all races, colours, genders and religions, united in their determination to end apartheid. The UDF posed an enormous threat to the National Party's grip on South Africa.

Opposition from individuals

Individuals also voiced their opposition to apartheid. Father Trevor Huddleston and Bishop Ambrose Reeves of the Anglican Church are two of the best known white opponents of apartheid. One of the best known black opponents of apartheid is Archbishop Desmond Tutu, who was awarded the Nobel Peace Prize in 1984 in recognition of his non-violent campaign against apartheid.

However, the most powerful opposition to apartheid came from outside South Africa. This is explained further in the following section.

6 EXAM PRACTICE

These questions test Section B of the examination paper.

OPPOSITION WITHIN SOUTH AFRICA

Study the information below and then answer the questions which follow.

INFORMATION

Injured black South Africans lie on the ground while white South African police stand by after protest is violently suppressed, 1961. In 1961, following anger at the way black people were treated, the Umkhonto We Sizwe, usually known as MK, was formed by Nelson Mandela.

EQ Exam Questions

1 **a** Describe the activities of the MK (the Spear of the Nation). [2]

b Explain why there was a massacre at Sharpeville in 1960. [4]

c How important was the African National Congress (ANC) in the campaign to end apartheid in South Africa? [5]

2 **a** Describe what happened at Soweto in 1976. [3]

b Explain the importance of Nelson Mandela in the period 1960–90. [4]

3 Was violence the only way to successfully oppose apartheid within South Africa during the 1970s and 1980s? Explain your answer fully. [7]

In what ways did international pressure contribute to the ending of apartheid in South Africa?

OPPOSITION FROM THE BRITISH COMMONWEALTH

The term 'Commonwealth' was first used after the First World War to describe the special relationship between Britain and its dominions (former colonies). In 1931 the Statute of Westminster declared these dominions fully independent but allowed them to remain loyal to the British crown as members of the British Commonwealth of Nations. The South African government chose its fiftieth anniversary to announce a referendum to change from dominion status to a republic separate from the Commonwealth.

Relations between South Africa and the Commonwealth remained uneasy throughout the 1950s. Verwoerd argued that the Commonwealth had become dominated by newly-independent African states that were hostile to South Africa. In 1960 the British prime minister Harold Macmillan ended a tour of Britain's African dominions in South Africa where he delivered his 'Wind of Change' speech which was directed against white rule and the system of apartheid.

In October 1960, 52 per cent of white people voted to establish a republic. Verwoerd had planned to remain in the Commonwealth but strong criticism of his government's apartheid policy from other Commonwealth members led him to withdraw South Africa on May 31 1961.

OPPOSITION FROM THE UNITED NATIONS

The United Nations charter also aimed to reaffirm faith in basic human rights and in 1948 it passed a resolution which recognised that people of all races were equal (see Source A).

SOURCE A

The inherent dignity and equal rights of all members of the human family in the foundation of freedom, justice and peace ... all are born free without distinction of race, colour, sex, language, religion, political or other opinion.

An extract from the UN resolution on human rights, 1948.

UN action against South Africa

After 1945, South Africa was the subject of much debate in the UN on two counts:

1 its policy of apartheid
2 South African control of South West Africa (Namibia).

The shootings at Sharpeville in March 1960 brought strong criticism for the South African government and the UN Security Council passed a resolution stating that South Africa's policies led to 'international friction thereby endangering peace and security'. As newly-independent African countries took their places in the UN in the 1960s and 1970s, condemnation of the South African government became more widespread.

SOURCE B A pro-apartheid poster of South Africa in the late 1950s.

South Africa's involvement in South West Africa (Namibia)

South West Africa had been a German territory and after 1919 it became a mandate of South Africa (mandates were to be 'looked after' by other countries as they prepared for independence). South Africa shamelessly exploited the region and by 1945 had put a programme of apartheid in place. When the UN demanded that the mandate be given up, South Africa refused and took steps to integrate South West Africa.

In 1960 an opposition group, the South West African People's Organisation (SWAPO) was set up to encourage guerrilla-type resistance to South Africa's presence. In 1971 the UN declared South Africa's presence illegal and in 1973 recognised SWAPO as the true representatives of Namibia. South Africa continued to resist UN directives. Over 30 years of brutal fighting between SWAPO and the South African army achieved little until 1989 when international pressure succeeded in achieving popular elections in Namibia. On 21 March 1990, Namibia became the last African colony to gain independence.

OPPOSITION FROM THE OAU

As they had been banned in South Africa, the ANC and PAC extended their activities outside South Africa by establishing offices in Dar-es-Salaam, London, Cairo, Algiers and elsewhere. Together with other expelled African political groups from Namibia and Southern Rhodesia they established the Organisation of African Unity (OAU) in May 1963. The organisation set out to put pressure on the UN in an attempt to isolate South Africa through sanctions as a start towards the overthrow of white rule. However, maintaining sustained opposition among OAU countries proved difficult because South Africa pursued a clever policy of developing trading relations with emerging African nations, many of whom relied on its wealth for their economic survival. This meant that they were in no position to impose sanctions.

Q Questions

1 How and why did the Commonwealth, United Nations and the OAU oppose South Africa?

2 What was South Africa's reaction to the opposition?

ECONOMIC SANCTIONS

In 1962 the UN voted to impose economic sanctions (trade restrictions) on South Africa and urged member states to break off diplomatic relations and close airports and harbours to South African planes and ships. In 1963 the Security Council of the UN resolved to ban sales of arms to South Africa. The Organisation of Petroleum Exporting Countries (OPEC) banned oil sales to South Africa in 1973. It was hoped that these actions would put pressure on South Africa to change its policies towards black South Africans.

In the aftermath of Soweto, a US civil rights worker, the Reverend Leon Sullivan, urged US firms to withdraw from South Africa. The Sullivan Code began a wave of international action that escalated in the 1980s when the world witnessed pictures of South African security forces in action:

- The European Community imposed economic sanctions in 1985.
- In 1986 the US Senate banned new investments and loans in South Africa and banned the import of uranium, coal, iron and steel.
- Large companies like General Motors, IBM and Coca-Cola closed down their operations in South Africa.
- Scandinavian countries imposed a total ban on South African goods.
- In October 1989 all Commonwealth countries apart from Britain proposed a three-tier plan to stiffen sanctions. The first phase would end all agricultural and manufactured imports from South Africa; the second phase would establish oil and arms embargoes and the banning of exports of computer and electronic equipment; the third phase would place sanctions on South African gold exports.

How effective were economic sanctions?

A country of such huge wealth was unlikely to be seriously damaged by sanctions and they were never uniformly and effectively imposed. Many developing African economies found it difficult to sever trade links with South Africa. South Africa was also too valuable to the West as the main supplier of manganese, platinum and chrome as well as gold and diamonds, so businesses with an eye on profits sought to evade sanctions. However, the South African economy suffered a serious downturn after western banks stopped loans to South Africa in 1985.

The most controversial issue was the supply of arms to South Africa. Opponents of apartheid argued that these would be used by the white South African government against black Africans, but Britain and other countries saw an armed South Africa as a barrier to Soviet (communist) ambitions in Africa.

Q Questions

1. Explain why sanctions were imposed on South Africa.
2. How effective were economic sanctions?

SPORTING BOYCOTTS

While economic sanctions were imposed by some countries, others used boycotts to protest at the system of apartheid. For example, in 1969 Basil d'Oliviera was selected to tour South Africa as part of the English national cricket team. As a classified 'coloured' he was disqualified from playing in a white English team against white South Africans.

SOURCE C Kenyon's Cartoon from the *Daily Despatch* makes fun of the inconsistencies of the new-model apartheid sports policy devised by Dr Koornhof.

The tour was cancelled, which began an international move to ban South Africa from sport, both at home and away fixtures.

In 1968 African countries had threatened to boycott the Mexico Olympics and in 1970 South Africa was expelled from the Olympic movement. In 1976 action was extended to any country maintaining sporting relations with South Africa. In 1977 all Commonwealth nations cut off sporting links. In the same year the UN passed the 'International declaration against apartheid in sport'.

SOURCE D

We are not prepared to receive a team thrust upon us by people whose interests are not the game, but to gain political objectives. The team is not the team of the MCC selection committee but of the political opponents of South Africa.

John Vorster, Prime Minister of South Africa, speaking in 1969.

How effective were sporting boycotts?

Despite the declaration of boycotts some sporting tours went ahead, especially in the game of rugby. In 1980 British teams toured South Africa and in 1981 the Springboks (the South African rugby team) visited New Zealand in a tour that caused many demonstrations and protests. Unofficial rebel cricket tours continued and in 1982 English cricketers received a three-year suspension for breaking the boycott. Other players respected the boycott, notably Ian Botham who refused to play in South Africa as a mark of respect to his friend, Viv Richards, and the footballer Kevin Keegan, who turned down £250,000 to play there.

Questions

1 How effective were sporting boycotts?

2 How useful is Source D to someone studying apartheid in South Africa? Explain your answer using the source and your own knowledge.

OPPOSITION TO APARTHEID BY ORDINARY PEOPLE

The Anti-Apartheid Movement (AAM) emerged in the late 1950s and proved important in the fight against apartheid by encouraging ordinary people to protest. By the mid-1970s branches had been set up in most European countries and the movement was especially strong in the Nordic countries who used their positions in the UN to voice their anti-apartheid stance. The AAM consisted of international, national and local bodies and developed a range of actions from public boycotts to UN sanctions, the provision of humanitarian assistance to refugees and military aid to liberation movements.

The AAM was also instrumental in promoting public opinion and public action against apartheid especially in countries that collaborated with South Africa. Many of the UN resolutions originated from the AAM. For example, in November 1972 the UN passed resolution 2923E (see Source E).

SOURCE E

[The UN] commends the activities of anti-apartheid movements, trade unions, student organisations, churches and other groups which have promoted national and international action against apartheid.

Extract from resolution 2923E of the United Nations Organisation.

6 EXAM PRACTICE

These questions test Section A of the examination paper.

INTERNATIONAL OPPOSITION TO APARTHEID

Study Sources A–D and then answer the questions which follow.

SOURCE A

A cartoon from a South African newspaper. Verwoerd is the small man in the cartoon, the other character is President Kennedy of the USA. The caption reads 'Aw gee Sheriff, I feel kinda silly being a bastion of the West without no shooting irons.'

SOURCE B

In 1968 various African countries threatened to boycott the Mexico Olympics if South Africa took part. The response was almost a foregone conclusion. South Africa was excluded and later expelled from the Olympic movement in 1970. The African bloc was able to force South Africa out of many competitions by indicating that it would withdraw if South Africa were included. In 1976, 21 countries boycotted the Montreal Olympic Games in protest at a rugby tour of South Africa undertaken by New Zealand – whose athletes had taken part in the games.

From a textbook, *The Readers Digest Illustrated History of South Africa.*

SOURCE C

In this solidarity movement, it can be said without any exaggeration, the Anti-Apartheid Movement in Britain and its leaders played a very significant role, at the national and international level and had a greater impact than its members perhaps realise. That is why the AAM became the target of South African intelligence and terrorism more than any group other than the liberation movement.

The views of E. S. Reddy, a member of the AAM, expressed in the paper, 'The Anti-Apartheid Movement: a 40-year Perspective', published in London in 1999.

SOURCE D

The foreign action that did South Africa the most damage occurred in 1985 when western banks refused to make any new loans and called in existing ones. South Africa was forced to repay US $13,000 million by December 1985. As a result, the Rand, the South African currency, lost 35 per cent of its value in thirteen days. From 1989 to 1992 South Africa went through a serious recession, which saw its national income fall by 3 per cent every year.

From a modern school textbook.

EQ Exam Questions

1 What information does Source A give about the supply of arms to South Africa? [3]

2 Use the information in Source B and your own knowledge to explain the use of sporting boycotts against South Africa [4]

3 How useful is Source C as evidence to an historian studying the role of AAM in the fight against apartheid in South Africa? Explain your answer using the source and your own knowledge. [5]

4 In Source D the author is saying that economic pressure was the most effective form of international opposition to South Africa. Is this a valid interpretation? *In your answer you should use your own knowledge of the topics, refer to the other relevant sources in this question and consider how the author came to this interpretation.* [8]

How and why did apartheid come to an end in South Africa?

P. W. BOTHA AND A 'NEW REALISM'

In 1978 P. W. Botha became Prime Minister and took over the government of a country which was experiencing serious problems:

- The economy was depressed, foreign investment was being withdrawn and sanctions and boycotts imposed.
- A population increase had led to a rise in unemployment, and finding work for so many uneducated and unskilled people would be difficult.
- The collapse of colonial (white) rule in Mozambique and Zimbabwe meant that South Africa was vulnerable to guerrilla attacks.

Botha saw the need for change, but did not want to give up apartheid and white control. As part of his 'Total Strategy' he aimed to:

- Create a black African middle class in order to increase competition among non-whites – coloureds against black South Africans, and middle-class black people against working-class black people. A new black middle class with extra rights, education and skills would also counter black activists in the townships.
- Stop ANC attacks from neighbouring states and the homelands by making those countries economically dependent on South Africa.
- Involve black people in politics and enable them to have a say in how taxes in townships were raised and spent.

In addition, Botha planned to remove many aspects of 'petty apartheid'. This meant that many of the restrictions on black South Africans were lifted:

- discriminatory signs were removed from public places
- desegregation was permitted but not made compulsory
- employers were allowed to employ skilled black workers and unions were legalised
- in 1985 the Mixed Marriages Act and laws preventing sexual relations between blacks and whites were repealed
- in 1986 the Pass Laws were abolished.

SOURCE A P.W. Botha (centre), with other South African parliamentarians, after becoming Prime Minister in 1978.

These measures were designed to continue apartheid but make some concessions in the hope of staying in power.

Changes to the constitution

In 1984 a parliament with three chambers – white, Asian and coloured – was created. MPs were to sit in separate chambers but any laws passed by the Asian or coloured houses had to be approved by the white chamber. This change further extended apartheid by dividing parliament on racial lines while excluding black Africans.

Botha's 'reforms' were attacked by anti-apartheid supporters, who argued that they had not gone far enough, and by white right-wing supporters, who felt that the reforms had gone too far.

Q Questions

1 Explain why Botha introduced changes to the apartheid system after 1978.

2 Botha's changes have been described as 'tinkering with the edges of apartheid'. How far do you agree with this statement?

THE GROWTH OF BLACK RESISTANCE

Botha's plan to exclude black Africans from parliament led to the setting up of the United Democratic Front (UDF) in August 1983 under the presidency of Dr Allan Boesak. The UDF attracted over 2 million members of all races and classes and adopted the Freedom Charter (1955) as the basis of its beliefs. It was joined by the more radical National Forum and by the ANC who called for its followers to make South Africa ungovernable.

Serious unrest flared up in the townships of the Transvaal as a result of a government decision to set up black African councils there as part of the policy of Total Strategy. The councils were unpopular and the townships set up their own community organisations. Peaceful protest turned to bitter violence.

Seven thousand troops entered Sebokeng township and began a search of 20,000 houses. After the killing of 20 Africans at Uitenhage, the government declared a state of emergency as parts of the country descended into virtual civil war. By March 1986 over 750 people had been killed, 20,000 injured and 14,000 arrested. Much of the violence resulted from clashes between ANC members and followers of Inkatha ya KwaZulu, a Zulu tribe nationalist movement led by Chief Mangosuthu Buthelezi. ANC leaders were angered that Buthelezi had accepted a Zulu homeland (KwaZulu) and accused him of co-operating with the National Party.

Botha's Rubicon speech

In August 1985, in an attempt to stop the violence, Botha gave his 'Rubicon' speech. Botha was expected to announce major reforms to the apartheid system, a 'crossing of the Rubicon' (a Rubicon is a point of no return), and the world's media gathered to listen to him. However, instead of the expected change of heart, they saw that Botha had no intention of bringing about major reforms and he also dismissed the idea of majority rule. However, Botha's Rubicon speech proved unpopular around the world and resulted in many major banks pulling out of South Africa, as well as an Anti-Apartheid Act in the USA.

Total Onslaught

Botha was convinced that South Africa was threatened by a 'Total Onslaught' or communist threat directed from Moscow and from within the country by the ANC. State security was stepped up and intelligence gathered on black activists. By the end of 1990, however, the Cold War was over and the Soviet Union was no longer seen as a threat to South Africa.

Questions

1 What were the causes of civil unrest after 1983?

CHANGES UNDER F. W. DE KLERK

In 1988 South Africa was in a state of deadlock. With sanctions causing economic difficulties and the main African political parties banned there seemed little hope of progress. The break came from an unlikely source – the National Party itself. In 1989 Botha had a stroke and resigned as leader of the party, so the leadership passed to F. W. de Klerk.

Dismantling apartheid

De Klerk accepted that apartheid could not survive and that concessions would need to be made with, at best, power sharing between black and white people.

THE ROLE OF BLACK CHURCH LEADERS

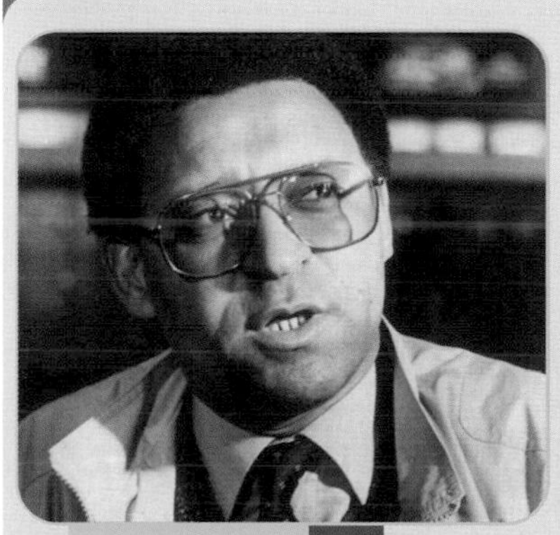

SOURCE B

Allan Boesak.

Allan Boesak, an ordained minister of the Dutch Reformed Church, was critical of the Church for its support of apartheid. He believed that apartheid was a heresy (an opinion or doctrine contrary to Church teachings). In 1983 Boesak became President of the UDF (see page 188) and he served as Vice-President of the South African Council of Churches from 1984 to 1987. In August 1985 he called for a march on Rollsmoor Prison to demand the release of Nelson Mandela, but was imprisoned by security forces. His detention attracted international interest and, when an attempt was made to start the march, the police intervened. In two days of clashes, 30 people were killed and 300 injured.

Desmond Mpilo Tutu, an Anglican priest, became the first black Secretary of the South African Council of Churches. In 1986 he became the first black Archbishop of Cape Town and titular head of the Anglican Church in South Africa.

Tutu was a vigorous critic of apartheid, and was awarded the Nobel Peace Prize in 1984. Tutu argued that apartheid cut across God's will since God had decreed all Africans to be equal. He urged world leaders to impose tough sanctions on South Africa. His crusading zeal was successful during the presidency of de Klerk.

SOURCE C

Archbishop Desmond Tutu

In his opening address to parliament on 2 February 1990 he legalised the ANC, PAC and Communist Party, ordered the release of many political prisoners, reduced emergency detentions to six months and suspended the death sentence.

The release of Nelson Mandela

The release of Nelson Mandela nine days later began a chain of events that few had anticipated.

- The government and the ANC began talks in May 1990; by June the state of emergency had been lifted and the ANC had agreed to a ceasefire.
- In 1991 the Acts which restricted land ownership, specified separate living areas and classified people by race were all repealed. South Africa had taken its first real steps towards becoming a multiracial society.

Backlash

De Klerk's reforms led many pro-apartheid supporters to leave the National Party and join the Conservative Party, which was against many of the reforms. It also provoked a resurgence of opposition from the white far–right Afrikaner Resistance Movement.

Violence also continued between Inkatha and the ANC fuelled by the revelation that the government had given economic and military aid to Inkatha.

TOWARDS RECONCILIATION

De Klerk's integrity had been challenged, Mandela was criticised by his more radical followers and Buthelezi was seen as a collaborator with apartheid. Spiralling violence finally brought them together in September 1991 when they signed a National Peace Accord.

CODESA

In December 1991, 19 political parties came together in the Convention for a Democratic South Africa (CODESA) to discuss a new constitution. They agreed to a motion to 'bring about an undivided South Africa with one nation sharing the common citizenship, free from any form of discrimination or domination under a liberal democratic constitution'.

Whites-only referendum for peace

De Klerk decided to gamble on a whites-only referendum on the peace process, to try and head off right-wing opposition. Mandela, determined that the process should not be derailed, urged his followers not to disrupt events. In a high turnout, 68 per cent of white people gave their support: the most serious barrier to reform had been swept away.

Beginnings of co-operation

In June 1992 hostel workers hacked, stabbed and shot 45 people to death in a brutal act of violence at Boipatong, Transvaal. The killings were seen at the time as part of the conflict between the African National Congress and the Inkatha Freedom Party.

Then, in September 1992, tens of thousands of ANC supporters marched on Bisho, Ciskei, in an attempt to overthrow the military government there. Soldiers responded by shooting at demonstrators. Thirty people died and some 200 were injured.

The double tragedy of Boipatong and Bisho, together with an economic slump, made politicians realise that co-operation was needed. De Klerk promised an investigation of the role of the security forces in the Boipatong and Bisho massacres. In April 1993 talks resumed, with the PAC and the 'white right' joining in, although Inkatha refused to take part.

On 10 April 1993, white right-wing activists assassinated the popular young ANC member Chris Hani. Mandela appealed for calm and channelled his anger and energy into plans for a general election.

Q Questions

1 Describe the parts played by de Klerk and Mandela in dismantling apartheid.

2 What events led to the speeding up of the peace process?

THE ROAD TO CONSTITUTIONAL DEMOCRACY

First election under universal suffrage

The interim constitution under which the election was held provided for a two-chamber parliament holding power with nine provincial legislatures. Candidates would be elected by proportional representation and the country would be ruled by a president elected by the national assembly heading a government obtaining 200 or more seats.

The Electoral Commission faced a massive exercise in organising a poll ten times bigger than ever before. On 27 April 1994 South Africa's first elections based on universal suffrage represented a defining moment in the country's history.

→ The ANC won an outright victory with 62.6 per cent of the vote and 252 of the 400 seats in the national assembly. However, it did not secure a two-thirds majority which would have allowed it to write its own constitution: this gave some reassurance to whites and other minorities.

SOURCE D Tens of thousands of ANC supporters march on Bisho, Ciskei, in an attempt to overthrow its military dictator, September 1992.

- The National Party gained 20.4 per cent of the vote taking 82 seats.
- Inkatha took 10.5 per cent of the vote and 43 seats.

Nelson Mandela as President

On 10 May 1994 Mandela was inaugurated as president of South Africa with Thabo Mbeki (chairman of the ANC) and de Klerk as deputy presidents. Buthelezi was made minister of home affairs. In a colourful ceremony in Pretoria the new government was sworn in. The occasion was hailed as one of the greatest acts of national reconciliation ever.

International acceptance

As the system of apartheid was abolished, the international isolation of South Africa began to break down:

- Sanctions were lifted in October 1993.
- Sports and cultural links were resumed.
- International trade missions began to explore investment possibilities.
- Talks began about relations with the European Union and the possibility of rejoining the Commonwealth.

6 EXAM PRACTICE

These questions test Section A of the examination paper.

THE END OF APARTHEID

Study Sources A–D and then answer the questions which follow.

SOURCE A A cartoon from a British newspaper, 1988. P.W. Botha is the white man in the cartoon.

SOURCE B

Let me remind you of three little words. The first word is 'all'. We want all our rights. The second word is 'here'. We want all our rights here in a united, undivided South Africa. We do not want them in impoverished homelands. The third word is 'now'. We want all our rights, we want them here and we want them now. We have been jailed, exiled, killed for too long.

The Reverend Allan Boesak speaking at the launch of the United Democratic Front (UDF), 20 August 1983.

SOURCE C

The ANC urges the assassination of black town councillors, policemen, members of the defence force and any other individual who disputes them. Part of its programme is to wipe out Inkatha and other black groups who oppose them. Such people have been hacked to death, they have been necklaced, their houses burned to the ground. One can only expect violent reaction to such violent attacks.

Chief Buthelezi, a Zulu leader, in a letter to the British newspaper the *Guardian*, 15 November 1986.

SOURCE D

In Parliament on 2 February 1990, de Klerk made a dramatic move. He announced the unbanning of the ANC and in the following weeks released Nelson Mandela. This move was partly brought about by popular protest and international criticism though the main factor was the economic crisis facing the country.

Extract from Nigel Worden's *The Making of Modern South Africa*, 1994

EQ Exam Questions

1 What information does Source A give about opposition to apartheid in South Africa in 1988? [3]

2 Use the information in Source B and your own knowledge to explain the aims of the UDF. [4]

3 How useful is Source C as evidence to an historian studying apartheid in South Africa? Explain your answer using the source and your own knowledge. [5]

4 In Source D the author is saying that apartheid was ended mainly because of the economic problems facing South Africa. Is this a valid interpretation?
In your answer you should use your own knowledge of the topic, refer to the other relevant sources in this question and consider how the author came to this interpretation. [8]

7 GERMANY, 1919–91

In 1900 Germany was one of the most powerful countries in Europe. It went to war confidently in 1914 but defeat in 1918 brought chaos to the nation.

In 1918 Germany's new government, the Weimar Republic, became associated with surrender and was forced to accept the humiliating terms of the Treaty of Versailles. The republic faced much opposition and, though it did experience some success in the mid-1920s, an economic depression made possible the rise of Hitler and the Nazi Party.

German society was drastically changed in the 1930's, brought about by the Wall Street Crash in October 1929, and Hitler's aggressive foreign policy led to war in 1939. Defeated in 1945, Germany was occupied by Britain, the USA, France and the Soviet Union but problems between the Allied powers saw Germany split into two separate countries – East Germany and West Germany.

Under the leadership of Konrad Adenauer, West Germany experienced an 'economic miracle' which transformed it into a prosperous industrial nation. While West Germany prospered, life in East Germany remained harsh under communist rule. As the Cold War raged, Berlin became a focal point in the tension. It was blockaded by the Soviet Union in 1948 and became a divided city in 1961 when a wall was built through it.

Relations between East Germany and West Germany improved in the 1980s and, when communism collapsed in Eastern Europe, the Berlin Wall came down and Germany was reunified in 1990.

TIMELINE OF EVENTS

1919 Treaty of Versailles

1929 Wall Street Crash

1933 January: Hitler becomes Chancellor

1934 Hitler declares himself Führer

1936 German occupation of the Rhineland

1938 *Anschluss*

1939 Invasion of Czechoslovakia and Poland

1941 Operation Barbarossa

1945 Yalta and Potsdam Conferences

1947 Truman Doctrine and Marshall Plan

1948 Berlin blockade and airlift

1949 September: Western zones combine to create Federal Republic of Germany (FDR)
October: East Germany becomes German Democratic Republic (GDR)

1955 West Germany joins NATO
East Germany becomes a member of the Warsaw Pact

1957 Treaty of Rome: West Germany a founding member of the European Economic Community (EEC)

1961 Building of the Berlin Wall

1968 Student riots in West Berlin

1972 Basic Treaty between East Germany and West Germany

1989 Border between FDR and GDR opened; Berlin Wall pulled down

1990 3 October: East Germany and West Germany officially reunited

What were the main factors responsible for bringing about political and economic change between 1919 and 1991?

GERMANY AND THE FIRST WORLD WAR

In 1900 Germany was the leading industrial nation in Europe. The Kaiser (emperor) ruled an empire stretching across Europe with colonies in Africa and the Pacific. By 1914 over half of the German population worked in factories but they endured low pay and poor conditions. Many turned to socialist parties to try to improve things. They argued that the Kaiser held too much power and that the Reichstag (parliament) should have more say.

When Germany went to war in 1914 most people were confident of victory. However, by November 1918 Germany was a defeated nation, the Kaiser had abdicated (given up the throne) and a new government had been set up.

The impact of the war on Germany

The war had cost 2.4 million German lives. It had been funded by loans and prices had soared. There was widespread starvation throughout Germany.

THE WEIMAR REPUBLIC

On 9 November 1918, Friedrich Ebert, leader of the Social Democratic Party, declared a new German republic. The 'wretched criminals' or 'November criminals', as Hitler viewed them, became associated with surrender. Germany had been 'stabbed in the back' by its leaders.

SOURCE A

> So it had all been in vain ... the sacrifice ... the hours in which, with mortal fear we did our duty. In vain the deaths of two millions. Had they died so that a gang of wretched criminals could lay hands on the Fatherland?
>
> Adolf Hitler, *Mein Kampf*, 1924.

The Weimar Constitution

The new constitution was a brave experiment in democracy.

- Men and women over the age of 20 were given the vote (previously only men over 25 had voted) and all citizens were to enjoy free speech and freedom of political and religious beliefs.
- Voters chose members for the two houses of parliament.
- The Chancellor was appointed by the President who had to be supported by a majority in the Reichstag.
- The President as head of state was elected by the people. He had control of the armed forces and could dismiss parliament.

Voting was by proportional representation: each party received seats in direct proportion to the number of people who voted for that party. The system resulted in a large number of small parties, with no one party having the majority. Parties therefore had to group together to achieve a political majority: there were nine coalition governments in the first four years of the republic.

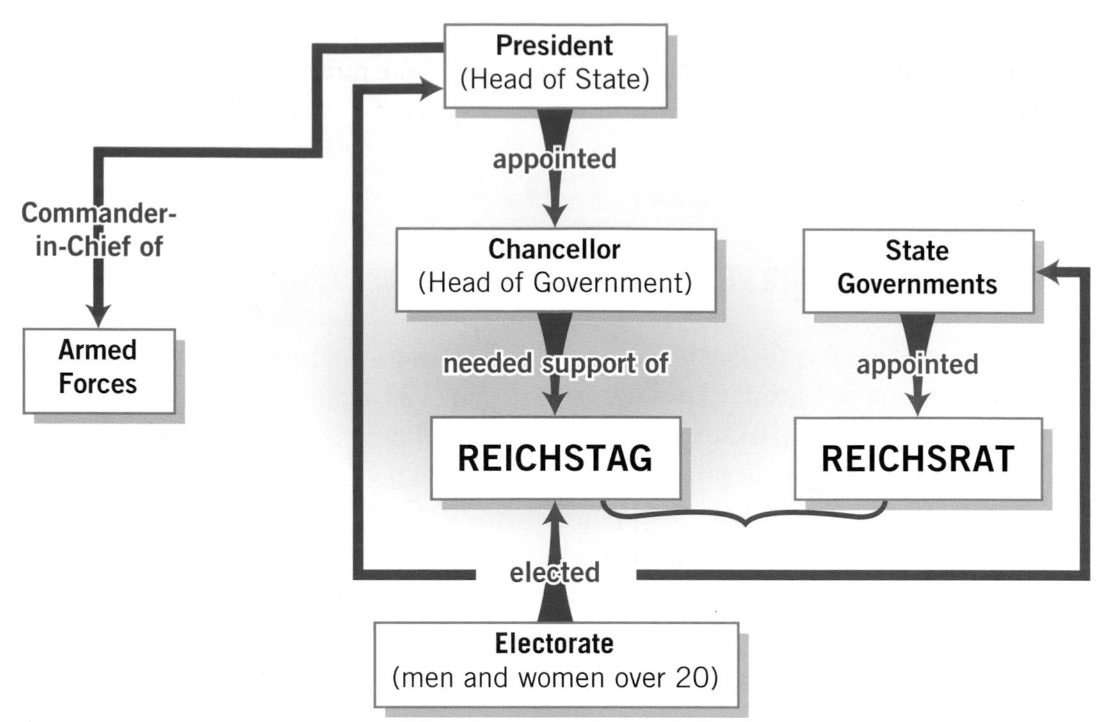

The organisation of the Weimar Republic.

When faced with serious political problems, the various members of the coalitions often fell out, resulting in weak government. Also, in times of crisis coalitions could be challenged by extreme left-wing groups (communists) or by right-wing groups (nationalists). Article 48 of the constitution was used in times of emergency to suspend democracy and rule by decree.

Germany had little experience of democracy. Many preferred the strong government of the Kaiser and felt that the army and the upper classes were the rightful rulers.

Questions

1 Why was the First World War a turning point in German history?

2 What were the weaknesses of the Weimar constitution?

WHAT PROBLEMS DID THE WEIMAR REPUBLIC FACE?

Threats from the left

The Spartacus League (later the German Communist Party) led by Rosa Luxemburg and Karl Liebknecht aimed to set up a communist state in Germany. They opposed the Weimar government and in January 1919 they rose in revolt in Berlin but were defeated by Ebert, with the help of groups of Freikorps (soldiers returning from war). Thousands were killed and Luxemburg and Liebknecht were shot.

Threats from the right

Nationalists protesting against the terms of the Treaty of Versailles marched on Berlin in March 1920 and proclaimed Dr Wolfgang Kapp leader of Germany. He set up a right-wing government, but the displaced government called a general strike of workers in the gas, water, electrical and transport industries.

Unable to govern, the Kapp *putsch* (revolt) failed and Kapp fled abroad.

The Treaty of Versailles

In June 1919 the republic had been dealt another huge blow when the Allies imposed a peace treaty. When the Germans signed the armistice to end the First World War, they hoped for fair peace terms. However, the German government was not allowed to take part in the negotiations at Versailles and when they were presented with the terms of the treaty, they were horrified. Germany was blamed for starting the First World War, a fact that the German population found humiliating and bitterly resented. The Allies used this War Guilt Clause to demand huge economic reparations from Germany to cover the costs of the war. This crippled an already struggling German economy. By the terms of the treaty, Germany also lost land and its colonies, and its military was severely restricted.

A storm of protest greeted the treaty and mass demonstrations were held in Germany. The German government insisted that it had no choice but to accept the terms of the treaty. The popular press, however, called for revenge. The Weimar Republic had got off to a bad start and the new government were seen as traitors by many Germans. Many did not forgive the government for signing the Treaty of Versailles.

The impact of the Treaty of Versailles on Germany was huge, and it was to dominate the history of Germany until the Second World War. The terms of the treaty can be grouped under four headings:

1 War guilt

Under Article 231 of the treaty, Germany had to accept total responsibility for the war.

2 Economic terms

Germany had to accept responsibility for the war and was forced to pay for the damage. The payments (or reparations) amounted to £6600 million.

3 Territorial (land) losses (see map on page 134)

- Alsace-Lorraine was returned to France.
- The Saar region, a rich coal area, was given to France for 15 years; then its inhabitants would vote for which country they wanted to belong to.
- Newly-created Poland was given a corridor to the sea. The 'Polish Corridor' cut off East Prussia from Germany.
- Germany was forbidden to unite with Austria (*Anschluss*).
- Belgium gained Eupen and Malmedy.
- Denmark gained Northern Schleswig.
- Upper Silesia was given to Poland.
- Germany lost its colonies.

4 Military terms

- The army was reduced to 100,000 volunteers.
- The navy was reduced to six battleships, six light cruisers and a few smaller craft. There were to be no submarines.
- There was to be no military airforce.
- All wartime weapons were to be scrapped.
- The Rhineland was demilitarised. No German soldiers were allowed within 50 kilometres of the right bank of the Rhine. The Allies were to occupy the zone for 15 years.

Economic problems, 1921–3

As a result of the treaty, Germany lost 10 per cent of its coal, 48 per cent of its iron, 15 per cent of its agricultural production and 10 per cent of its manufacturing industries. Unemployment worsened as soldiers returned from war. The Germans stopped reparation payments and in January 1923 France reacted by occupying the Ruhr valley, a rich industrial area. The German government ordered the workers out on strike. To pay them, more money was printed. The effect was dramatic – money became worthless in a period of hyperinflation.

THE 'GOLDEN AGE OF STRESEMANN'

Economic stability

In 1923 the German economy lay in ruins, yet it soon recovered and entered a period of stability and prosperity. Much of the success was due to Gustav Stresemann. His first act was to introduce a new currency, the Rentenmark. This brought stability to the economy and people felt confident enough to deposit money in banks. Inflation was controlled, unemployment reduced and industry was revitalised using new US methods of production. To prevent future economic collapse, Stresemann turned to the issue of reparations. He argued that repayment should resume, which led to the French withdrawing from the Ruhr. This made him unpopular and he was forced to resign as Chancellor.

In 1924 Stresemann agreed the Dawes Plan with the USA, Britain and France, which relaxed the system of reparation payments based on Germany's ability to pay. As part of the treaty the USA also agreed to loan Germany 800 million gold marks. The Young Plan of 1929 further eased repayments by extending the deadline until 1988 (although payments actually stopped in 1930). By 1929 Germany was out-pacing Britain and France in industrial production, all this despite the damaging terms of the Treaty of Versailles.

Political stability

Stresemann's political diplomacy was an important factor in keeping the coalition governments together. The Republic was now more stable and the German people were more content during this time, voting for moderate parties like the Social Democrats. The result was a decline in the fortunes of the Nazi Party, which did badly in the Reichstag elections, gaining only 14 seats in December 1924 and 12 seats in 1928.

International relations

As Foreign Secretary, Stresemann did more than anyone to make Germany acceptable again to the European powers.

- In 1925, Germany signed the Locarno Pact with Britain, France, Belgium and Italy, in which they agreed never to try to change the borders between them.
- In 1926, Germany was allowed to join the League of Nations.
- In 1928, Germany signed the Kellogg–Briand Pact with over sixty other countries. This was a declaration that the countries would not go to war against each other.

In 1926, Stresemann was awarded the Nobel Peace Prize for his diplomatic work.

Questions

1. How might a proud German argue a case for rejecting the Treaty of Versailles?
2. Describe the problems faced by the Weimar government. Which was the most serious problem?
3. What part did Stresemann play in the recovery of 1923–9?

HITLER AND THE RISE OF THE NAZIS

SOURCE B Adolf Hitler, painted by Heinrich Knirr in 1937.

Origins of the Nazi Party

After the First World War, Hitler was employed by the army as a propaganda agent. His job was to visit political meetings where a chance encounter with the German Workers Party (DAP) changed his life. Hitler joined the party and in 1920 he and the party leader, Anton Drexler, put together the Twenty-five Point Programme. The party was renamed the National Socialist German Workers Party (Nazi Party for short) and by 1921 Hitler had become leader. The party became far more aggressive with an emphasis on discipline and loyalty to the leader.

SOURCE C

1 We demand the union of all Germans in a greater Germany.
2 We demand equality of rights for the German people in its dealings with other nations.
3 We demand land and colonies to feed our people and to settle our surplus population.
4 Only those of German blood ... may be members of the nation. No Jew may be a member of the nation ...
8 All non-German immigration must be prevented ...
17 We demand a land reform suitable to our national requirement ...
22 We demand ... the formation of a people's army.
25 We demand the creation of a strong central state power for the Reich.

Some of the points outlined in the Twenty-five Point Programme of the Nazi Party.

Hitler founded the Sturmabteilung (Stormtroopers or SA), a brown-shirted paramilitary organisation. The SA attracted ex-soldiers and members of the Freikorps who intimidated opponents of the Nazis, especially the communists. The swastika became the symbol of the party.

Hitler attempts to take power: the Munich putsch, 1923

In 1920 a right-wing group seized power in Munich. The Nazis were able to flourish in the right-wing atmosphere and by 1923 numbers had swollen to 35,000. With the discontent caused by the French occupation of the Ruhr, Hitler felt the time was right to take power. On 8 November 1923 the SA burst in on a meeting of the Bavarian government and Hitler declared himself leader.

Hitler planned to march on Berlin the next day and take over the German government. The marchers were met by armed police and 16 were killed. Hitler was arrested and put on trial for treason.

Hitler used his trial as an opportunity to put forward his ideas. He portrayed himself as a patriot who wanted the best for Germany. Hitler faced the death sentence but he received the minimum sentence of five years of which he served only nine months.

While in prison, Hitler dictated the first part of his book *Mein Kampf* (My Struggle) which outlined many of his ideas and became the bible of the Nazi movement. It was in prison that he realised that he would have to take power legally by the 'ballot not the bullet'.

SOURCE D

Instead of working to achieve power by an armed coup, we will have to hold our noses and enter the Reichstag against Catholic and Marxist members. If outvoting them takes longer than outshooting them, at least the result will be guaranteed by their own Constitution. Sooner or later we shall have a majority, and after that – Germany!

From a letter written by Hitler while in Landsberg Prison in 1924.

The nature of Hitler's appeal

Hitler appealed to the nation as a whole. He declared that Germans deserved to live with pride in a new nation free from the burdens imposed by the Treaty of Versailles and safe from people he believed to be inferior such as the Jews.

He also appealed to different sections of society. The working classes were promised jobs and farmers would receive state aid. German businesses would be protected from the evils of communism. Since over half of the population were women, Hitler was keen to stress the role women would play in Nazi Germany. The Nazis portrayed themselves as the party of family values.

How successful were the Nazis in the period 1923–9?

On his release from prison in 1924, Hitler went about reorganising the party. Regional branches were set up throughout Germany. Each branch, or *gau*, was placed under the control of a party leader, or *gauleiter*. Mass meetings were grand affairs and were well attended. The SA paraded in the streets and seemed to represent order and discipline.

However, this was not reflected in election success, with the Nazis achieving only 32 seats in the election of May 1924, a figure which fell to only 14 seats in December 1924. After 1927 the Nazis saw some signs of hope when unemployment began to rise. Yet it would take something far more dramatic to change Nazi fortunes.

Q Questions

1 Was the Munich *putsch* a complete failure? Explain your answer.

2 Look again at Source C. Who do you think the programme would appeal to?

DEPRESSION IN GERMANY, 1929–33

In October 1929 the Wall Street Crash plunged the USA into chaos which in turn triggered a European depression. The USA called in its loans and, with less money to invest, German factories cut back on production and sacked workers. Many businesses went bankrupt and in 1932 unemployment in Germany peaked at over 6 million. In Germany the Depression led to the collapse of democracy. By January 1933 Hitler was Chancellor; by August 1934 he was a dictator with total power.

Political crisis

The financial crisis called for a politician of skill and vision. Stresemann had died three weeks before the Wall Street Crash. The parties in the government found it difficult to work together and, without the support of a majority, Chancellor Brüning resorted to Article 48 (see page 196). There were fewer meetings of the Reichstag: in reality democracy had all but come to an end by 1930. With no jobs or food, support for parties from the extreme left and right – the Communists and the Nazis, began to grow.

Hitler's election machine sprang into action. Goebbels (see page 153) ran a 'Hitler over Germany' campaign and propaganda posters played on the misery of the people, promising that Hitler would make people's lives better. The SA disrupted meetings of opponents of the Nazis. Jews and communists became convenient scapegoats and were blamed for Germany's misery. By 1930 the Nazis had won 107 seats in the Reichstag and were the second largest party.

Hitler becomes Chancellor

In March 1932 Hitler challenged Hindenburg for the presidency. Hitler came second with 13.4 million to Hindenburg's 19.4 million votes. In the Reichstag elections of the same year the Nazis gained 230 seats, becoming the largest party but lacking an overall majority. Hindenburg disliked Hitler but in January 1933 invited him to become Chancellor with von Papen as Vice-Chancellor. Hindenburg and von Papen had little faith in Hitler's ability. They underestimated the new Chancellor. Hitler now called an election for March 1933, hoping to gain the majority necessary to control the Reichstag.

SOURCE E A *Punch* cartoon showing Hitler with Hindenburg and von Papen.

Q Questions

1. How was the German economy affected by the Depression of 1929?
2. Why did support for the Weimar government fall after 1929?
3. How did Hitler use the financial crisis to increase support for the Nazi Party?
4. What factors led to Hitler becoming Chancellor in 1933?

FROM CHANCELLOR TO DICTATOR

Hitler was appointed Chancellor by President Hindenburg in January 1933. His rise to power had been partly due to the crisis experienced by the Weimar Republic after 1929. It was also due, however, to Hitler's skill in converting the Nazi Party from a tiny and insignificant party in 1919 to the largest party in the Reichstag by 1932.

Violence

Violence was a significant feature of the Nazi rise to power. The SS was the main security force, under the leadership of Heinrich Himmler. Herman Göring (see page 149) set up the Gestapo in 1933 and dealt ruthlessly with any opposition. He controlled two-thirds of the police forces throughout Germany and absorbed 50,000 SA members into the force. Political opponents were intimidated and pressure put on 'true' Germans to vote for the Nazi Party.

The Reichstag fire, 27 February 1933

A week before the election of 1933 the Reichstag buildings burned down. Hitler immediately blamed the communists.

SOURCE F

> This is a signal from God. If this fire turns out to be the work of the communists then there is nothing that shall stop us from crushing out the murderous pest with an iron fist.
>
> Hitler's reaction to the Reichstag fire.

The police found 24-year-old Dutchman Marinus Van der Lubbe at the scene. He was mentally unstable and may have been forced to confess to starting the fire, but he had been a communist and that was enough for the Nazis. Hitler argued the fire was the signal for a communist uprising; the communists argued that the Nazis had started it to discredit them.

Hitler persuaded Hindenburg to sign an emergency decree under Article 48 of the constitution. The police could now arrest and imprison people without trial. Left-wing newspapers were banned and political meetings restricted.

The Enabling Act, 1933

The Nazis won the election of 1933 but failed to gain a majority. In March 1933 Hitler therefore introduced the Enabling Act which allowed the government to introduce its own laws without consulting the Reichstag. A further law made Germany a one-party state – and by legal means.

The 'Night of the Long Knives'

The SA led by Ernst Röhm had served its purpose in getting Hitler to power and had been loyal to Hitler. But Röhm was a committed socialist who wanted the second socialist revolution that Hitler had promised. In addition, Hitler now wanted to merge the SA with the army, but this was unpopular with the army whose support Hitler needed. On 29–30 June 1934 the SS began a round-up of 'suspected' SA traitors and rivals to Hitler. Several hundred, including Röhm, were killed on what became known as the Night of the Long Knives.

Hitler becomes Führer

In August 1934 Hindenburg died and Hitler became both President and Chancellor of Germany. He added the position of Supreme Commander of the Armed Forces and called himself 'Führer' (leader). He had become a dictator of Germany. His power was total.

SOURCE G A British cartoon about the Night of the Long Knives, called 'They salute with both hands now!'

Q Questions

1. Look at Source G.
   - a Who are figures A, B and C?
   - b Explain the significance of figure A's armband.
   - c Who are forces D, E and F?
   - d What is the reference to the paper on the ground?
   - e Explain the significance of the caption.
2. How did Hitler achieve total power by August 1934?

THE NATURE OF POLITICAL CONTROL

Hitler used two methods to control the population. Propaganda – the spreading of ideas – was used to great effect. For those who resisted, the Nazis used terror tactics.

Propaganda

Propaganda was used to indoctrinate (or brainwash) the German people. Various techniques were used:

- → The Nazis controlled radio stations and flooded the market with cheap radios. By 1939, 70 per cent of families had a radio.
- → The Nazi film industry churned out adventure and comedy films all with a Nazi message. The most spectacular film, *The Triumph of the Will*, emphasised the grandeur of Nazi achievement.
- → All news came from a Nazi press agency and newspapers that criticised Hitler were closed down.
- → Books were censored. Libraries were ransacked and banned books were burnt in public.
- → All aspects of cultural life were controlled by the Reich Chamber of Culture.

- Rallies were a feature of Hitler's rise to power. Every year a huge rally was held at Nuremberg to emphasise Nazi achievement.

SOURCE H

> It is the task of state propaganda to simplify complicated ways of thinking that even the smallest man in the street may understand ... The fundamental principle of all propaganda is the repetition of effective arguments.
>
> The Nazi government's views on propaganda.

The police state

If persuasion failed then force was used. The SS carried out a highly organised terror campaign and was given unlimited powers to deal with the opposition. The Gestapo had powers to arrest people merely on suspicion and without charge. 'Confessions' were often extracted by torture. The Gestapo became the most feared organisation in Germany.

The courts

If a case did get to trial it was unlikely that the defendant would receive justice. In 1934 the People's Court was set up to try opponents for crimes against the state. All judges had to swear an oath of loyalty to Hitler.

Concentration camps

'Criminals of the state' were sent to concentration camps for 'correction'. The first camp was established in Dachau in 1933 and others followed throughout Germany. 'Undesirables' – communists, intellectuals, homosexuals, gypsies, alcoholics, Jehovah's Witnesses and Jews – were brutally treated. Some concentration camps became extermination camps during the Second World War.

ECONOMIC POLICY IN NAZI GERMANY

With the Nazis in power the economic problems now needed to be addressed.

'Brot und Arbeit' (bread and work)

Economic policy from 1934 to 1937 was directed by Dr Hjalmar Schacht. His first task was to reduce unemployment:

- The National Labour Service was set up to provide jobs for men between 18 and 25 on public works schemes.
- Hitler's rearmament programme and compulsory military service also brought employment to many.
- People were sent to forced labour camps, removing them from the job market.
- Women were made to leave their jobs and run their homes.
- In October 1934 the Labour Front was set up, taking the place of trade unions. It imposed discipline on workers.

Autarky (self-sufficiency)

Germany needed to be self-sufficient and not dependent on foreign trade. In 1936 a Four-Year Plan was introduced by Göring. However, it soon became evident that self-sufficiency could not be achieved. Germany simply needed to help itself to the materials and goods of 'lesser' countries. Therefore, German economic policy became linked to an aggressive foreign policy (see pages 221–3).

THE IMPACT OF THE SECOND WORLD WAR ON GERMANY

The *Blitzkrieg* (lightning war) tactic was used to devastating effect in the early part of the war (see pages 223–4). As country after country fell to Germany a wave of optimism and expectancy swept the nation.

However, by 1942 defeats in North Africa and Stalingrad in the Soviet Union saw the war turn against Germany. As armaments minister, Albert Speer set about organising the economy for 'total war'. Workers were forced to work longer hours and had their rations cut. The hardships endured by the civilian population were worsened by an extensive Allied bombing campaign (see page 217). By 1945 most Germans were weary of war. In April the Red Army linked up with the Allies in Berlin and in May 1945, after Hitler's suicide, Germany surrendered.

How did the war affect the Jews?

In their advance on Germany Allied troops liberated the extermination camps (see map on page 161), revealing the horrific story of the Holocaust. The Second World War had given Hitler the opportunity to carry out his plan to exterminate a whole race of people. At the Wannsee Conference in Berlin in January 1942 plans for the 'Final Solution' had been put forward for the systematic murder of 13 million Jews. By April 1945 over 6 million had perished. The revelation of the Holocaust to the German people added to the misery and psychological impact of defeat.

Q Questions

1 How did Hitler gain political and economic control of Germany?

2 What impact did the war have on Germany?

POST-WAR PROBLEMS

The war had claimed over 8 million lives and 7.5 million Germans were homeless. Factories and communication points were destroyed and shops were empty. By 1946 Germany was producing only 25 per cent of the output of 1936. The Allied powers had to decide what to do with defeated Germany.

The Yalta Conference

In February 1945, before Germany's surrender, the Allied leaders met at Yalta to decide how Europe would be organised after the war. They decided that:

- Those responsible for war crimes should be punished.
- Germany should be rid of Nazism (denazification) and democracy restored.
- Germany should be totally disarmed and demilitarised.
- Germany should pay compensation for damage done in the war.
- Germany should be divided into separate zones of Allied occupation.

The Potsdam Conference

In May 1945 the Germans surrendered and the Allied leaders met again at Potsdam near Berlin. On 2 August 1945 the proposals made at Yalta were reaffirmed. In 1919 the Allies had imposed a harsh treaty on Germany, which laid the seeds of resentment. In 1945 revenge was not the issue. The Potsdam declaration laid the blame on the Nazi government and not the German nation.

Relations between the Allies worsen

In April 1945 the US President, Roosevelt, had died. He was replaced by Truman who was suspicious of Stalin. At the conference Truman told Churchill and Stalin that the USA had successfully tested an atomic bomb. When Stalin heard this he became more suspicious of the West.

The USA was concerned about Russian expansion westwards at the end of the war. Rather than setting up free elections for democratic governments in the countries they liberated from Nazi control, Soviet troops simply remained. The USA, Britain and France had intended to weaken Germany but now realised that a strong Germany could act as a buffer against communism. They began to aid German economic recovery. Reparations would be ended and a new currency introduced. Their zones would be returned to democracy. From 1945 the Western zones and the Soviet zone were run in their own separate ways. Out of these zones emerged two countries, West Germany and East Germany.

The Nuremberg trials, 1945–6

There was one important example of co-operation between the four powers – the treatment of war criminals. Twenty-one Nazi leaders were put on trial for: planning an aggressive war; war crimes; and crimes against humanity.

Three – Schacht, von Papen and Fritzsche (Commander-in-Chief of the army) – were found not guilty. Seven were jailed and the rest received death sentences. Göring committed suicide, as had Goebbels, but the others were hanged.

Q Questions

1. How and why did the peace agreement of Yalta and Potsdam differ from the Treaty of Versailles?
2. Why was German economic recovery important to the West?
3. What caused the suspicion between the Allies after 1945?

WEST GERMANY AND EAST GERMANY

The Federal Republic of Germany

Stalin viewed the idea of a separate West German state as a violation of the Potsdam agreement, which could lead to German rearmament. His response was to blockade all links between West Berlin and western Germany (see page 227). There seemed little hope of a unified Germany and the Allies arranged for the ministers – presidents of the *Länder* (provinces) – to draw up a new constitution on federal, democratic lines.

On 21 September 1949 the Western zones officially combined to form the Federal Republic of Germany (FDR):

- → Military occupation ended and a civilian agency, the Allied High Commission, replaced the military governors (West Berlin remained occupied).
- → The Federal Parliament (consisting of an upper house, Bundesrat, and a lower house, Bundestag) would meet at the new capital, Bonn.
- → The president would be elected for five years and could stand only once. He or she did not control the armed forces and had no powers to declare a state of emergency or appoint and dismiss chancellors.
- → The key political figure was the chancellor, who was elected by the Bundestag.

The German Democratic Republic

In eastern Germany communists were appointed to local offices and a Soviet-style system was established. Banks, factories and farms were seized and reorganised. People who opposed the communists were arrested and imprisoned.

In 1946 the communists forced the Social Democrats to join them in the formation of the Socialist Unity Party and Walter Ulbricht became first secretary (later general secretary). In the first elections the Unity Party was the only party allowed to put forward candidates. On 7 October 1949 the German Democratic Republic (GDR) was created with East Berlin as its capital.

DEVELOPMENTS IN WEST GERMANY

Economic expansion

The first Chancellor of West Germany was Konrad Adenauer. A Rhinelander, Catholic and staunch anti-communist, he became the embodiment of the nation. He served as Chancellor from 1949 to 1963, longer than all 21 chancellors in the Weimar Republic. His aims were to:

- repair the physical damage done
- transform Germany from a post-war occupied zone into a respected independent nation
- instil a moral rebirth after the brutality of Nazism.

SOURCE I Konrad Adenauer.

In the 1950s there was industrial expansion in West Germany unparalleled elsewhere in Europe. There were several causes:

- West Germany had inherited a well-established tradition of industrialism and rebuilding the war damage meant that factories could be equipped with the latest technology.
- Adenauer's minister for economic affairs, Ludwig Erhard, encouraged economic development.
- West Germany received $1300 million of Marshall Aid (see page 226).
- The demand for industrial equipment caused by the Korean War (1950–3) gave the economy a massive boost.
- Trade unions discouraged strikes and the absence of strikes helped stabilise the economy.

Economic and political problems

The 1960s, however, saw a decline in industrial output and a rise in unemployment. In the mid-1970s unemployment rose to 1 million, consumer demand decreased, inflation rose and strikes became more commonplace.

Cracks began to appear on the political front when the National Democratic Party (NDP) began to score victories in local government elections. This neo-Nazi Party, founded in 1964, was anti-American, anti-Russian and hostile to foreign 'guest workers' (immigrant workers).

A more immediate threat came from student protest groups, who campaigned against the Vietnam War and the building of nuclear power stations. In 1968 riots broke out in West Berlin. A real threat to the state was the outbreak of terrorism associated with the Baader–Meinhof gang.

The gang launched bomb attacks, and kidnapped and murdered leading politicians and businessmen. The anti-terrorist measures of the government of Willy Brandt (Chancellor 1969–74) stopped the violence but led some Germans to question police handling of the problems.

EAST GERMANY AFTER 1949

Industrial unrest

East Germany faced enormous problems after 1949:

- It possessed only 30 per cent of former German industrial capacity and was desperately short of raw materials.
- The attraction of better living conditions in West Germany induced many skilled workers to leave. There was a shortage of consumer goods because emphasis was placed on rebuilding heavy industry. The economic situation worsened as the Soviet Union continued to demand reparation payments.
- Poor wages led to industrial unrest and the government's response was to raise working quotas.

On 16 June 1953 workers marched in protest in East Berlin demanding an improvement in living conditions, free speech and free elections. The next day 300,000 workers responded to the call for a general strike. The Soviet army put down the troubles killing 21 people, blaming Western agitators for the events.

The Berlin Wall

A great deal of land and industry in East Germany had been transferred from private hands into state control and, by 1955, 82 per cent of production came from state-owned industry. Unemployment was reduced and by the 1970s East Germany had the highest living standards in the Eastern bloc (Soviet-controlled Eastern Europe). However, this did not stop the steady flow of refugees to the West. The government response was to strengthen its frontiers with West Germany and in 1961 a wall was built through Berlin (see pages 218–9). The erection of the wall was ordered by Erich Honecker who later succeeded Ulbricht in 1971. He continued government control of industry and by 1972 the state was virtually the sole employer.

East Germany did experience social and economic development after the Second World War but one aspect did not change. The Unity Party's grip over all aspects of life was probably tighter and state security services more powerful than in any other Eastern bloc country.

SOURCE J

An unattractive, fear-inspiring police state which screws foreign currency out of its unhappy children and locks its critics either in or out, a state in whose coat of arms is not the hammer and compass but the bludgeon and muzzle.

The GDR as described by the singer Wolf Biermann, who was deprived of East German citizenship for his criticism of the state.

Q Questions

1. Why were there two Germanies in 1949?
2. What were Adenauer's goals as Chancellor of West Germany?
3. Did life improve for people in East Germany after 1949?

WEST GERMANY IN EUROPE

As the split between East and West became more pronounced, Adenauer saw the importance of political, economic and military co-operation with the Allies. To Adenauer, West Germany's future lay in a united Europe. The first step was made in 1947 when the Organisation for European Economic Co-operation (OEEC) was set up to administer Marshall Aid. In May 1949 the Council of Europe was established at Strasbourg; Adenauer saw it as a European parliament.

The European Coal and Steel Community (ECSC)

In 1950 Robert Schuman, the French Foreign Minister, put forward a plan that has been described as the 'most audacious and constructive since the war'. Coal and iron ore are needed to make steel. The Saar region of Germany is rich in coal, and France has large iron ore deposits. Schuman's plan was to bring the two together without the fuss of customs duties. In 1953 France, Belgium, Italy, Luxemburg, the Netherlands and West Germany formed the ECSC.

SOURCE K A British cartoon commenting on the Schuman Plan, 1950.

The European Economic Community (EEC)

The ECSC was a huge success: in its first decade, member countries saw their trade increase by 170 per cent in the atmosphere of free trade. It seemed logical to expand the activities and in 1957 the countries signed the Treaty of Rome, which established the European Economic Community (EEC), or Common Market. Its principal aim was to remove trade barriers between European countries.

HELMUT KOHL AND THE REUNIFICATION OF GERMANY

In 1982 Helmut Kohl became West German Chancellor. As West Germany emerged as a prominent economic power in the 1980s it also took on more responsibility on the international front. The fall of East Germany's communist government in 1989 significantly altered relations between the two Germanies. Kohl pushed hard for the reunification of Germany and on 3 October 1990 East and West Germany were officially reunited. On 2 December the first all-German elections since 1933 were held. Kohl scored a substantial victory and became Chancellor of a unified Germany.

Q Questions

1 Why did Germany join the ECSC and the EEC?

2 What were the main political and economic developments after 1949 in:
  - **a** West Germany
  - **b** East Germany?

In what ways did the lives of the German people change between 1919 and 1991?

THE IMPACT OF THE ECONOMIC PROBLEMS OF THE WEIMAR REPUBLIC

In January 1919 nine German marks could be exchanged for one US dollar; by November 1923 that rate was 4.2 million million marks to the dollar. Germany was in the grip of hyperinflation (rapidly rising prices).

The French occupation of the Ruhr in 1923 had triggered the inflation but huge government borrowing to pay for the First World War had contributed to the problems (Germany had been confident that it would recover the money from the defeated nations). As a temporary measure, the government printed more money, forcing up prices. Food queues began to lengthen.

SOURCE A German children playing with piles of worthless money, 1923.

Occupation of the Ruhr

The Allies fixed the amount of reparations in 1921 at £6600 million to be repaid over 66 years. The Germans scraped together the first payment, but when they failed to make another the French prime minister Raymond Poincaré persuaded the Belgians to join France in an invasion of the Ruhr. The Ruhr was the industrial heartland of Germany: it produced 80 per cent of the nation's coal, iron and steel. In January 1923, 60,000 French and Belgian troops invaded, taking over the mines, factories and railways in the region.

The German government ordered the workers to carry out a programme of passive resistance. They were to go on strike, refuse to collaborate with the French and carry out acts of sabotage. The French reacted with force: 150,000 people were expelled and 132 were shot.

Hyperinflation

The workers still had to be paid and coal was having to be imported from abroad. The German government again simply printed more money, which meant inflation spiralled further out of control. Money lost its value and workers took their wages home in wheelbarrows. People resorted to bartering.

Losers

- Hardest hit were people on low, fixed incomes such as pensioners.
- The middle classes saw their savings disappear as banks went out of business.

SOURCE B A German poster from 1932. It reads *Hands off the Ruhr!*

Winners

- From the outset businessmen had calculated and sold their goods in gold value (the value of gold is often more stable) but paid their workers in inflated marks. Business debts had been wiped out as the value of money diminished.
- Farmers survived because inflation had pushed up food prices.
- Foreigners exploited the exchange rate. Small amounts of foreign currency could be traded for millions of marks.

ECONOMIC RECOVERY

Chancellor Stresemann brought stability to the economy (see page 198). He called off the strike in the Ruhr and a new currency was introduced. The situation was further helped by the Dawes Plan of 1924 and the Young Plan of 1929.

Living standards began to improve and by the end of the 1920s German people were buying as many luxury goods as they had in 1913. Car ownership had risen by over 400 per cent by 1927. Much of Germany's success in the period 1924–9 was the result of massive US investment and a heavy reliance on loans. However, the collapse of the Wall Street stock exchange in October 1929 had a devastating effect on Germany.

Q Questions

1. What were the causes and effects of hyperinflation in Germany?
2. How far had Germany recovered by 1929?

CRISIS RETURNS: THE IMPACT OF THE DEPRESSION ON THE GERMAN PEOPLE

Following the Wall Street Crash US investment dried up and loans were called in. As the effects of the collapse rippled around the world, German exports could no longer be sold, which meant that businesses closed down and unemployment rose sharply. People unable to meet mortgage payments or pay rent set up shanty towns and became dependent on soup kitchens. Benefit payments were cut back to save government revenue. The middle classes found their savings lost as banks collapsed. Taxes were increased, which put businesses under more pressure. By 1932 unemployment had risen to 6 million, and Germany was again gripped by social discontent.

WHAT ECONOMIC CHANGES TOOK PLACE IN GERMANY 1933–9?

Hitler brought full employment to Germany by setting up a National Labour Service (*Reichsarbeitsdienst* or RAD), and by rearming and introducing conscription (see also page 204). By the start of war in 1939 there was a labour shortage.

Hitler's priority was to increase production of industrial, mainly military goods, rather than that of consumer goods. However, this increased productivity came at a price.

- Germany's national income, the total value of all goods produced, was higher in 1938. This increase in production was not reflected in a rise in wages. The average working week had increased from 45 hours per week in 1928 to 50 hours per week in 1938, and to over 60 hours per week by the end of war in 1945. People were working longer hours for less money.
- As the priority was to produce industrial and not consumer goods, people had less money to spend and little to spend it on. By 1936 the price of food had risen and taxation had increased.

Year	Unemployed (millions)
1928	1.8
1932	6.0
1933	4.8
1934	2.7
1935	2.2
1936	1.6
1937	0.9
1938	0.5

German unemployment figures, 1928–38.

Year	Index of wages	Wages (% of national income)
1928	125	62
1933	88	63
1934	94	62
1936	100	59
1938	106	57

Index of wages and wages as a percentage of national income in Germany, 1928–38.

The German Labour Front

One reason for increased productivity was the total absence of strikes. Trade unions had been abolished in May 1933 and replaced by the Labour Front headed by Dr Robert Ley. Its function was to control workers: they could not negotiate better wages or leave their jobs without the permission of the Labour Front.

If the workers of Germany were not better off they had to be made to think that they were. The Labour Front set up two movements for the benefit of the workers:

- Beauty of Labour (*Schönheit der Arbeit*, or SdA) promoted better conditions at the workplace. Health and safety standards were improved and hot meals provided.
- Strength through Joy (*Kraft durch Freude*, or KdF) was set up to keep the workforce happy by organising leisure activities. Workers were offered cheap holidays. Entertainment was controlled by the KdF and subsidised sport was provided along with theatre and opera trips.

Workers were persuaded that life was better by clever advertising. The industrious and hardworking could aspire to car-ownership with a Volkswagen, the 'people's car' (see Source C).

Questions

1. How were the people of Germany affected by the Depression?
2. How successful were Hitler's measures to reduce unemployment and increase production between 1933 and 1939?
3. Were Germans better off under the Nazis? Explain your answer.

SOURCE C

The advert suggests that a car could be bought by saving 5 marks a week (an average worker earned 30 marks a week). Millions of marks were paid into the scheme yet not one car was made for a customer. When war came the Volkswagen factory at Wolfburg became an armaments factory.

CULTURAL CHANGES, 1919–39

As prosperity returned in the mid-1920s, many Germans began to look optimistically to a new age. The 1920s have been described as one of the greatest periods of expression and experimentation in the arts. Writers and artists thrived in this atmosphere of creativity.

Art, design, architecture and literature

The upheaval of the First World War encouraged artists like Paul Klee, Otto Dix and George Grosz to view the world in a different way. Grosz used his art to pour scorn on the issues and personalities he despised, such as Germany's government and its military past. In 1929 Erich Remarque wrote *All Quiet on the Western Front*, an anti-war novel that vividly portrayed the horrors of war.

The Bauhaus school of architecture and design was founded in Weimar by Walter Gropius in 1919 and its influence is still seen today in many aspects of modern design. The school attracted avant-garde designers who produced beautiful objects for mass production using tubular metal and plastic. In 1925 it moved to Dessau but was closed down by the Nazis in 1933 because they felt it was too decadent. Gropius and many leading Bauhaus teachers emigrated.

The Nazis criticised these works for being unpatriotic and immoral. Many Germans viewed such works as part of the decline in decency. Berlin, the hub of artistic creativity, was seen as a hotbed of debauchery with its sleazy clubs full of the 'wrong types'.

SOURCE D

The Party by George Grosz. It shows the decadent night club life of the Weimar Republic.

German 'culture', 1933–9

The Nazi Chamber of Creative Art laid down guidelines for artists, sculptors, writers and musicians. In order for art to be seen or music performed it had to conform to Nazi beliefs. Many writers were banned and public book burnings of 'unacceptable' literature took place. By controlling the arts the Nazis stifled individuality and reduced it to a dull, simple level.

Q Questions

1. Which Germans were better off under the Nazis? Explain your answer.
2. Why did the Nazis declare some art forms degenerate?

WOMEN IN NAZI SOCIETY

The Weimar years had witnessed a significant move towards equal rights for women. However, Hitler had very firm ideas about the place of women in society – their purpose was to produce children and keep house.

The Law for the Encouragement of Marriage, 1933

Under this law each newly-married family qualified for a loan of 1000 marks (about nine months' pay), repayment of which would be reduced by 250 marks with the birth of each child. After the fourth child the loan would be cleared and the term 'family' could officially be used. Women were rewarded with a gold Motherhood Cross for eight children, silver for six and bronze for four. Birth control was banned and infertile families were forced to divorce.

Shortly after Hitler came to power, he ordered some women to leave the workplace and female doctors, civil servants, lecturers and teachers were dismissed. In 1936 women were barred from sitting as judges on the grounds that they were incapable of logical thought. They were also denied freedom of expression. Even their appearance was dictated. Hair was to be worn in a bun or in plaits. Trousers, high-heeled shoes and make-up were banned.

Opposition to Nazi policy

Most women accepted this, believing they were valued by the state but also because they had no choice. Others joined illegal political organisations, like the communists and social democrats, in protest. However, by 1939 women were being employed in factories because men were called up into the armed forces.

SOURCE E *The Family*, a painting by the Nazi artist Walter Willrich.

Children in Nazi society

The aim of Nazi educational policy was to indoctrinate the young and to train them to be loyal to the state.

- Teachers were forced to join the German Teachers League; children were encouraged to inform on 'unsafe' teachers who failed to toe the Nazi line.
- All lessons began and ended with a Nazi salute and every subject was taught with a Nazi bias. Geography lessons taught about the territorial wrongs of Versailles. Biology emphasised the need to purify the 'master race'. History textbooks praised a mythical and glorious German past.
- Emphasis was placed on character rather than intelligence. For boys it was military training while for girls it was domestic science and preparation for motherhood. The most promising boys were sent to elite Adolf Hitler Schools to be trained as future leaders.

SOURCE F

We start our work when the child is three. As soon as he begins to think a little flag is put into his hand. Then comes School, the Hitler Youth Movement and the Stormtroops. After, there is the Labour Front.

A description of how the Nazis trained children.

The Hitler Youth

The Hitler Youth or *Hitler Jugend* movement was set up in 1925 but by 1936 membership was compulsory. There were over 2 million members in 1933, rising to just over 7 million in 1939. Propaganda newsreels showed the excitement of life in youth camps, but discipline was severe and physical training harsh. Boys were trained to march 80 kilometres (50 miles) on minimal rations.

Age	Boys	Girls
6–10	**Pimpfen** (Little Fellows)	
10–14	**Deutsche Jungvolk** (German Young People)	**Jungmädel** (Young Maidens)
14–18	**Hitler Jugend** (Hitler Youth)	**Bund Deutsche Mädel** (League of German Maidens)

Different groups within the Hitler Youth.

Opposition groups

While many youngsters enjoyed the activities on offer, others opposed the regimentation and strictness. In a mood of self-expression some young people adopted outrageous hairstyles and listened to jazz music from the USA. (Hitler had banned jazz on the basis that it originated from black people, who were seen as undesirables.)

More serious resistance came from organised gangs which sprang up in the late-1930s. The Navajos Gang, the Kittelbach Pirates and the Edelweiss Pirates attacked Hitler Youth members and during the war became involved in resistance movements. When captured they were treated brutally by the Gestapo.

Q Questions

1. Did the lives of women change for the better or for the worse under the Nazis?
2. How did the Nazis affect the lives of young people in Germany?

THE CHURCH IN NAZI SOCIETY

Hitler claimed to be Catholic but did not trust the Church because its teachings conflicted with Nazi beliefs. In the 1930s the Nazis attempted to replace Christianity by introducing a Faith Movement based on pagan ideas, though with little effect. Hitler's vision for religion in Germany can be seen in the rules for the National Reich Church, which he set up in 1933.

SOURCE G

In the National Reich Church ... only national Orators of the Reich will be allowed to speak ... The National Reich Church demands an immediate stop to the printing and sale of the Bible in Germany ... The National Reich Church will remove from the altars of all churches the Bible, the cross and religious objects. On the altars there must be nothing but *Mein Kampf*, and to the left of this a sword.

From the rules for the National Reich Church.

Relations with the Catholic Church

The Catholic Church was prepared to support Hitler in the early years of his rule because he appeared to represent family values and morality after the decadence of the Weimar Republic. Nazism also formed a barrier against communism, which argued that there was no place for organised religion in the state. In 1933 Hitler signed a Concordat with the Catholic Church, in which the church agreed to keep out of politics if the Nazis did not interfere in church matters.

The Protestant Church

The Protestant Church showed early support for Hitler but, when details for the National Reich Church emerged, many leading churchmen spoke out in protest. Dietrich Bonhoeffer was arrested for his views and hanged in April 1945.

THE JEWS IN NAZI SOCIETY

Hitler stated in *Mein Kampf* that the German race had to be kept pure and protected from race polluters such as Jews. Jews became a convenient scapegoat for all Germany's problems and, on coming to power, Hitler set about persecuting them.

Persecution

In April 1933 Hitler ordered the SA to ensure people boycotted Jewish-owned shops. Windows of shops owned by Jews had to show the Star of David, and so became targets for vandalism. Jewish civil servants and doctors were dismissed and Jewish doctors were not allowed to treat Aryan Germans. In 1935 Jews were banned from parks, restaurants, trains and buses. Even more serious were the Nuremberg Laws of the same year. Jews were declared to be no longer members of the German state. They were denied the vote and were not protected by the law. Marriages between Jews and non-Jews were made illegal.

On 7 November 1938 a young Jewish student shot dead a German government official at the embassy in Paris. A fine of 1 billion marks was imposed on the Jews for the murder and Hitler ordered the SS to carry out a campaign of terror on the Jewish population. The night of 9 November 1938 became known as *Kristallnacht* (the Night of Broken Glass) because of the great number of windows smashed. Synagogues were burned down and 8000 shops and homes looted. Over 100 Jews were killed and 30,000 arrested and sent to concentration camps.

SOURCE H

The sign reads 'Germans! Protect yourselves! Do not buy from Jews!' An SA guard makes sure that no one enters the Jewish-owned shop.

The Holocaust

From 1941 the Nazis developed plans to deal with the 'Jewish problem'. Jews and other 'undesirables' were to be shot by mobile murder units or sent to concentration camps to be exterminated. Approximately 6 million Jews were killed during the Holocaust.

Questions

1 How did Hitler attempt to replace organised religion in Germany?

2 How did the Nazis' treatment of Jews change between 1933 and 1939?

THE HOME FRONT IN THE SECOND WORLD WAR

Early victories from 1940 were greeted with great enthusiasm by the Germans. Nazi propaganda films celebrated victory over the French and rejoiced at revenge for the harsh Treaty of Versailles. The spoils of war – raw materials, land, slave workers – opened up the prospect that Germany would become a very rich and powerful country. Defeats in 1942 saw the war turn against Germany. The population was told to prepare for total war – sacrifices would have to be made and hardships endured.

The German people now began to realise how hard war was when you're not winning. Supplies were needed for the armed forces and sacrifices had to be made at home. Goebbels stepped up his propaganda campaign to raise morale and ask for sacrifices. When a call went out for warm clothing for troops in the Soviet Union, the German people donated 1.5 million fur coats. German factories were forced to work longer hours and food rations were cut. Women were increasingly drafted into factories to keep up production.

From 1942, the Allies began bombing raids on German cities. These were intended to knock out important factories and disrupt production of goods for the war. Civilians were also targeted, in an attempt to reduce morale. Round-the-clock 'carpet bombing' reduced cities and towns to ruins. The most notorious and controversial raid came in February 1945 when Dresden was virtually destroyed. It is estimated that at least 150,000 men, women and children were killed in two days of bombing raids.

By the end of the war more than three million civilians had been killed. This, coupled with food shortages and an army in retreat, meant that many Germans were happy to see an end to the war.

SOURCE I

Wednesday morning, 28 July 1943
There was no gas, no electricity, not a drop of water, neither the lift nor the telephone was working. It is hard to imagine the panic and chaos. There were no trams, no Underground, no rail-traffic to the suburbs.

A German eyewitness account of Hamburg on the morning after a heavy bombing raid.

Q Question

1 How were the lives of German civilians affected by the Second World War?

ADENAUER'S 'ECONOMIC MIRACLE'

The economic miracle was the transformation of West Germany from a devastated and demoralised post-war country into a prosperous industrial state. In the confusion of post-war Germany, the economy had been flooded with worthless money and there was a thriving black market. On 20 June 1948 a new Deutschmark was introduced and the *Wirtschaftswunder* (economic miracle) can be dated from this point.

Adenauer's first task was to rebuild Germany physically. Ludwig Erhard was appointed Federal Economics Minister and much of the credit for the miracle must go to him. The new Germany was to operate a free-market economy with a greater sense of social responsibility for the unemployed, the sick, young and old. The success of this welfare state would depend on industrial recovery.

Erhard utilised Marshall Aid very efficiently, rebuilding old 'smokestack' industries into modern ones with hi-tech machinery. Firms were taxed heavily but rebates were given to those who ploughed money back into research and development. In 1952 a tax of 50 per cent was levied on wealthier Germans. The revenue was used to build 2 million homes and, at the end of Adenauer's first term of office, living standards had improved and unemployment declined.

Demand was high for luxury goods such as Leica cameras and Mercedes-Benz cars. The huge Volkswagen plant at Wolfburg returned to producing the 'People's Car' and by the mid-1950s the VW Beetle was rolling off the assembly lines at a price that Germans and other countries could afford. West Germany was now second only to the USA in the manufacture of cars. By 1960 it was the second largest producer of steel after the Soviet Union and between 1948 and 1964 industrial production increased by 600 per cent. Unemployment dropped from 9 per cent to 0.4 per cent between 1952 and 1965 and foreign guest workers (*Gastarbeiter*) were brought in from Turkey, Italy and Greece to help rebuild the German economy.

Adenauer had talked of a moral rebirth of the nation. One issue required particular attention – the Jewish survivors of the Holocaust. Though no amount of money could compensate for the horrors of Nazi policy, Adenauer considered it a symbol of Germany's resolve never to forget the atrocities. A reparations agreement was concluded in 1953 which provided support to German Jews beginning to rebuild their lives.

LIFE IN GERMANY DURING THE COLD WAR

After 1945 West Berlin became the 'shop window of the West' as Allied co-operation and investment led to its reconstruction. At first people could move between zones easily but, when the Berlin blockade (see page 227) ended in May 1949, some 3.5 million East Germans left for a better life in West Germany. Life remained difficult in East Germany. Poor pay and increased work quotas led to an uprising in Berlin in June 1953 (see page 208).

The Berlin Wall, erected on 13 August 1961, made it more difficult to escape to the West.

The border between the two Germanies was heavily fortified. Many Berliners found themselves cut off from family, friends and work.

Border guards and machine-gun posts made escape to the West hazardous: between 1961 and 1989, 86 people were shot trying to cross to the West. Peter Fechter was one such casualty. On 17 August 1962 he tried to cross into West Berlin to join his sister. He was shot by border police as he climbed the barbed wire on the eastern side and fell back into the narrow strip between East and West (see Source J). He could be heard crying for help and shouting his sister's name as he slowly bled to death. Fechter was only 300 metres from the West Berlin border post, and as crowds on the western side witnessed the awful spectacle, they begged the Americans to rescue him. But the soldiers were told by their officers not to intervene. An hour later, East German guards collected Fechter's body. Life in East Germany and East Berlin remained hard.

SOURCE J The body of Peter Fechter, an 18-year-old bricklayer from East Germany who was shot trying to cross the Berlin Wall in 1962.

SOURCE K

When you leave, searches sometimes include the X-raying of luggage. A long stick may be poked into the fuel tank to make sure someone is not hiding in there. The back seats are folded down for inspection and the undercarriage examined with mirrors set in the road surface. It may take 20 minutes for such an inspection, 20 minutes wait and 20 minutes for passport control.

Observations of a Western visitor to East Germany in the 1970s.

SOURCE L

It was like going back twenty years. There weren't many cars on the road. Many of the buildings looked as if they hadn't been touched since the war. There were political slogans and red flags on many buildings. Many young people wore jeans, but the clothes had a strange outdated look about them.

Comments of a British tourist about a visit to East Germany

Q Questions

1 What impact did Adenauer's economic policy have on the people of West Germany from 1949 to 1963?

2 Why did people want to leave East Germany to go and live in the West?

3 Why did Berlin become a focal point in the Cold War?

What changing role did Germany play in world affairs between 1919 and 1991?

THE IMPACT OF THE TREATY OF VERSAILLES ON GERMANY

Look at the map on page 134 and read the terms of the Treaty of Versailles on page 197.

Germany's hopes of a moderate and fair peace treaty rested with President Woodrow Wilson of the USA. His aim was to ensure that war could never happen again and he looked to a 'new order' where the nations of the world would co-operate and live in peace. He believed that to punish Germany harshly would create a desire for revenge in the future. French Prime Minister Georges Clemenceau wanted revenge and security against a future German invasion. Prime Minister David Lloyd-George of Britain privately agreed with Wilson, but he had just been elected on a 'make Germany pay' ticket.

The terms of the treaty shocked the German nation. Germany had not been part of the negotiations and was made to take full responsibility for the war. The treaty was viewed as a *diktat* or dictated peace, intended to shame and weaken Germany.

Germany lost 65,000 square kilometres of territory, 6.5 million people and vast amounts of raw materials. These territorial losses together with the military and economic clauses considerably weakened Germany as a world power. Most humiliating of all, however, was the war guilt clause by which Germany was held responsible for starting the First World War and forced to pay reparations totalling £6600 million.

SOURCE A Cartoon of Wilson's new order c.1919.

Treaty of Rapallo

One consequence of the peace settlement was a drawing together of 'outcast' nations. In 1922 Germany and Russia signed the Treaty of Rapallo by which Germany recognised the new Soviet government.

The occupation of the Ruhr, 1923

Towards the end of 1922, Germany failed to make a reparations repayment. In response, in 1923 French and Belgian troops occupied the industrial heartland of Germany – the Ruhr – to take the value of the missing payments in goods. The German government ordered a policy of passive resistance and German workers went on strike. Although this meant that the French and Belgians could not take the goods they wanted, it also brought about the collapse of the German economy. The German mark became worthless and many people lost their life savings or pensions.

STRESEMANN'S FOREIGN POLICY

Between 1924 and 1929 Germany began to regain international respect and its status as a great power, largely thanks to Gustav Stresemann. His aim was to make Germany great again by freeing it from the terms of the Treaty of Versailles: this would be done by co-operation and diplomacy. He wanted Germany's lands restored and the removal of the war guilt clause. Entry into the League of Nations would lead to greater German involvement in Europe. He approved of secret rearmament, not in order to pursue an aggressive foreign policy but to get equality with other European powers.

Stresemann's success as a diplomat

Stresemann scored a great diplomatic victory in 1925 with the signing of the Locarno Pact. Germany, France and Belgium agreed not to attack each other or adjust each other's boundaries. Germany accepted the permanence of its western boundaries and the demilitarised status of the Rhineland.

Stresemann's next move was to steer Germany into the League of Nations in 1926, for which he was awarded the Nobel Peace Prize. Germany was given permanent membership on the Council of the League implying recognition as a great power. In 1928 Germany, along with over 60 other nations, signed the Kellogg–Briand Pact, which renounced war as a means of settling disputes.

Stresemann's last success came in 1929 when the Allies withdrew their remaining forces from the Rhineland and Germany agreed to settle the reparations question as part of the Young Plan. Before the terms were completed, Stresemann died.

Q Questions

1 How did the Treaty of Versailles weaken Germany as a world power?

2 How did Germany respond to the occupation of the Ruhr in 1923?

3 To what extent did Stresemann improve Germany's international relations after 1919?

GERMANY AND THE CAUSES OF THE SECOND WORLD WAR

Did Hitler's foreign policy lead directly and deliberately to war in 1939? In many ways Hitler's foreign policy was the same as Stresemann's. However, while Stresemann hoped to achieve his aims through diplomacy, Hitler chose an aggressive foreign policy. He promised to unite all German-speaking people into one Reich and to expand eastwards for *Lebensraum* (living space).

Historians disagree about Hitler's aims:

- A. J. P. Taylor has argued that Hitler did not deliberately set out for a war to end civilisation. He was an opportunist and made gains by bluff and nerve.
- Hugh Trevor-Roper has argued that Hitler planned a programme of eastern colonisation and a war of conquest in the west. This *Stufenplan* (step-by-step policy) led to war.

  Step 1: a moderate policy up to 1935
  Step 2: increased activity in 1935–7
  Step 3: a more confident foreign policy based on the idea that there would be little opposition after 1937.

HITLER DISMANTLES THE TREATY

Germany leaves the League of Nations

Rearmament had begun before Hitler came to power. It was generally felt throughout Europe that Germany had been treated unfairly at Versailles and Hitler sought to use this to his advantage. At the Disarmament Conference of the League of Nations he argued that Germany would disarm if other countries did the same. France refused and Hitler quit the conference and the League.

Germany rearms

In March 1935 Hitler announced that Germany had an airforce (*Luftwaffe*) and introduced conscription. The navy was expanded with the building of battleships and submarines. This clear rejection of the Treaty of Versailles caused Britain, France and Italy to sign an agreement (the Stresa Front) denouncing his actions, but they took no military action.

The Saar rejoins Germany

In 1935 the people of the Saar voted overwhelmingly to return to Germany. Hitler promised not to make any further territorial claims on France, including Alsace and Lorraine.

Germany reoccupies the Rhineland

On 7 March 1936 German troops entered the Rhineland in a deliberate breach of the Treaty of Versailles. Hitler later admitted that he did not have the military resources to withstand opposition. France could have driven him back, but it would not act without Britain. The attitude of the British government was that Hitler was only 'marching into his own backyard'.

Hitler makes allies

Even though he had not met with any resistance to his actions so far, Hitler saw the need to form alliances.

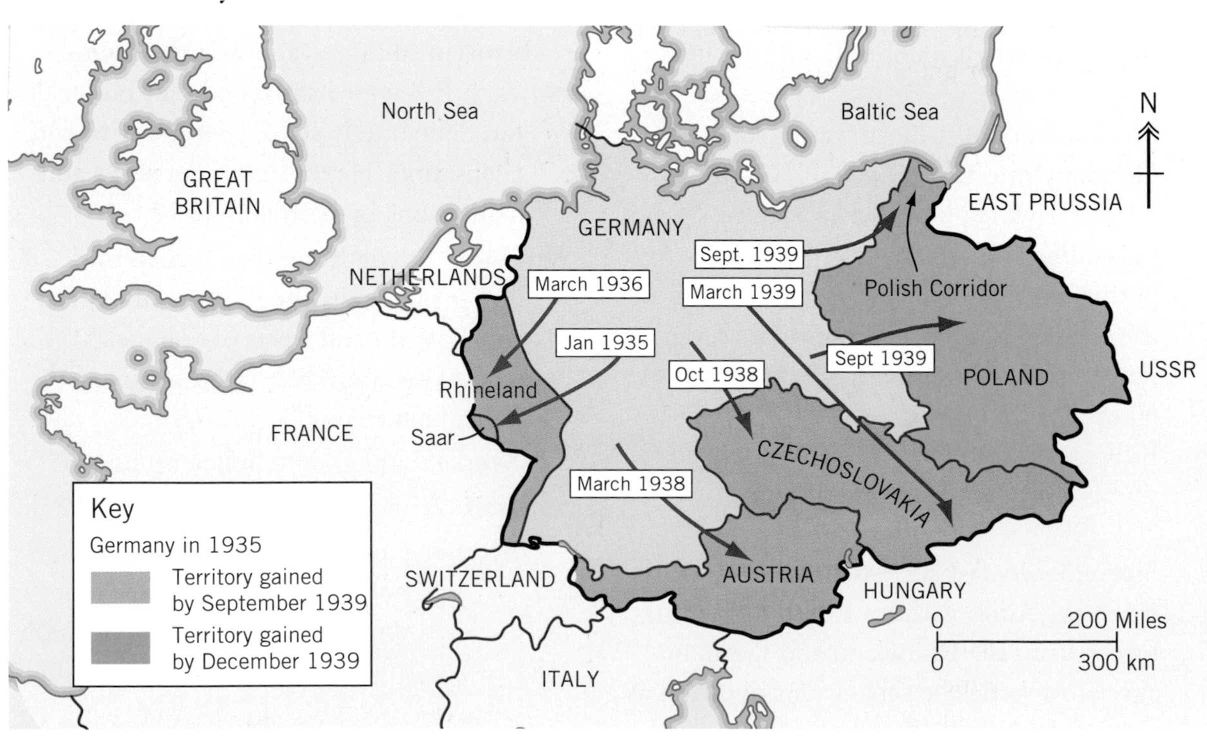

Hitler's territorial gains, 1935–9.

- **Spain**: when civil war broke out in Spain in 1936 Hitler sent his crack air force division to fight alongside the nationalist leader General Franco.
- **Italy**: in 1936 he agreed the Rome–Berlin Axis with Mussolini, dictator of Italy.
- **Japan**: the Anti-Comintern Pact of 1936 brought Germany and Japan together in opposition to the Soviet Union. Italy joined in 1937. A full military alliance between Germany and Italy – the Pact of Steel – was signed in 1939. Japan joined in 1940.

Hitler invades Austria: the Anschluss

Hitler now turned his attention to Austria, in a further move forbidden by the Treaty of Versailles. In 1938 he ordered the Austrian Nazi Party to begin a programme of disruption to undermine the government of Chancellor Schuschnigg, whose resignation he demanded. Schuschnigg was replaced by Seyss-Inquart, a Nazi supporter, and German troops invaded on 12 March 1938. A plebiscite (vote) was held on 10 April and 99.75 per cent of Austrians voted in favour of the *Anschluss*, or union with Germany.

Hitler turns to Czechoslovakia

Czechoslovakia is rich in deposits of coal and lignite and possessed the huge Skoda armaments factory. Czechoslovakia also had 3.5 million Germans living in the Sudetenland near the borders with Germany and Austria. Most of the Sudeten Germans supported a Nazi-style Party led by Konrad Henlein. Henlein organised demonstrations and riots, and in April 1938 German troops massed on the Czech border.

The British prime minister, Neville Chamberlain, met Hitler to discuss the crisis. Hitler made it clear that if he could not occupy the Sudetenland by 1 October 1938, he would invade Czechoslovakia. Chamberlain was prepared to sacrifice the Sudetenland to avoid war. This policy of appeasement was agreed at a four-power conference in Munich attended by Chamberlain, Hitler, Mussolini and Daladier, the French prime minister. But in March 1939 Hitler also marched into Czechoslovakia claiming the western half. Hungary and Poland seized the rest.

Hitler in Poland

Hitler now demanded the restoration of Danzig and the return of the Polish Corridor. Britain and France now realised that Hitler could no longer be appeased and agreed to defend Poland. In August, Nazi Germany and the Soviet Union signed a non-aggression pact – a promise not to fight each other. Hitler could now invade Poland without worrying about the Soviet Union. On 1 September 1939 German tanks crossed the Polish frontier. Britain therefore declared war on Germany on 3 September 1939, followed shortly after by France. Europe was at war again.

Q Questions

1. What were Hitler's aims for Germany?
2. How successful was Hitler in his attempt to undo the terms of the Treaty of Versailles?
3. How did other European countries respond to Hitler's foreign policy between 1935 and 1939?

GERMANY AND THE MAIN EVENTS OF THE SECOND WORLD WAR

The *Blitzkrieg* tactic was unstoppable in the early years of the war. Poland fell within three weeks and Hitler turned his forces on Western Europe. Denmark, Norway, Holland and Belgium fell quickly; France was Hitler's next target.

The fall of France, May 1940

The French had built an impressive set of fortifications – the Maginot Line – along their border in the hope of preventing a German invasion. However, the Germans simply went round it and moved rapidly towards the coast.

In the face of the German thrust the British and French forces retreated to the Channel port of Dunkirk and were surrounded. From 27 May to 4 June 1940 the *Luftwaffe* attacked the beaches of northern France and the British navy began the evacuation of troops. Small, privately owned vessels crossed the Channel and ferried troops to larger ships. In all, 340,000 men were rescued in what Churchill called the 'miracle of Dunkirk'.

Within a month Paris was captured and, under the terms of the armistice of 22 June 1940, Germany occupied the northern and western parts of France while a pro-German government controlled the south.

The Battle of Britain, 1940

Hitler was confident that Britain would fall to Germany but he underestimated the mood of its people, the inspiration of its leader and the bravery of its air force. Hitler needed control of the air if his invasion was to succeed. The battles that raged from July 1940 in the Battle of Britain were crucial for the whole course of the war. The British had the advantages of a better fighter plane (the Spitfire) and radar. In mid-September 1940 Hitler postponed the invasion, but he continued aerial attacks on Britain in the 'Blitz'.

The invasion of Russia, 1941

Despite signing the Nazi–Soviet Pact in 1939, it was always Hitler's intention to invade the Soviet Union. He wanted to destroy communism, but in the short term Hitler needed the grain and oil resources to help the war effort. His plan to invade in April 1941 was delayed while he helped Mussolini, who had entered the war and suffered defeats in North Africa and Greece. Meanwhile, German armies captured Yugoslavia, Greece and Crete.

On 22 June 1941 Operation Barbarossa began. By November the Germans had reached Moscow, Leningrad and Kiev.

The Soviets retreated and adopted a 'scorched earth' policy, destroying everything that could be used by the advancing Germans. The weather then came to the aid of the Soviet Union. One of the worst winters arrived early catching the Germans in summer uniforms and halting the German advance in its tracks. In spring 1942 Hitler's armies swung south to seize the Caucasian oilfields and attack Stalingrad. The war had reached a crucial stage. At the Battle of Stalingrad (1942) the German forces met with heavy resistance. General von Paulus requested retreat but Hitler refused. With supplies running low, von Paulus disobeyed orders and surrendered in January 1943. The Red Army began to push back the German forces to Poland.

Q Questions

1 How successful was the German *Blitzkrieg* tactic?

2 Why did Hitler invade the Soviet Union?

3 Why was Hitler defeated in the Soviet Union?

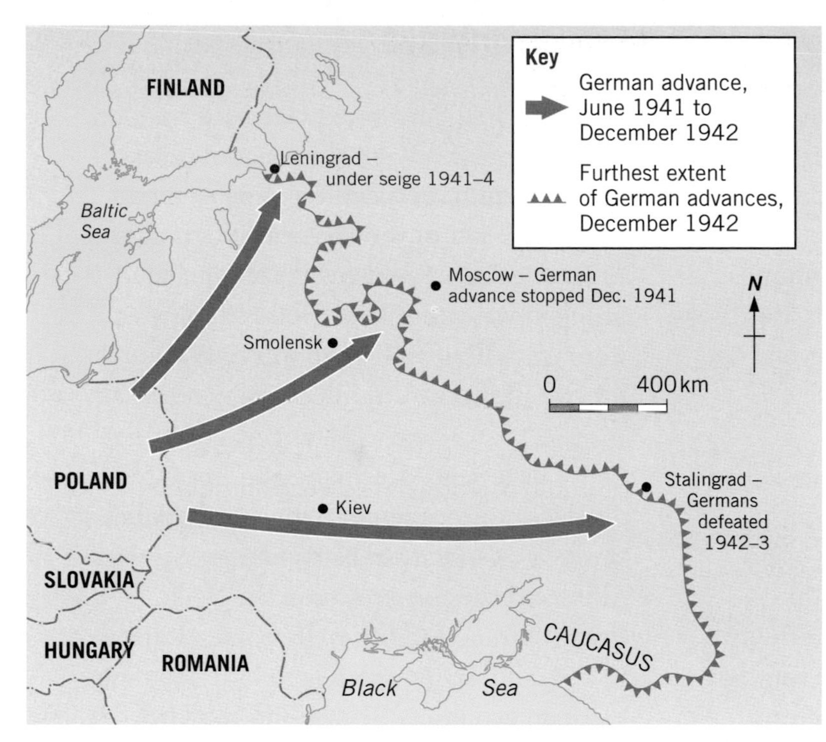

Germany's invasion of the Soviet Union, 1941–2.

El Alamein, October 1942

The Suez Canal was a vitally important shipping route for Britain in controlling access to the Middle East oil reserves. From September 1940 to June 1942 the British and Axis (German and Italian) armies battled for control of the Mediterranean. The decisive battle was fought at El Alamein in Egypt in October 1942. The British Eighth Army under General Montgomery defeated the Axis forces. With the arrival of US troops General Rommel requested a withdrawal, but Hitler refused. By May 1943, 130,000 Axis troops had surrendered. The Allies crossed into Italy and began the push towards Germany.

The D-Day landings, 6 June 1944

Hitler argued that, whatever happened elsewhere, German armies were invincible in *Festung* Europe (Fortress Europe). However, the first failure occurred when the Allies landed in Sicily on 9 July 1943. Hitler now faced war on three fronts. More defeats followed when the Allies landed in France as part of the D-Day invasion on 6 June 1944.

Hitler had expected the invasion on his western front to take place at Calais, but the Allied landings in Normandy surprised the Germans. By the end of the first day, 156,000 US, British and Commonwealth troops had landed and began pushing the German army back to the River Seine. On 25 August 1944, General Charles de Gaulle entered Paris and was declared Prime Minister.

Hitler attempted a new offensive and in December 1942 attacked US troops in the Ardennes in the Battle of the Bulge. After initial successes he was forced to withdraw.

By early-1945 Soviet troops had advanced on to German soil and the Allies had crossed the Rhine. Hitler retreated to his underground bunker in Berlin, where he committed suicide on 30 April 1945. On 7 May Germany surrendered unconditionally and the four Allied powers took control of Germany. The Reich which Hitler had claimed would last a thousand years had lasted just twelve years.

Q Questions

1 What events led to the German defeat in 1945?

2 Why did Hitler's 'war on all fronts' fail?

GERMANY AND THE COLD WAR

In capitalist countries like the USA and Britain businesses and industries are run with the aim of making profits for the owners. This is believed to create competition and efficiency. In communist countries businesses and industries are run by the state for the benefit of everyone and do not make a profit.

Capitalist USA and communist Russia had allied themselves against Nazism during the Second World War, but when war ended the old suspicion and hostility returned. The differences between the two sides might previously have led to war, but the invention of atomic weapons meant that both sides shied away from a 'hot war' of mass destruction. Instead, both sides reverted to a 'cold war', a war which stopped short of actual fighting.

SOURCE B A cartoon from a British newspaper, published in July 1946. The foreign ministers of the wartime allies are arguing over what should be done to Germany now that the war is over.

GERMANY DIVIDED

Total war had devastated Germany and, on top of the psychological impact of defeat, the German nation had to come to terms with the cloud of the Holocaust (see page 217). For most Germans the immediate problem was more basic: food supplies were dwindling and there was only enough for two months in the Western zones.

As we have seen, Germany and Berlin were divided into four zones between the Allies. Problems soon arose between the Western Allies and the Soviet Union. In 1947 Britain, France and the USA agreed that they would work together to kick-start the German economy. Britain and the USA joined their zones into a bi-zone or 'Bizonia' and France joined, forming a tri-zone. Stalin felt threatened by this action.

The Truman Doctrine and Marshall Aid

In a speech in March 1947 the US President Truman offered help to any government that felt threatened by 'internal or external forces'. He saw countries devastated by war as breeding grounds for communism and offered economic aid to promote recovery. Marshall Aid put the Truman Doctrine into practice. The US Secretary of State George C. Marshall offered over $13 billion in aid and 16 countries applied. Countries such as Britain, France, Germany and Italy received aid. Stalin viewed the plan as a US plot to dominate Eastern Europe and insisted that communist countries refuse aid.

SOURCE C

> Our policy is not directed against any country or doctrine, but against hunger, poverty, desperation and chaos. Any government that is willing to assist in the task of recovery will find full co-operation on the part of the United States government.
>
> From a speech in which George C. Marshall, US Secretary of State, explains Marshall Aid.

The Soviet zone

The food shortage was more acute in the Soviet zone than in the Western zones. The Soviets had stripped it of capital equipment which it sent to the Soviet Union to rebuild its war-ravaged economy. Nazi land and large farm estates were broken up and given to labourers. A communist state was emerging.

The Berlin blockade

In an attempt to combat inflation, the Western Allies introduced a new currency into their zones in June 1948. Stalin was concerned about the threat from a prosperous Germany. Berlin lay in the Soviet zone and he saw it as a capitalist base in Eastern Europe. On 24 June 1948 Soviet troops cut off all road, rail and canal links between the West and Berlin.

Stalin planned to starve Berliners and the Western powers into submission. The Americans considered using their army but this could have escalated into war, so instead they decided to get supplies in by air. The Allies used three air corridors over the Soviet zone and the airlift began. By September 1948 aircraft were landing every three minutes. Stalin could do little: to shoot down planes would be an act of war. From June 1948 to May 1949 over 27,000 trips were made and 2 million tonnes of supplies airlifted in.

SOURCE D 'The Bird Watcher', a *Punch* cartoon about the Berlin blockade from July 1948.

Stalin eventually gave way and lifted the blockade on 12 May 1949. The Berlin blockade hardened the hostility between East and West. There was now no prospect of uniting Germany; West Germany (FDR) and East Germany (GDR) came into being (see page 206). The crisis also demonstrated the need for the Western powers to combine their military strengths in order to combat communism in Europe.

Q Questions

1. Why did Stalin reject Marshall Aid?
2. Why was the Berlin blockade a significant event in the Cold War?
3. What does the Berlin blockade say about Germany's importance as a world power?

NATO and the Warsaw Pact

In May 1955 West Germany became a member of the North Atlantic Treaty Organisation (NATO) which had been set up in 1949. NATO had come into being as an alliance of 12 Western powers which would come to the defence of others if one was attacked. The move stemmed from the Soviet acquisition of the atomic bomb. A direct result of German entry into NATO was the setting up, also in 1955, of the Warsaw Pact, a military alliance of the Soviet Union and its allies.

The Berlin Wall

The Western presence in Berlin was a huge embarrassment to the USSR. US economic aid helped transform the city into a showpiece of capitalism. While people in the west of the city were able to buy luxury goods, those in East Berlin worked long hours and suffered from food shortages. Even more embarrassing for the USSR was the huge numbers of East Berliners who escaped to the West. On 13 August 1961 the GDR authorities began to build a wall to divide East Berlin physically from West Berlin to prevent 'spies and diversionists' from entering their capital. In reality it was to stop the steady stream of highly-skilled professionals fleeing to the West.

The Wall separated families and friends. Anyone caught trying to cross the Wall would be shot. Even so, many people were desperate enough to try and in the first year of the Wall, 41 Berliners were shot trying to cross. Later in the year the East German government began creating problems at crossing-points in the city. For a time Soviet and US tanks faced each other muzzle to muzzle.

BRANDT AND THE POLICY OF *OSTPOLITIK*

Relations between the two Germanies throughout the 1950s were not good. Adenauer's policy of 'maintained tension' discouraged contact with East Germans.

When the Cuban Missile Crisis of 1962 brought the world to the brink of war many West Germans saw the need for peaceful co-existence. Chancellor Erhard proposed a reduction of nuclear weapons and an agreement with East Germany to renounce the use of force to settle disputes. As mayor of West Berlin Willy Brandt had witnessed the building of the Berlin Wall, but as a Social Democrat he was convinced that East and West Germany could be reconciled. He made *Ostpolitik* (the opening of relations with the Eastern bloc) the major election issue of 1969. On election Brandt concluded a number of agreements with East Germany.

On 21 December 1972 the two Germanies signed the Basic Treaty, in which they agreed to develop good understanding as normal neighbours and to respect each other's independence. This allowed them to be admitted to the United Nations in 1973 and represented a thaw in the Cold War. Travel between the two Germanies and within Berlin was made easier and communications were improved. Trade tripled throughout the 1970s.

Q Questions

1 Why was the Berlin Wall built?

2 How did relations between East and West Germany improve after 1962?

A REUNIFIED GERMANY

However, relations became strained following the Soviet Union's invasion of Afghanistan in 1979, which led to a deepening of the Cold War. By 1985 the Soviet economy was in crisis. Mikhail Gorbachev, the new General Secretary of the Communist Party, argued that too much money was being spent on the arms race and the war in Afghanistan. His policies of *perestroika* (economic restructuring) and *glasnost* (openness) relaxed tensions between the East and the West.

By 1989 the Cold War was at an end and Soviet control of Eastern Europe was beginning to collapse. In March 1989 Gorbachev informed the leaders of communist Eastern Europe that the Red Army would no longer be able to defend them and help them crush internal opposition. People soon began to demonstrate against communist regimes. In May 1989 Hungary removed its barriers with Austria and hundreds of East Germans fled into the West. By mid-September 1989 the number of East German refugees had swollen to 50,000 and, as East Germans demonstrated for more freedom, the hardline leader Honecker was forced out. On 9 November 1989 the East German government announced that it would open the borders and allow free travel. The next day East Germans marched to the Berlin Wall and pulled it down (see Source E).

After November 1989 the West German government injected huge amounts of money to help support the East German economy and in July 1990 the economies were merged. Negotiations were held between the foreign ministers of the two Germanies along with the Allied powers of the Second World War, who still had rights of occupation. On 21 August representatives of East and West Germany signed a treaty for reunification which finally took place in October 1990. Berlin was unified and became the capital of the new Germany. The Christian Democratic Coalition, led by Helmut Kohl, won a decisive victory in the election for the new German government and Kohl became Chancellor of a reunified Germany.

SOURCE E In November 1989 the Berlin Wall was breached and the people of East and West Germany were reunited.

Q Questions

1. Why was Berlin a focal point of the Cold War?
2. How did relations between East and West Germany improve in the period 1949–90?

7 EXAM PRACTICE

THE DEVELOPMENT OF GERMANY, 1919–91

Study the information below and answer the questions which follow.

INFORMATION

This poster shows a figure representing the Weimar Republic in 1924 pulling Germany away from the dark years at the end of the First World War.

EQ Exam Questions

1 **a** What was the Weimar Republic? [2]

b Describe the work of Gustav Stresemann between 1924 and 1929. [4]

2 Explain why the Nazis came to power in Germany. [6]

3 Why were the Yalta and Potsdam Agreements important for the development of Germany? [8]

4 How successful was Germany, both politically and economically, during the period 1919–91?
In your answer you may wish to consider the Weimar Republic, the Nazi years, Adenauer, the situation in 1991 and any other relevant factors. [10]

THE LIVES OF PEOPLE IN GERMANY, 1919–91

Study the information below and answer the questions which follow.

INFORMATION

In the 1930s and 1940s the Nazis attempted to indoctrinate the youth of Germany in the ideas of the Third Reich. The picture shows Hitler addressing young people at a Nazi-run youth camp.

EQ Exam Questions

1 **a** What was meant by reparations? [2]

b Describe the impact of the Depression on the German people between 1929 and 1933. [4]

2 Explain why the Nazis wanted to keep women in the home. [6]

3 Why was Berlin such an important city during the Cold War? [8]

4 Did life for for the Germans improve during the period 1919–91?
In your answer you may wish to consider the impact of the wars, the Depression, Nazism, the situation in 1991 and any other relevant factors. [10]

GERMANY AND THE WIDER WORLD

Study the information below and answer the questions which follow.

INFORMATION

This photograph shows Berlin as a divided city during the Cold War.

EQ Exam Questions

1 **a** What was the Treaty of Versailles? [2]

b Describe what happened during the *Anschluss*. [4]

2 Explain why Germany became involved in the Second World War. [6]

3 Why did Germany help to establish the EEC? [8]

4 Was Germany important in world affairs throughout the period 1919–91?
In your answer you may wish to consider the Nazi years, the Second World War, the Cold War, the situation in 1991 and any other relevant factors. [10]

8 THE UNITED STATES OF AMERICA, 1929–90

The economic boom of the 1920s came to an end with the Wall Street Crash in October 1929, plunging the USA into the Great Depression. By 1933 unemployment stood at 13 million. On his election in 1932, President Roosevelt promised a New Deal for the American people and pumped huge amounts of money into this programme. He set the USA on the road to recovery, but it was the US entry into the Second World War in 1941 that ultimately pulled the nation out of the Depression.

After victory in 1945 the USA emerged as the world's leading nation. Many Americans enjoyed improved living standards but poverty remained a problem. The USA remained a nation divided by race. By 1968, civil rights legislation had been passed, but racism remained an issue.

After 1945 the USA saw itself as the defender of democracy and promised to contain communism. This was achieved in Korea (1950–3) but it brought the world to the brink of nuclear war over Cuba in 1962. In March 1965 US combat troops arrived in Vietnam and entered an unwinnable war. Defeat still affects the nation today. Since the 1970s the USA has sought better relations with the USSR and China in an attempt to achieve world peace and stability.

Popular culture has played an increasingly prominent role in the lives of Americans. Hollywood remains the capital of the global film industry and US films are shown worldwide, turning their actors and actresses into international stars. American television programmes and music are also exported worldwide, having a far-reaching influence.

After the Second World War, teenagers began to emerge as a distinct cultural group and many young Americans became disenchanted with American society. Confronted by the nuclear age, students demonstrated against war and hippies experimented with alternative lifestyles. The feminist movement achieved significant changes for women.

TIMELINE OF EVENTS

1929 Wall Street Crash

1932 F.D. Roosevelt elected President

1933 Beginning of the New Deal

1941 Japanese attack on Pearl Harbor; US enters Second World War

1945 US atomic bombs dropped on Hiroshima and Nagasaki

Yalta and Potsdam Conferences

1947 Truman Doctrine and Marshall Aid

1948 Berlin airlift

1949 USA joins NATO

1950 Outbreak of Korean War

1953 End of Korean War

1960 U2 spy plane incident

1962 Cuban missile crisis

1963 Nuclear Test Ban Treaty

Assassination of President Kennedy

1965 Outbreak of Vietnam War

1972 Strategic Arms Limitation Talks end in SALT 1 agreement

1973 US withdraws from Vietnam War

1974 Watergate scandal: Richard Nixon resigns as US President

1975 Helsinki Accords

1987 Immediate Nuclear Forces Treaty (INF)

In what ways did American society change between 1929 and 1990?

THE GREAT DEPRESSION

The 1920s was a time of unparalleled prosperity and excitement. The writer F. Scott Fitzgerald called the period the 'Jazz Age' but argued that society had turned away from the real issues. The Republicans were in office throughout the period and believed that they had created a 'new economic era' where soon all Americans would live in comfort.

What caused the Great Depression?

The Great Depression was caused by several interconnected factors:

- The USA was a divided society – 5 per cent of the people owned 33 per cent of the country's wealth.
- Old traditional industries and agriculture had suffered in the 1920s.
- Republican thinking was based on the idea of *'laissez-faire'* (the government should not interfere in people's lives, especially in the economy).
- High tariffs on imported goods led to a drop in demand for US goods overseas.
- The huge output of manufactured goods generated by assembly lines was no longer matched by consumer spending.
- The better-off over-speculated on the stock exchange; the poor over-extended themselves on credit.

The collapse of the US economy: the Wall Street Crash, October 1929

Investors on the stock exchange, thinking that the prosperity boom would soon end, became nervous and began selling shares. Prices began to fall and panic set in. On Tuesday, 29 October 1929 (Terrifying Tuesday), 16.5 million shares were sold. By the end of 1929 the value of all shares had dropped by $40,000 million.

The 'cycle of depression'

The cycle of depression.

Many Americans lost everything in the Crash. Banks had speculated with investors' money and 9 million people lost their savings as 5000 banks went out of business. By 1932 over 100,000 businesses had gone bust and there were 13 million unemployed, about 25 per cent of the workforce. Many town dwellers became homeless and were forced into makeshift shanty towns or 'Hoovervilles' (so called because the unemployed blamed President Hoover for their position). With no system of social security many people were forced to rely on handouts from private charities or to beg and scavenge on rubbish tips.

The 'Bonus Army'

In the summer of 1932 a 'Bonus Army' of unemployed war veterans marched on Washington DC to demand early payment of bonuses of about $500 scheduled to be paid in 1945. They set up a huge Hooverville opposite the White House. President Hoover ordered troops to drive them out and burn down the shanty town.

Agricultural depression

The Depression also brought ruin to the countryside. As demand for farm produce fell, many farmers went bankrupt and were evicted from their properties. The situation was worsened by over-intensive farming, which led to soil infertility and erosion. Thousands of farmers set off across the USA in search of a new life.

ROOSEVELT AND THE NEW DEAL

The 1932 election campaign

During the election campaign people threw eggs at Hoover and made placards that said 'Hang Hoover' and 'In Hoover we trusted. Now we are busted'. Voters nicknamed Roosevelt the 'Champ' – he was the man to trust. His slogan was 'Happy days are here again'. The American public voted for the man who promised action and Roosevelt won 42 of the 48 states in a landslide election victory and was elected President.

SOURCE A A 'Hooverville' in the centre of New York.

Hoover's policies.

Roosevelt's policies.

The 'three Rs'

Roosevelt proposed a New Deal for the US people which was based on 'three Rs'. These were: **relief** – aimed at the homeless and the unemployed; **recovery** – aimed at rebuilding the economy; and **reform** – aimed at creating a fairer society.

The key to the New Deal was direct federal action. The first 'Hundred Days' of Roosevelt's presidency therefore saw the setting up of many government bodies to tackle the USA's problems. These organisations became known as the 'Alphabet Agencies' (see information boxes on pages 236–7 which explains the role each agency played). These agencies were designed to help Americans get back to work, which would give people money to pay off debts and start spending again.

Roosevelt's first move to stabilise the economy was to allow only solvent banks to stay in business. These received government backing and so helped restore the public's faith in the banking system.

Successes of the New Deal

- The income of farmers doubled between 1932 and 1939 as a result of the AAA.
- The TVA improved the lives of 7 million people (see page 236).
- 2.5 million people were employed in the CCC (see page 236).
- 4 million people were employed on public works schemes created by the PWA and WPA.
- Workers were protected by codes of practice and trade unions introduced by the NRA and Wagner Act.

Government spends money on Alphabet Agencies
more jobs created
more money to spend on goods
increased demand for goods
increased production

The cycle of recovery.

Criticisms of the New Deal

- The AAA paid farmers to produce less food – 'shoot the cows and milk the government'. This failed to help sharecroppers and farm workers.
- Unemployment did fall but it was the USA's entry into the Second World War in 1941 that ultimately lifted the country out of the Depression.
- Some argued that Roosevelt's recovery projects were only short-term solutions that provided cheap labour, for example, employing men as pigeon scarers.
- Many viewed trade unions as un-American and some firms employed thugs to beat up members. Paying benefits to workers went against the belief in 'rugged individualism'.
- The rich objected to paying taxes to help poorer people.
- Black people benefited because they were poor, not because they were black, so still faced a great deal of discrimination (see page 249). Women benefited only if they were married.

Some felt that Roosevelt's New Deal interfered too much in the affairs of the American people. In 1935 the Supreme Court declared the NRA unconstitutional. In 1936 the AAA was also declared unconstitutional. In retaliation, President Roosevelt tried to fill the Supreme Court with judges sympathetic to his views. He eventually withdrew the plan, but the Supreme Court was now more cautious about blocking Roosevelt's policies.

THE TWO PHASES OF THE NEW DEAL

The first New Deal

Agency	Purpose	Action
Federal Emergency Relief Administration (**FERA**)	Federal money to individual states to help the unemployed and homeless	One dollar given by the government for every three spent by the state: $500 million given in total
Civilian Conservation Corps (**CCC**)	Conservation work for unemployed young men aged 18–25 years	Workers given $30 a week (of which $25 was to be sent home) in return for food and shelter
Agricultural Adjustment Administration (**AAA**)	To help farmers to increase profits	Subsidies for farmers to destroy crops and slaughter animals to push up prices
Tennessee Valley Authority (**TVA**)	To provide aid to the poverty-striken Tennessee Valley	21 dams built, hydro-electricity produced
National Industrial Recovery Act (**NIRA**) (i) National Recovery Administration (**NRA**) (ii) Public Works Administration (**PWA**)	(i) To encourage employers to improve conditions at work (ii) To put skilled unemployed workers on large-scale construction projects	(i) Codes of practice drawn up on minimum wages, hours and conditions. Participating companies were allowed to display the Blue Eagle symbol (ii) Slum clearance, house building. Schools and hospital built

Other opponents of the New Deal argued that it did not go far enough to help people. Huey Long, Governor of Louisiana, was an outspoken critic of Roosevelt's policies. He proposed a 'Share Our Wealth' campaign which would confiscate all personal fortunes of over $3 million so that every family would receive $4000–5000. Dr Francis Townsend argued that Roosevelt had not done enough for old people and proposed a pension of $200 a month for everyone over 60. In return they had to spend their money within the month, which would increase demand for goods and therefore provide further employment.

Questions

1. What were the causes and effects of the Wall Street Crash in 1929?
2. What were the main features of the New Deal?
3. How successful was the New Deal? Explain your answer.

HOW DID THE SECOND WORLD WAR AFFECT AMERICAN SOCIETY?

The Second World War broke out in 1939. Although the USA did not enter the war until 1941, from 1939 the USA continued to supply European countries fighting in the war.

The second New Deal (The second New Deal emphasised workers' rights.)

Agency	Purpose	Action
Works Progress Administration **(WPA)**	To consolidate all agencies involved in job creation	People put to work building roads, schools and airports. Writers and artists employed on creative projects
National Labour Relations Act **(Wagner Act)**	To replace codes declared illegal by the Supreme Court by giving workers the right to join trade unions	National Labour Relations Board set up. Workers able to negotiate better pay and conditions. Stopped employers sacking union members
Fair Labour Standards Act	To regulate hours and conditions of work	Tightened up laws against child labour and minimum wages
Social Security Act	To set up a national system of social security	Benefit provided for unemployed, pensions for people over 65, aid to the disabled, widows and orphans
Soil Conservation Act	Replaced the AAA, which was declared illegal by the Supreme Court (see page 236)	Provided subsidies for farmers

American people experienced various changes during the Second World War. After 1941, the USA concentrated its entire manpower, industrial and agricultural resources on the war effort. Conscription (compulsory military service) of men between 18 and 45 accounted for over 15 million people by 1945 and millions of workers found employment in munition factories. In 1942 the War Production Board (WPB) put US industry on a war footing and by 1945 industrial production had doubled. Unemployment fell from 9.5 million in 1939 to 670,000 in 1944. In this way the Second World War brought an end to the Great Depression.

People were encouraged to produce 'victory gardens' in which they grew their own vegetables, and 'to give an hour a day for the USA'. Farmers also benefited from the war: a guaranteed market for their produce saw profits increase. US foodstuffs supplied the US armed forces and were transported to war-ravaged Europe. The need for factory workers meant that many women entered the workplace (see page 246).

The war years also witnessed a massive internal migration of some 27 million people between 1941 and 1945. Most went in search of better jobs, especially to armament factories in California. Not all Americans moved out of choice: 112,000 Japanese Americans were interned (imprisoned) during the war years in a wave of anti-Japanese feeling. Many lost their homes and businesses and 1000 were transported back to Japan. (The US government made a formal apology to the Japanese in 1988 and paid compensation to the 60,000 still alive.)

Q Question

1 What impact did the Second World War have on the American people?

THE AFFLUENT SOCIETY

In April 1945 Harry Truman became President. He put forward a 21-point development programme called the 'Fair Deal', a continuation of the New Deal. Unemployment remained low but rising inflation meant trade unions demanded higher wages and Truman had to deal firmly with strikers. His main concern was social policy: he raised the minimum wage from 40 cents to 75 cents an hour and built 1 million low-cost houses.

In 1952 the Republican Dwight Eisenhower became President. Eisenhower did not backtrack on the New and Fair Deals and encouraged economic expansion while fostering the interests of the middle classes, on whose support the Republicans relied. The USA enjoyed unprecedented prosperity throughout the 1950s and, by the end of the decade, it was producing half of the world's manufactured goods.

Life in suburbia

During the 1950s, an increase in car ownership and road improvements together with long-term, low-interest mortgages resulted in some 19 million Americans moving out of the cities for a life in the suburbs.

By 1960, 25 per cent of Americans lived in suburbia. Television sets, record players, swimming pools and the car (or two) became status symbols.

Consumer goods were bought on 'time payments' or credit, which increased by 800 per cent between 1945 and 1957. Between 1945 and 1960 car ownership increased from 25 to 62 million. The Model T had long been overtaken by 'gas guzzling' Cadillacs and Pontiacs.

McCARTHYISM

While this period was a happy and prosperous one for many Americans, others continued to face discrimination. In the early-1950s Senator Joseph McCarthy helped to whip up anti-communist feeling by claiming to have a list of 'known communists' in the State Department, the army and other walks of life. Hundreds of people were accused, without proof, of secretly working for the USSR. The Communist Party was subsequently banned in the USA.

McCarthy helped to ruin the lives and careers of many Americans as a result of his 'witch hunt'. However, after accusing 45 army officers of being communist agents, McCarthy was challenged and asked to provide evidence to support his accusations. The Army–McCarthy hearings were televised. He was eventually dismissed from office in 1954 when his 'evidence' was exposed as no more than rumours. Television had influenced public opinion and McCarthy's reputation lay in ruins.

AFFLUENCE FOR ALL?

By 1960 the standard of living of the average American was three times that of the average Briton. The USA was well out of the Depression. However, the division of wealth across the US meant that not all Americans shared in this affluence.

SOURCE **B** An American family watches television at home, 1956.

Michael Harrington, in *The Other America* (1962), estimated the number of poor at 30 per cent of the population (50 million). Included in this list were the 'hill-billies' of the Appalachian Mountains; Hispanic workers in the west; and black people in the city ghettos in the north. These groups greatly influenced the policies of President Kennedy and, later, President Johnson.

Questions

1. What were the main features of life in suburbia?
2. Did all Americans experience prosperity in this period? Explain your answer.

JOHN F. KENNEDY AND THE NEW FRONTIER

SOURCE C President Kennedy speaking in the 1960s.

In November 1960 John F. Kennedy, a Democratic, was elected president. He called for a New Frontier which was aimed at destroying the twentieth-century evils of poverty, inequality and deprivation.

At this time there was no doubt that US prosperity would continue. However, problems that had begun to appear in the 1950s were continuing to cause divisions in the 1960s. These were: urban decline associated with unemployment, poverty and a rising crime rate; the issue of civil rights (see pages 250–4); and the USA's role in foreign affairs such as the war in Vietnam (see pages 264–6).

Kennedy aimed to introduce far-reaching reforms to society and the economy. He proposed an ambitious system of state health insurance called Medicare, together with a Medical Help for the Aged Bill and a Civil Rights Bill. He also aimed to get an education law passed to inject more money into schools especially in the run-down poverty-stricken inner cities.

The verdict on Kennedy

For all his charm and charisma, President Kennedy was unable to handle Congress: he failed to gain enough support from senators and his bills were rejected. He did, however, succeed in increasing social security and raising the minimum wage, and he was also successful in setting up training schemes for the unemployed.

Kennedy's hopes for the nation were ended on 22 November 1963 in Dallas when he was assassinated. As you can see from Sources D and E, there have been very different opinions about Kennedy's performance as President.

SOURCE D

What was killed in Dallas was … the death of youth and the hope of youth, of the beauty and grace and the touch of magic … He never reached his meridian: we saw him only as a rising sun.

James Reston in the *New York Times*, 1963.

SOURCE E

> In the administration of John F. Kennedy, activity was mistaken for action … toughness was mistaken for strength, articulacy was mistaken for clarity, self-confidence was mistaken for character.
>
> H. Fairlie writing in *The Kennedy Promise*, 1973.

Kennedy's death united a society in grief and allowed the new President, Lyndon B. Johnson, to continue to build on and develop Kennedy's ideas. Johnson's 'Great Society' was a vision of a country with high living standards and a sense of community. He won the 1964 election on a ticket of 'war on poverty'. The creation of an Office of Economic Opportunity provided new job opportunities for the poor and the unemployed and a jobs corps similar to Roosevelt's WPA was set up. Operation Headstart provided extra funds to inner-city schools in an attempt to motivate and challenge poorer students. In 1966 he persuaded Congress to agree to a Medical Care for the Aged Act that gave free medical treatment to the elderly.

Q Questions

1. Was the New Frontier policy successful? Use Sources D and E in your answer
2. How did Kennedy's New Frontier build on Roosevelt's New Deal?

RICHARD NIXON AND WATERGATE

During Johnson's presidency the issues of civil rights, inner-city poverty and anti-Vietnam feeling merged, giving rise to violent protest which was often brutally put down by the authorities.

The Republican presidential candidate for 1968, Richard Nixon, made the most of the problems of law and order and the previous government's failure to secure an honourable withdrawal from Vietnam. Nixon's appeal was to the middle classes who did not favour reform. He did not reverse the civil rights legislation (see page 254) and most of the changes to the social security system, health and education came from Congress where the Democrats had a majority.

The Nixon administration saw the first man land on the moon in July 1969, an initiative that had come from Kennedy in 1961 and had cost $25,000 million. In 1972, *Time* magazine voted Nixon 'man of the year' but a year later, as a result of the Watergate scandal, he was impeached (charged with misconduct in office) and became the first US President to resign.

Watergate

At midnight on 17 June 1972, five men were arrested inside the Democratic Party offices in an apartment block called Watergate. They were trying to plant listening devices and it was later revealed that they were working for the Republican Committee for the Re-election of the President (CREEP). When Nixon heard that some of his advisers had been involved, he ordered a cover-up. Nixon strongly denied any knowledge of the incident and was re-elected in a landslide victory.

The timeline on the next page shows the main events of the Watergate scandal. The day after Nixon resigned Gerald Ford was sworn in as President. He promised to 'heal the wounds' of Watergate but kept most of Nixon's administration on and was severely criticised when he pardoned the shamed ex-President.

WATERGATE: A TIMELINE OF EVENTS

1973

7 February Senate establishes a select committee to investigate the incident

21 March $1 million 'hush money' given to the burglars by Nixon

30 April Nixon's top aids, Haldeman and Ehrlichman, resign; John Dean, Nixon's lawyer, is sacked

25 June Dean testifies to the Watergate Committee and states that Nixon is part of the cover-up

23 July The prosecution demands tape recordings of the President's conversations

25 July Nixon refuses to hand over the tapes

10 October Vice-President Agnew resigns

23 October Demands made in Senate for Nixon's impeachment (removal from office)

21 November Tapes handed in but some are missing and others contain gaps

1974

30 April Nixon supplies transcripts of the missing tapes. They showed that he had ordered the CIA to halt the investigation of the Watergate burglary

27 July The impeachment process begins

8 August Nixon resigns the presidency

6 September President Ford pardons Nixon for his part in the scandal

SOURCE F The television broadcast of President Nixon's resignation speech, August 1974.

'Jimmy Who?'

Watergate cast a long shadow over the political scene. Many people of America felt that they could no longer trust their most senior politician. In the presidential election of 1976, the Democrats chose a largely unknown candidate, Jimmy Carter, as their nominee. Carter attempted to restore faith in the government and included more black Americans and women in his administration. He served for only one term, at a time of high petrol prices resulting from an oil crisis, and he was heavily criticised for his handling of the situation involving US hostages in Iran in 1979.

THE REAGAN YEARS

In 1980 the Republicans nominated Ronald Reagan, the Governor of California, to stand against President Carter. Reagan had been a famous Hollywood actor before entering politics. Reagan secured a decisive victory, coming to office at a time of high inflation (15 per cent) and rising unemployment (7.5 per cent). His solution was to slash income taxes while reducing social welfare, emphasising the old virtues of 'rugged individualism'. In 1981 his Economic Recovery Tax Act reduced individual and business taxes by about $33 billion, the largest tax cut in US history.

SOURCE G Republican president, Ronald Reagan.

However, when recession struck in the mid-1980s Congress adopted tax increases totalling $91 billion, the largest tax increase in US history. By late-1982 unemployment was at its highest since 1941, although there followed a rapid recovery and by 1984 the economy was thriving. Reagan's economic policy was dubbed 'Reaganomics'.

'You ain't seen nothing yet'

Reagan and his Vice-President, George Bush (Senior), easily won the Republican nomination for the 1984 election. Reagan emphasised the country's economic growth, the decline in unemployment and the fall in inflation.

In his second term of office, Reagan continued his policy of tax cuts, but government spending was dominated by a $26 billion research programme to investigate the feasibility of a space-based defence system (nicknamed Star Wars) to protect the USA from nuclear attack (see page 268).

Q Questions

1 What was President Nixon's role in the Watergate scandal?

2 What were the results of the Watergate scandal?

3 How successful were the economic policies of President Reagan?

HOW DID POPULAR CULTURE CHANGE BETWEEN 1929 AND 1990?

Music

Music played an important part in the social revolution of the 1920s. 'Ragtime', an Afro-American music, in turn inspired jazz. In the 1920s and 1930s it spread throughout the USA, popularised by bandleaders like Louis Armstrong and Duke Ellington. Also popular in the period was country music. It too originated in the south, but whereas the blues reflected the lives of poor black people, country music dealt with the disadvantaged rural life of poor white Americans.

Throughout the 1940s the musical was strengthened by the work of Rogers and Hammerstein. Broadway musicals like *Oklahoma*, which was made into a film in 1955, portrayed a sugar-coated, optimistic USA. Then, in the 1950s, rock and roll hit the USA. This combined elements of both blues and country and western music.

SOURCE H Elvis Presley in the 1950s.

In 1956, 21-year-old Elvis Presley exploded onto the scene becoming a national sensation. This 'white boy who sang like a black man' shattered the calm of the 1950s with his energetic dancing and upfront sexuality.

The 1960s produced many important bands, such as the Beachboys, and folk-singers such as Bob Dylan voiced anger over the Vietnam War. Performers also came together in free open-air concerts – the biggest was Woodstock in August 1969. Disco dancing took off in the 1970s, while the 1980s witnessed the development of rap and hip hop.

The movies

The 1920s had seen the building of thousands of cinemas and, by 1930, 80 million Americans were weekly visitors. The first 'talkie', *The Jazz Singer*, created a sensation in 1927, and in 1928 Walt Disney issued *Steamboat Willy*, an animated short film using sound. The film introduced a character who was to become a US star – Mickey Mouse. Broadway musicals and gangster films offered a form of escapism during the Great Depression. Hollywood contributed to the war effort by dramatising the war in films like *Casablanca* (1942).

Movie-going steadily decreased throughout the 1950s as people preferred to relax in front of their television sets. In the early-1970s film companies began releasing films in hundreds of cities at the same time, supported by national TV advertising. As a result, films like *The Godfather* (1972) became huge box-office successes. The 1970s saw the emergence of talented directors like Steven Spielberg and George Lucas with films like *Jaws* (1973) and *Star Wars* (1972). In the 1980s and 1990s, developments in technology led to increasingly spectacular special effects, seen in films such as *The Terminator* (1984) and *Ghostbusters* (1984).

The star system

The success of movies also led to the huge successes of the actors and actresses that starred in them, with many being idolized by fans. Stars of the pre-war period included the cinema legends Bette Davis and James Cagney. Marilyn Monroe, Marlon Brando and James Dean were huge stars in the 1950s and 1960s; Harrison Ford, Tom Cruise and Meg Ryan have proved popular stars of the 1980s and 1990s. Star appearances add to the appeal of Hollywood films, and film stars have been able to charge increasingly large fees for movie appearances.

Youth culture

In the late-1940s 'bobbysoxers', as they were known, began playing music loudly but this represented a safe phase of youth culture. During the Second World War a new group began to emerge as a distinct part of society – the teenager. The teenager by the 1950s had more money and free time than ever before.

Writers in the early-1950s began to question the cosy values of suburbia. The hero in J. D. Salinger's novel, *The Catcher in the Rye* (1951), is a school drop-out who becomes alienated in a phoney adult world. Jack Kerouac, leader of the 'beat' movement of the 1950s and 1960s, emphasised spiritual freedom through sex, drugs and Zen religion. As rock and roll shattered the calm of the 1950s, and Elvis Presley and Little Richard became heroes of a new youth culture, American youths became more rebellious and promiscuous. Juvenile delinquency increased and much of the older generation was shocked by the behaviour of young people. The generation gap had arrived.

The hippy movement

During the second half of the 1960s many young people rejected their parents' lifestyles and values. They opposed the Vietnam War, racism and the 'safe' route from high school to a decent job. Hippies wore ethnic-style clothes and grew long hair, took drugs recreationally, followed mystical religions and engaged in 'free love'. 'Flower power' became a symbol for their peaceful beliefs; they settled in communes and San Francisco became the hippy capital.

SOURCE I Hippies at a concert during the 1960s.

Student protest

In the late-1960s students staged demonstrations on college campuses: they demanded a greater say over what they were taught and an end to restrictive rules. The most serious protests were against the Vietnam War, which was televised and so the horrors of war were seen by civilians. In May 1970 a peaceful student protest at Kent State University, Ohio, against President Nixon's decision to bomb Cambodia, ended in disaster. National Guardsmen were called to disperse the 600 students but the students refused to go. Tear gas was used and shots were fired, killing four students and injuring 11 others.

Q Question

1 What were the main features of popular culture in the period 1929–90.

THE CHANGING ROLE OF WOMEN AT HOME AND AT WORK

The 1920s were a time of liberation for many women. They cut their hair into short 'bobs', wore shorter skirts and some behaved outrageously. However, in terms of their economic or social status, little changed. Most worked as domestic or clerical workers, teachers or nurses. They were often paid less for doing the same jobs as men. Sexual discrimination actually got worse during the Great Depression, when women were seen as occupying the jobs of unemployed men and Roosevelt's measures to tackle unemployment positively discriminated against women. The NRA (see pages 236–7) allowed women to be paid less then men and the Social Security Act of 1935 gave no protection to women.

Women and the Second World War

SOURCE J

A poster showing Rosie the Riveter, part of the US government campaign to encourage women to work in factories during the Second World War.

Women's contribution in the First World War had resulted in their getting the vote and increased employment opportunities. The Second World War again increased opportunities in the workplace as 6 million women entered factories as machinists and toolmakers, and nearly 200,000 joined the armed forces. The war gave women a sense of independence and, after the war, some were not prepared to relinquish it.

A woman's place

Despite women's contribution to the Second World War, the majority of people felt that a woman's place was in the home (see Source K). However, boredom with the domestic routine and increased freedom because of labour-saving devices and convenience foods encouraged women to enter the workplace although again often in stereotyped occupations.

SOURCE K

> A 32-two-year-old pretty and popular suburban housewife, mother of four, who had married at age sixteen, an excellent wife, mother, hostess, volunteer, and home manager who makes her own clothes, hosts dozens of dinner parties each year, sings in the church choir, works and is devoted to her husband. In her daily round she attends club or charity meetings, drives the children to school, does the weekly grocery shopping, makes ceramics, and is planning to study French. Of all the accomplishments of the American woman the one she brings off with the most spectacular success is having babies.

Description of the ideal woman in *Life* magazine, 1956.

Feminism

SOURCE L Members of the Women's Liberation Group demonstrating in August 1970.

The 1960s witnessed a significant change in attitudes towards women. The publication of Betty Friedan's *The Feminine Mystique* in 1963 proved a milestone in the women's rights (feminist) movement. Friedan wrote that women should have political, economic and social rights equal to those of men. She also ridiculed the common belief that women were only suited for low-paid jobs and that female achievement could only be measured by their success as wives and mothers.

In 1966, Frieden and others set up the National Organisation for Women (NOW). They demanded an equal rights amendment to the US Constitution and the 'right of women to control their reproductive lives' (abortion was then illegal in all US states).

During the 1960s, American women became proactive in the campaign for sexual equality, using petitions, strikes and legal action to push forward their views. The Civil Rights Act of 1964 was the first legislation to explicitly ban discrimination based on sex as well as race. By the mid-1970s laws were passed that allowed women equal treatment in employment and admission to higher education, equal pay and equal access to credit. In 1973 the Supreme Court legalised abortions.

However, in 1989 women's earnings were still only 70 per cent of men's and by 1990 women were six times as likely to be living in poverty than men. Female-headed families made up nearly half of poor American families.

Q Questions

1. What types of discrimination did American women face before the 1960s?
2. How did the lives of women change between 1929 and 1990?

How did the lives of black people in America change between 1929 and 1990?

WHAT WAS THE STATUS OF BLACK PEOPLE IN THE USA IN 1929?

Segregation and the Jim Crow laws

Under the constitution of the USA, all US citizens are born equal and should enjoy equal rights and opportunities to lead a full life. After the abolition of slavery in 1863 and further legislation, black people had equal civil rights including the right to vote – or did they? In the south, state laws were devised to maintain white supremacy and to deprive black people of their rights, forcing them to live separately. This was called segregation.

These laws were called the Jim Crow laws after a line in a plantation song. Black people were forced to use separate schools, buses, trains, theatres, hospitals and churches. The Supreme Court in 1896 declared that segregation was legal as long as the facilities were separate but equal. If a black person felt that they were not, he or she would have to take the case to a white-controlled court. The Jim Crow laws also denied black people the right to vote. They were stopped from registering to vote by:

- poll taxes: most black people were too poor to pay the taxes and so could not register to vote;
- literacy (reading) tests: they were asked to read difficult passages to prove them incapable of voting.

If these measures failed, then intimidation and violence were used to prevent black people from voting.

SOURCE A

A Negro in the Deep South who tried to register might lose his job or his credit. He might be beaten, have his house set on fire, or be killed. 'I don't want my job cut off', one man explained. Another was more blunt: 'I don't want my throat cut', he said.

A report by a civil rights worker for the National Association for the Advancement of Colored People (NAACP).

Black people had the lowest standards of education and the poorest paid jobs. Many worked as share-croppers, a system by which landowners would not pay workers until the harvest had been gathered. Workers would keep one-third of the crop but easily fell into debt and so become tied to the landowner for as long as he needed them. The industrial boom of the 1920s encouraged thousands of black people to migrate north in search of a better life. Segregation did not exist in the north to the same extent but they were still given the poorest jobs and lived in the worst housing. By 1940, 22 per cent of black people lived in northern US states.

The 'Harlem Renaissance'

Many talented black musicians and entertainers were 'discovered' by white 'patrons' during the 1920s from among the poverty and squalor of Harlem and other impoverished black areas in the northern states. Records brought black music into white homes across America, and proved extremely popular. However, when black musicians entertained white audiences, black people were banned.

The Ku Klux Klan

Another reason to head north was to escape the activities of the Ku Klux Klan (KKK), which was active in the southern states. The Klan was set up in 1865 after the Civil War as a means of maintaining white supremacy. Membership was open to White Anglo-Saxon Protestants (WASPS) who promised to defend the USA from black people, immigrants, Jews, Catholics, communists and socialists. Klansmen met in the evenings and paraded in white robes and hoods carrying blazing torches. Victims were beaten, tarred and feathered, raped or murdered, Klansmen then leaving a burning cross as their calling card. The most terrifying punishment was lynching (execution by a mob).

SOURCE B Ku Klux Klan members parading through the streets of a town c.1920.

In Georgia there were 135 lynchings between 1924 and 1925 but no one was convicted for these brutal crimes. If brought to trial it was difficult to find a jury that would convict Klansmen – sometimes as a result of Klan intimidation, but also because some police officers and even judges belonged to the Klan. By 1924 there were an estimated 5 million members, but numbers fell when the Klan's leader, D. C. Stephenson, was found guilty of the abduction and rape of a young girl in 1925. He was sentenced to life imprisonment.

The work of the NAACP

The National Association for the Advancement of Colored People (NAACP, see also page 103) had been set up in 1909. Its aims were abolishing segregation and achieving equal voting rights and educational opportunities for black people. Throughout the 1920s the NAACP fought against lynchings and tried to encourage black people to vote. However, many were scared to exercise their right to vote because of the threats they had received from groups such as the Ku Klux Klan.

Throughout the 1930s and 1940s the work of the NAACP increasingly used the legal system to challenge discrimination against black people. Political parties also began to recognise the importance of the votes of black people, particularly in the northern states. This growth in the political influence of black voters in northern US states was one of the factors in Roosevelt setting up a 'Black Cabinet'.

THE IMPACT OF THE DEPRESSION

Roosevelt's concern was for the poor and hungry: most black people came into those categories. Roosevelt's New Deal (see pages 234–7) brought some improvement to the lives of black people but the worst effects of the Depression fell on them. By mid-1934 over half of the black people living in the northern US cities were dependent on relief. Much of the New Deal programme was state administered and discrimination continued. However, over 1 million black people secured relief and employment through such schemes.

The Democrats captured the black vote in 1936 and there was an increase in the numbers of black people elected to local state and federal office. By 1940 about 100 black people had been brought into the service of the federal government.

Q Questions

1 In what ways were black people discriminated against in 1929?

2 How did the Great Depression affect black people?

HOW DID THE SECOND WORLD WAR AFFECT BLACK PEOPLE?

The USA entered the Second World War in 1941. The problem was, how could a 'Jim Crow army' fight a racist power like Nazi Germany while suffering racism at home? The Selective Service Act of 1940 forbade discrimination in the calling-up and training of black soldiers, but the War Department continued the practice of segregated regiments: black and white soldiers fought the same war separately.

SOURCE C

Along with the desire to fight for equal rights was the feeling that participation in the war effort would be rewarded. If we fight and die for our country, Afro-Americans argued, surely our country will no longer deny us our rights.

Neil Wynn writing in *The Afro-American and the Second Word War* (1976).

In Britain, where more than 1.5 million US servicemen were stationed, there was frequent trouble between black and white Americans. White US southerners could not accept that British pubs were open to black soldiers and that black men were attractive to local white girls.

At home

Black workers made an important contribution to the war effort at home. By the end of 1944 nearly 2 million were working in war factories. Some met with hostility. In Detroit, which had a large black community, racial tensions gave rise to large-scale rioting in 1943, which cost over 30 lives. However, service for their country generally led many black people to believe that change would happen after the war. Membership of the NAACP rose from 50,000 to 450,000 during the war.

A 'Fair Deal' for black people?

After the Second World War, the emergence of independent African and Asian states and the formation of the UN placed the US race question on a world stage. President Truman gave much attention to the issue of civil rights. In 1946, as part of his Fair Deal programme (see page 238), he set up a presidential committee. This proposed an anti-lynching bill and the elimination of the poll-tax requirement for voting. Although the US Congress rejected the proposals, Truman was able to end segregation in the armed forces. Truman's support for the civil rights of black Americans meant that the issue could not be suppressed for much longer.

THE CIVIL RIGHTS MOVEMENT

Segregation in education was a very emotive issue and one to which the NAACP directed its efforts after the Second World War. In 1954, twenty US states, including Washington DC, had segregated schools.

SOURCE D

> Segregation is the way in which a society tells a group of human beings that they are inferior to the other groups.
>
> Extract from a NAACP publication.

Challenges to the Constitution: through education

- **Kansas 1954.** Linda Brown, a 7-year-old black girl, had to walk 20 blocks to her school even though there was a school for white people just two blocks away. With the help of the NAACP her father took the Board of Education to court. On 19 May 1954, Chief Justice Earl Warren announced that segregation was illegal under the US constitution. The constitution was declared 'colour blind' and the Topeka Board of Education and all other authorities were ordered to end segregation. However, despite this decision, by the end of 1956 not one black child was attending an integrated school in the six southern states.
- **Little Rock, Arkansas, 1957.** In September 1957, at Little Rock Central High School, nine black students tried to enter the school to take their places. The Governor of Arkansas surrounded the school with National Guardsmen to prevent the black students from entering (see Sources E and F). The black community subsequently took the governor to court and the soldiers were withdrawn. President Eisenhower sent 1000 paratroopers to protect the black students for the rest of the school year. By 1960 only 2600 black school children out of a total 2 million went to integrated schools in Arkansas.

SOURCE E Elizabeth Eckford, 13, one of the nine black students arriving at Little Rock Central High School on 5 September 1957.

SOURCE F

> I walked up to the guard who had let the white students in. When I tried to squeeze past him, he raised his bayonet and then the other guards closed in and they raised their bayonets. Somebody started yelling 'Lynch her!' I tried to see a friendly face somewhere in the mob. I looked into the face of an old woman and it seemed a kind face, but when I looked at her again she spat on me. They came closer, shouting, 'No nigger bitch is going to get in our school! Get out of here!'
>
> Elizabeth Eckford speaking in an interview in 1957.

- **Mississippi, 1962.** James Meredith, a southern black student, qualified to enter the University of Mississippi in September 1962. When he arrived to register his way was barred by the Governor of Mississippi. Riots broke out and President Kennedy sent in troops who had to accompany Meredith to his lectures throughout his course.

Bus boycotts and freedom rides

- **Rosa Parkes and the Montgomery bus boycott.** On 1 December 1955 in Montgomery, Alabama, a 42-year-old black woman called Rosa Parkes defied the order of a bus driver to give up her seat to a white man when the bus became full, as was the law. She was arrested and jailed. As local secretary of the NAACP her ordeal prompted the black community to call a bus boycott. The Reverend Dr Martin Luther King, a young Baptist minister, led the campaign – the Civil Rights Movement was born. In November 1956 the Supreme Court ruled that segregation on buses was illegal and in December the bus company gave in.
- **The 'freedom rides'.** However, segregation still existed on interstate transport. Black and white people could sit together in bus stations and use the same facilities in states in the north, but not in the segregated south. Would black and white Americans be able to travel together the length and breadth of the country? In 1961 the Congress of Racial Equality (CORE) organised 'freedom rides' to test the new policy. There were ugly clashes and Attorney General Robert Kennedy had to send in 500 marshals to protect the freedom riders. However, Kennedy was able to get the Interstate Commerce Commission to end segregation in all bus and rail stations and airports. By 1963 this had extended to most other public facilities.

Q Questions

1. Did the Second World War change conditions for black people?
2. How much progress had the Civil Rights Movement made by the early-1960s? Explain your answer.

Martin Luther King

SOURCE G Martin Luther King.

SOURCE H

> I have a dream that one day this nation will rise up, live out the true meaning of its creed: 'We hold these truths to be self-evident that all men are created equal.' I have a dream that one day on the red hills of Georgia sons of former slaves and sons of former slave-owners will be able to sit down together at the table of brotherhood.
>
> Part of Martin Luther King's famous 'I have a dream' speech, August 1963.

It was with words like those in Source H that Dr Martin Luther King stirred the conscience of a nation. His ideas were based on non-violent civil disobedience, which Mahatma Gandhi had pursued in India before India gained its independence from British rule in 1947. Violence, he believed, was morally wrong and he favoured sit-ins, boycotts, freedom rides and marches as a way of protesting.

In 1962 the council of Birmingham, Alabama, closed all public recreational facilities to black people. In 1963 Martin Luther King led a freedom march to end segregation: 30,000 black Americans took part in sit-ins and 500 were arrested each day. Police Commissioner Eugene 'Bull' Connor used water cannons, dogs and baton charges on the peaceful protesters. These events were televised and stirred up public opinion against racist people like Connor. President Kennedy sent in troops and demanded that the Birmingham council end segregation, which it did. Kennedy later stated that the Civil Rights Movement had much to thank Connor for.

In August 1963 over 250,000 people, including over 50,000 white Americans, marched to the Lincoln memorial in Washington DC to demand civil rights for all. King made his famous speech (see Source H). In December 1964 Martin Luther King was awarded the Nobel Peace Prize. He was back in prison five days later in Selma, Alabama, after campaigning for changes to voting registration for black people. In the end, King's campaigning was rewarded when the new Voting Rights Act was passed in 1965 and a further 1 million black Americans were able to vote.

From non-violence to black power

Martin Luther King argued that non-violent civil disobedience should also be taken to the north and the west of the USA, and the headquarters of the Southern Christian Leadership Conference (SCLC) were moved to Chicago. However, many black people rejected King's pacifist (peaceful) and Christian approach.

The 1950s witnessed an increase in membership of the Nation of Islam, a black Muslim movement led by Elijah Muhammed. The Nation of Islam rejected white society and advocated race war. They discarded their 'Christian slave names' substituting the letter 'X' as a sign of their transformation.

The long-term aim of the Nation of Islam was to obtain a separate state for black Americans and to this end a violent black power movement grew up. The Black Panthers was one of the most militant groups, which called on black people to arm themselves in the struggle. Malcolm X was the movement's impressive leader: he called on his followers to be more self-reliant and aggressive.

SOURCE I Malcolm X.

In the mid-1960s a wave of riots took place in many cities. In 1964 there were riots in Harlem and New York. In the Watts district of Los Angeles in August 1965, 34 people died and 1072 were injured in six days of trouble. Malcolm X was shot dead in 1965 and the Black Power movement was taken over by Stokely Carmichael. Martin Luther King's non-violent methods came to an end in 1968 when he was assassinated by a white extremist.

Civil rights legislation

President Eisenhower's Civil Rights Acts of 1957 and 1960 had made discrimination illegal. They also guaranteed the right to vote for all Americans and declared the federal government's intention to end segregation.

President Kennedy's promise to push for better civil rights won him the black vote in 1960. However, he relied on the support of the southerners in Congress and had to proceed cautiously. In 1963 he proposed a package of reforms but before it could be passed he was assassinated.

Lyndon Johnson, Kennedy's successor, committed himself to the passage of Kennedy's civil rights programme. In 1964 the Civil Rights Act was passed.

- Racial discrimination was banned in employment.
- Black pupils were given equal rights to enter all public places and any bodies receiving government money, including schools.
- An Equal Employment Opportunities Commission was set up to investigate complaints of discrimination.

Johnson's presidency produced further legislation:

- 1965 – The Voting Rights Act stopped racial discrimination over the right to vote.
- 1967 – The Supreme Court declared that state laws forbidding interracial marriages were unconstitutional.
- 1968 – The Fair Housing Act made racial discrimination illegal in the property market.

THE ECONOMIC AND SOCIAL PROGRESS OF BLACK PEOPLE TO 1990

Civil rights legislation did lead to some integration in schools, but in the 1970s a backlash was directed against bussing children long distances in order to create racially balanced schools. Despite the Fair Housing Act of 1968, the majority of black people in 1990 trying to buy or rent housing still faced discrimination. Equal standards in education for black and white students, both in the north and the south, had not been achieved by 1990.

A black cultural movement in the late-1960s and 1970s sought to make black Americans proud of their racial and cultural heritage. Its logo was 'black is beautiful', an idea many had never had the chance to explore. In the 1980s, the films of Spike Lee and the novels of Toni Morrison continued to celebrate American black culture in this way.

Since the Civil Rights Movement of the 1960s, black people have played a more active part in American society. In 1967 Carl Stokes became the first black person to be elected mayor of a major city. The US government has also deliberately appointed black people to positions of prominence. The Reverend Jesse Jackson stood for the 1984 presidential election, and in 1989 Colin Powell became Chairman of the Joint Chiefs of Staff, the nation's highest military post. Black celebrities are seen more frequently in the media, for example, Eddie Murphy and Will Smith are famous film and TV personalities. However, discrimination against black Americans continues. In 1990 the average income of a black family was less than half that of the average white family.

Q Questions

1 What was Martin Luther King's contribution to civil rights in the USA?

2 How much had civil rights legislation achieved by 1968?

3 How near had the USA got to a racially equal and fair society by 1990?

What changing role did America play in world affairs between 1929 and 1990?

THE USA IN ISOLATION

Americans viewed themselves in geographical isolation. They also believed that they could withdraw from the rest of the world and focus on their own affairs. At the beginning of the twentieth century many Americans still held on to these ideas. The USA entered the First World War in 1917 and after the Treaty of Versailles in 1919 it reasserted its isolationist policy which then continued through the next two decades.

However, how could a country whose economy was so important to the prosperity of the whole world totally cut itself off? Isolationism did not mean that the USA had nothing to do with foreign affairs, it meant that it tried to avoid becoming involved in disputes that could lead to war.

Though the USA did not join the League of Nations it did involve itself with the rest of the world in the 1920s. US investment helped Europe recover after the First World War and the USA took the lead in disarmament meetings. In 1928 the USA signed the Kellogg–Briand Pact with over 60 other nations, which renounced war as a means of settling disputes.

The USA's priority in the early-1930s was to haul itself out of depression. As war loomed, events in Europe would divert it from this but Congress continued to support the policy of isolationism by passing a series of Neutrality Acts after 1935 (see table below). Roosevelt despised Hitler and Mussolini but could not risk his New Deal legislation by losing public support, which was strongly isolationist.

SOURCE A

There can be no objection to any hand our government may take which strives to bring peace to the world so long as it does not tie 130 million people into another world death march. I fear we are again being called upon to police a world that chooses to follow insane leaders.

Senator Gerald Nye, a leading isolationist, speaking in 1935.

THE NEUTRALITY ACTS

1935 Gave the president powers to stop US ships carrying US-made weapons to countries at war

1936 Extended the ban on loans to warring countries

1937 Set up the 'cash and carry' scheme. Congress decided that the only danger came from transporting goods, not their sale. Nations at war could buy US goods so long as they paid 'cash' and could 'carry' (ship) the goods themselves. When Britain and France declared war on Germany in September 1939 it was agreed that they could buy arms under the scheme. This caused opposition and the America First Committee was set up to prevent entry into the war.

The rising threat of Japan

Japan was rapidly transformed from a feudal country to an industrialised nation in the second half of the nineteenth century. The Japanese fought on the Allied side in the First World War but felt insulted at the exclusion of a statement in the Covenant of the League of Nations acknowledging racial equality. In 1921 at the Washington Naval Conference it was decided that Japan's navy was to be no more than 60 per cent that of Britain and the USA. Clearly Japan was not considered to be a great power, something which caused resentment among the Japanese.

The Japanese economy continued to expand in the post-war era but the collapse of the US stock exchange in 1929 saw the USA slide into depression and trade between the two countries fell dramatically. At this time the Japanese army was beginning to influence the Japanese government and calls came for a Co-prosperity Scheme, which involved extending Japanese control over other countries in Asia. If Japan could not get what it needed by trade, it would get it by war.

The invasion of Manchuria, 1931

Without government orders, the Japanese army attacked Manchuria (part of China) in 1931. China appealed to the League of Nations for help. Before it could respond, the Japanese had secured Manchuria and launched further attacks into China. The League condemned Japanese actions and ordered it to withdraw from China. Instead Japan simply withdrew from the League of Nations (see Source B).

The League had little power to enforce its decision because two of the most powerful countries – the USA and the Soviet Union – were not members of the League of Nations. Only two countries recognised the new Japanese state of 'Manchukuo' – Germany and Italy, who soon withdrew from the League themselves.

Help for Britain

In response to an appeal by Churchill, the USA agreed in March 1941 to a 'lend–lease' agreement which allowed Britain to receive armaments immediately but delay payment.

Early German successes in the Second World War gave Japan the confidence to extend its ambitions. With Holland, France and Britain sidetracked in a war against Germany, Japan could move in on their colonies in East Asia and the Pacific. Japanese troops were sent to take Indo-China from the French. The USA increased its aid to China and began to cut trade with Japan. In July 1941, the USA stopped all shipments of oil to Japan. Japan had imported 80 per cent of its oil from the USA so this ban led it to look towards the rich deposits in South East Asia. As a warning to Japan, the US government ordered its fleet to stay at Pearl Harbor – the major US base in the Pacific Ocean.

Q Questions

1. How isolationist was the USA in the period 1929–41?
2. How much of a threat to the USA had Japan become by 1941?

SOURCE B A cartoon commenting on Japan leaving the League of Nations in 1933.

THE END OF ISOLATION: THE USA AND THE SECOND WORLD WAR

Pearl Harbor

At dawn on Sunday 7 December 1941, the Japanese launched a surprise attack on the US fleet at Pearl Harbor in Hawaii. Eight battleships were sunk and ten other craft destroyed; 188 planes were destroyed and 159 damaged; and 2403 people were killed. The next day the USA declared war on Japan. There was nothing to make the USA declare war on Germany, instead Hitler declared war on the USA on 11 December 1941.

War in the Pacific

Following the attack on Pearl Harbor Japanese forces swept over South East Asia and the islands of the western Pacific. By March 1942 the British colonies of Hong Kong and Singapore and the US defenders of the Philippine Islands were forced to surrender. By mid-1942 the Japanese had conquered over 2.5 million square kilometres of land, much of it rich in raw materials. In the war in the Pacific, control of the sea and air spaces was vital. The naval war was fought from aircraft carriers protected by warships.

War in Europe

After the attack on Pearl Harbor, the US also sent troops to fight on the Western Front with British and Canadian forces. On 6 June 1944, the D-Day landings across the Normandy coast were the result of months of planning by the Allies. The Germans were not prepared for the attack, expecting the Allied invasion to take place at Calais. Germany put up a strong resistance, but the superiority of the Allies, in men and supplies, was overwhelming. Eleven months later, Germany surrendered on 8 May 1945.

The atomic bomb

By the summer of 1945 almost all Japanese conquests in the Pacific had been recaptured and Japanese forces were retreating. However, the Allies faced the prospect of an invasion of Japan itself which, it was believed, would result in massive casualties. US President Truman therefore decided to use the atomic bomb as a means of bringing the war to an end as quickly as possible. On 6 and 9 August 1945, atomic bombs were dropped on the Japanese cities of Hiroshima and Nagasaki (see page 259). A week later, the Japanese government surrendered.

War in the Pacific, 1941–5.

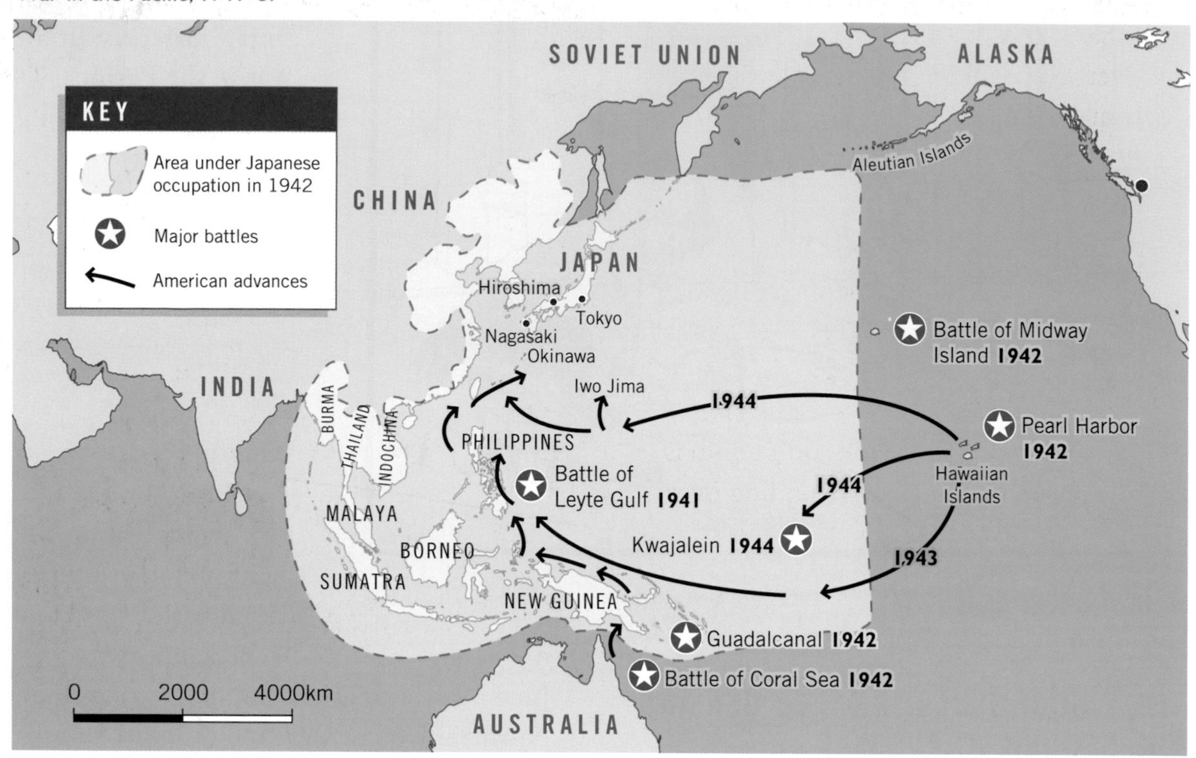

TIMELINE OF EVENTS

War in Europe

November 1942 Operation Torch – US and British troops invade Vichy-held Algeria and Morocco, a week after the Battle of El Alamein. The Allies press on to Tunisia.

September 1943 US troops invade Italy. It takes two years of bitter fighting to reach the north of the country.

June 1944 'D-Day' – Operation Overlord: on 6 June, 156,000 British and US troops land on the beaches of Normandy.

May 1945 Germany surrenders – the war in Europe is over.

War in the Pacific

May 1942 Japan's first defeat at the Battle of the Coral Sea.

June 1942 The Japanese attack the US base at Midway Island but are beaten. The Battle of Midway is seen as a turning point in the Pacific war.

August 1942 General MacArthur moves up to the Solomon Islands after a victory at Guadalcanal.

October 1944 General MacArthur invades the Philippines and in the Battle of Leyte Gulf, the largest sea battle in history, the Japanese lose four carriers and two battleships. The US advance on the capital, Manila.

February 1945 The island of Iwo Jima is captured by US marines at a cost of 4000 dead.

April 1945 US forces attack and take control of Okinawa and are well placed for an attack on Japan. The victory costs 12,000 lives.

August 1945 US bombers continue to destroy Japanese cities but the Japanese government refuses to surrender. On 6 August an atomic bomb is dropped on Hiroshima, killing over 70,000 people. The government still refuses to submit and on 9 August a second bomb is dropped on Nagasaki, killing over 40,000 people. On 15 August Emperor Hirohito announces the unconditional surrender of Japan.

SOURCE C A British cartoon of March 1946 about Churchill and the Iron Curtain.

1 Why did the USA become involved in the Second World War?
2 How did the USA justify the use of the atomic bomb on the Japanese cities of Hiroshima and Nagasaki?

THE USA AND THE COLD WAR

The USA and the Soviet Union had been united against Hitler, but when war ended the hostility returned. Previously the two sides would have gone to war to resolve their differences but atomic weapons now meant that war would lead to mass destruction. Instead a 'cold war' took place, a war which stopped short of actual fighting. In March 1946, in a speech in Fulton, Missouri, British Prime Minister Churchill spoke of an 'iron curtain' which had descended between Soviet-controlled Eastern Europe and Western Europe (see Source C).

The Truman Doctrine and Marshall Aid

The USA supported a policy of containment to prevent communist expansion in a 'domino effect' (meaning countries might fall to communism, one by one, like dominoes). This policy of containment was the opposite of isolationism and became the cornerstone of US foreign policy throughout the Cold War. In March 1947 President Truman of the USA offered help to any government threatened by 'internal or external forces'. By doing this, he hoped to continue to prevent the further spread of communism.

Marshall Aid put the Truman Doctrine into practice. Secretary of State George C. Marshall offered over $13 billion in aid to countries recovering from the effects of war. Stalin attacked it as a US plot to dominate Eastern Europe and refused to allow Soviet-controlled countries to accept the aid.

SOURCE D

I believe that it must be the policy of the United States to support people who are resisting attempted subjugation by armed minorities or by any outside pressures. I believe that we must help free peoples to work out their own destiny in their own way.

An extract from President Truman's speech on 12 March 1947.

In the late-1940s the USA took steps that revolutionised its foreign policy. It kept its military forces close to wartime levels and continued to build up its armoury including nuclear weapons. The National Security Act of 1947 centralised control over all branches of the military in a new Department of Defense and created the National Security Council (NSC) and the Central Intelligence Agency (CIA). The USA was put on a permanent state of emergency.

SOURCE E An American cartoon depicts the effects of the Truman doctrine on the Soviet Union.

Q Questions

1 What was the 'domino effect'?

2 What was the significance of President Truman's speech of 12 March 1945? Refer to Sources D and E in your answer.

CRISIS BERLIN

After the Second World War Berlin had been divided into four zones of occupation. The Soviets used their zone to help rebuild the worn-torn Soviet economy. Life in the Soviet zone was harsh. It was decided to make the Western zones more self-sufficient and to this end the American and British zones were merged into 'Bizonia'; later it was joined by the French zone. In June 1948 a new currency was introduced, which alarmed Stalin. He believed that a prosperous Germany would pose a threat and, because Berlin lay in the Soviet zone, he saw it as a capitalist base in Eastern Europe.

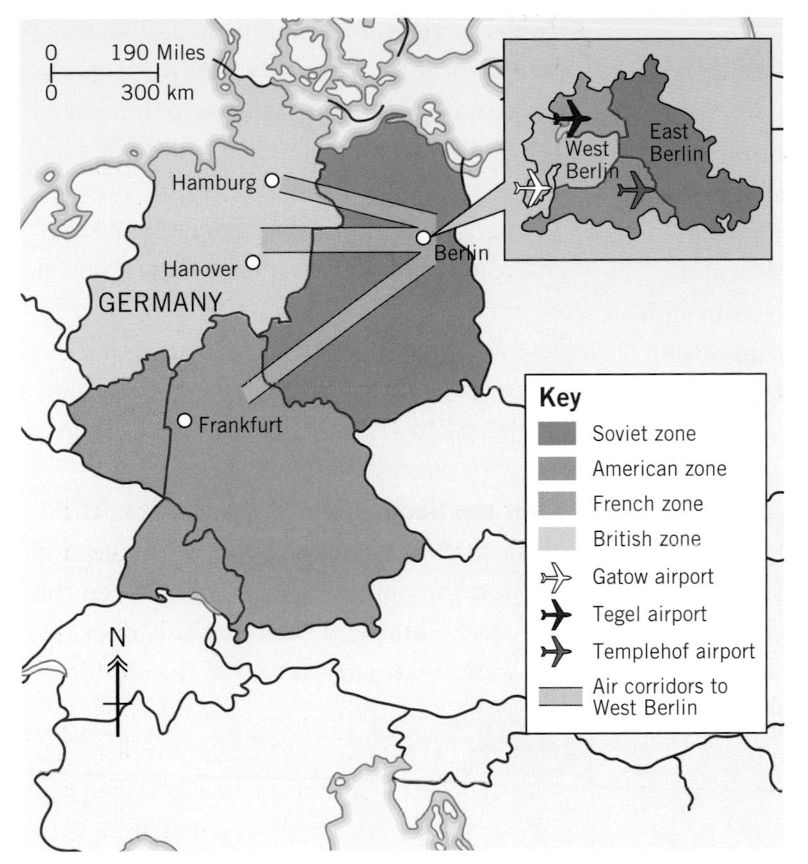

The division of Berlin after the Second World War.

On 24 June 1948 Soviet troops cut off all road, rail and canal links between the West and West Berlin. The Berlin blockade was an attempt to starve the Western powers into submission. Truman summed up the feelings of the Western powers: 'We are going to stay, period.'

The Berlin airlift

The Americans considered using their army to open up the routes but this would have represented an act of war. Instead, a massive airlift of supplies was organised, mainly by the USA. By September 1948 aircraft were landing every three minutes and Stalin could only sit and watch. To shoot down planes would be an act of war and, although American planes faced the hazard of Soviet planes 'buzzing' them, no actual attacks were made.

From June 1948 until Stalin reopened supply routes to the West in May 1949 over 27,000 trips were made and 2 million tonnes of supplies airlifted in.

The USA joins NATO

The events in Berlin led to a historic reversal in US foreign policy – for the first time in its history it joined a peacetime alliance. In September 1949 the North Atlantic Treaty Organisation (NATO) was signed by the USA and 11 other Western powers, each committed to the defence of the others. At the time of its signing the USSR announced that it had tested its first nuclear bomb.

THE KOREAN WAR

When Japan surrendered in 1945 Korea, a former colony, was occupied in the north by Soviet forces and in the south by the Americans. The countries were divided along the 38th parallel. The Soviets left a communist government in the north under Kim Il Sung while the USA established a 'democratic' government in the south under Syngman Rhee (who actually acted as a virtual dictator). Both governments claimed the right to rule over the whole country and in June 1950 Soviet-backed North Korean troops invaded South Korea. President Truman, fearful of the 'domino effect', sent in US forces and appealed to the UN for backing.

The USA's war?

Sixteen countries sent forces but the USA provided 50 per cent of land forces, 93 per cent of air forces and 86 per cent of naval forces. The Commander-in-Chief, General MacArthur, was appointed by Truman and reported to him. After initial successes, the communists were pushed back over the 38th parallel. The USA now sought to unite all Korea under a pro-American government.

Mao Zedong, ruler of China, warned the US to stay away from China's borders and, when a warning was ignored, sent thousands of Chinese soldiers to help the North Koreans. A further 300,000 Chinese troops secretly infiltrated Korea. The war now became a private affair between the USA and China. General MacArthur asked Truman to agree to an invasion of China and even advised using nuclear weapons. Truman rejected the idea: MacArthur's criticism of this decision led to his dismissal.

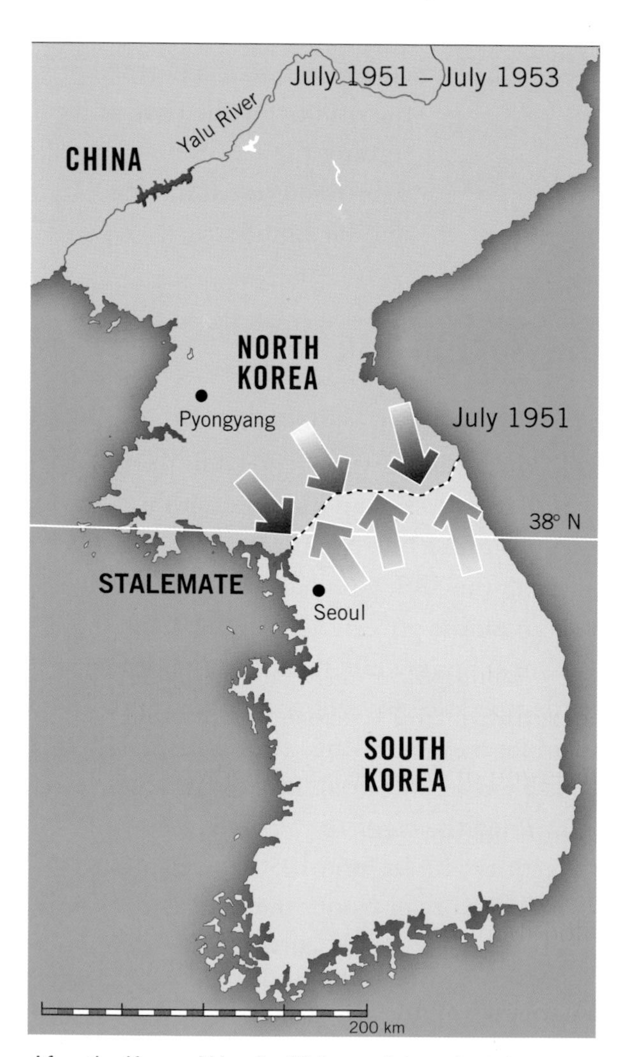

After the Korean War, the 38th parallel marked the border of North and South Korea.

The war dragged on and finally ended in stalemate in July 1953. The new border ran almost exactly across the 38th parallel and the USA continued to support – at great cost – the 'democratic' government in the south: 50,000 American soldiers had been killed in the fighting. Relations between the USA and China had been seriously damaged and were to remain poor until the 1970s.

Q Questions

1 Why was Berlin the focus of attention in the immediate post-war period?

2 Why has the Korean War been called 'the USA's war'?

THE BERLIN WALL

While the Cold War continued throughout the 1950s, relations between the two superpowers did improve slightly leaving many with a sense of optimism. The Soviet leader, Nikita Khrushchev, had made a successful visit to the USA in 1959 and, building on that, a summit meeting was arranged in Paris for May 1960 between the USA, USSR, Britain and France. It was hoped that the superpowers would use this meeting to talk about their differences. However, just two days before the meeting an American U2 spy plane was shot down over the Soviet Union. It had been carrying high-tech cameras.

Despite US attempts at a cover-up they had to admit to spying. Khrushchev said he would still attend the summit meeting if the US president Eisenhower apologised. Eisenhower refused and relations once again took a turn for the worse.

In August 1961 a 45-kilometre concrete wall was erected by the Soviets through Berlin to prevent refugees moving to the West. The Berlin Wall became a striking symbol of the Cold War. Tension increased and both superpowers started testing more powerful nuclear weapons.

THE CUBAN MISSILE CRISIS

In January 1959 the corrupt dictatorship of Fulgencio Batista was overthrown by a left-wing Cuban patriot called Fidel Castro. The USA, though suspicious of Castro's left-wing views, recognised his government. The USA had massive financial interests in Cuba. When Castro began a programme of social and economic reform it threatened US interests. Castro planned to nationalise US businesses and began making trade agreements with the Soviets. The USA began to fear the threat of a communist country just 150 kilometres from its mainland.

The newly-elected President Kennedy was convinced by the Central Intelligence Agency (CIA) that Castro should be overthrown. On 17 April 1961, a CIA-backed force of 1400 anti-Castro exiles invaded Cuba at the Bay of Pigs. The attempt was as a disaster, being put down by 20,000 Cuban soldiers. President Kennedy was severely embarrassed, realising he had been wrongly advised. In July, Castro nationalised all US industries and sought protection from the Soviet Union. He then declared himself a communist.

In October 1962 US spy planes photographed Soviet missiles in place on Cuba. With a range of 4000 kilometres almost every US city was in danger of attack. It seemed that Khrushchev had decided to use Cuba to put pressure on Kennedy to remove US missile sites in Turkey and even to withdraw from Berlin. Kennedy had several options:

- ➜ Do nothing and merely protest to Cuba and the USSR – this would have been seen as weakness.
- ➜ Ask the UN for help – the USSR would have vetoed any planned action.
- ➜ Invade Cuba and destroy the missile sites.
- ➜ Attack the Soviet Union.
- ➜ Blockade Cuba using the US navy – the missile sites would remain but it would put pressure on Khrushchev to respond.

The options to invade Cuba or attack the Soviet Union could lead to nuclear war and mass destruction.

SOURCE F

A cartoon from the *Daily Express*, October 1962. Kennedy and Khrushchev are shown as gunslingers waiting to see who will draw first. Castro is riding on a donkey.

TIMELINE OF EVENTS

The Cuban missile crisis, 1963

22 October Kennedy announces the blockade of Cuba and accuses the Soviets of 'provocation'.

23 October Soviets claim to be defending Cuba against US aggression.

24 October Soviet vessels reach the blockade – and turn back.

26 October Khrushchev sends a letter to Kennedy agreeing to remove the missiles if the USA lifts the blockade and promises not to invade Cuba.

27 October Khrushchev sends a second letter adding a condition that the USA remove missiles from Turkey. Kennedy agrees to the first letter in public and to the second in private.

28 October Khrushchev agrees to remove missiles from Cuba.

Consequences of the crisis

While both Kennedy and Khrushchev were accused of 'brinkmanship', both emerged with some credit. Kennedy had forced Khrushchev to back down and had avoided war. Khrushchev was praised by Western powers for his good sense, but was criticised by China for backing down.

Relations between the superpowers improved and a telephone 'hotline' was installed between the White House and the Kremlin to ease communication. In 1963 a Test-Ban Treaty was signed, outlawing nuclear weapons tests in the atmosphere, under the sea or in space.

Questions

1 What were the causes of the Cuban Missile Crisis?

2 Who gained the most from the Cuban Missile Crisis?

THE WAR IN VIETNAM

Between 1965 and 1973 the USA fought a difficult war against communism in Vietnam. However, the wealthiest and most powerful nation in the world was not able to defeat a much smaller guerrilla force of a developing country.

In 1954 the French had been driven out of their former colony of Indo-China by communist rebels led by Ho Chi Minh. The area was divided into four states: Cambodia, Laos, North Vietnam and South Vietnam. The north of Vietnam became communist under Ho Chi Minh while the south was controlled by the anti-communist government of Ngo Dinh Diem.

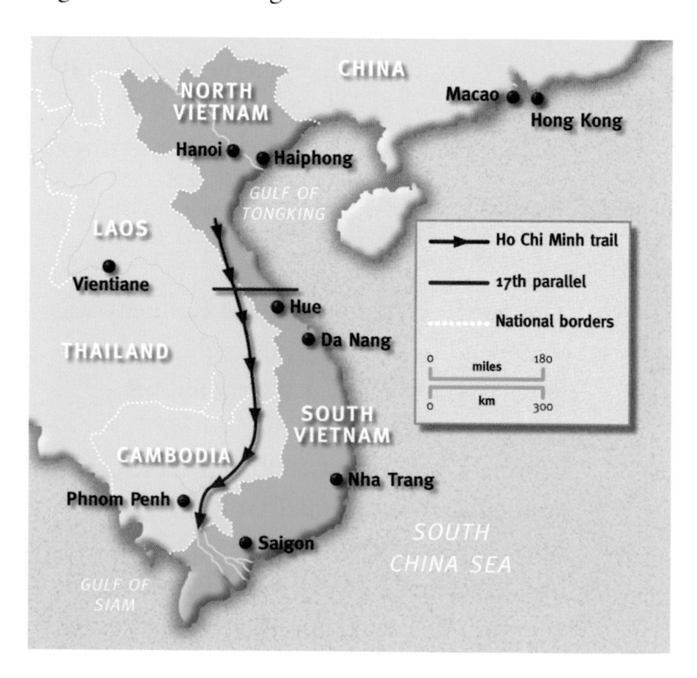

The division of Vietnam.

Ho Chi Minh wanted an independent, communist Vietnam and set out to achieve it by war. Presidents Eisenhower and later Kennedy sent weapons and 'advisers' to help the south as part of their policy of containment and to prevent the spread of communism. President Johnson later justified war as being necessary for economic recovery in the USA.

The USA steps up involvement

By 1963 the Vietcong (communist forces) had control of 40 per cent of the countryside in South Vietnam and Johnson decided to increase US support. In August 1964 North Vietnamese boats attacked US ships in the Gulf of Tonkin providing President Johnson with an excuse to step up the programme. Johnson launched Operation Rolling Thunder, a massive bombing offensive against North Vietnam, and committed 180,000 combat troops as a quick way of defeating the Vietcong. By 1968 over 540,000 'grunts', as they called themselves, were fighting in Vietnam. To bolster the Vietcong the Soviets and the Chinese sent weapons and supplies, and thousands more communist troops poured in along the Ho Chi Minh Trail, a series of jungle tracks (see map on page 264).

Vietcong tactics

The Vietcong fought a highly successful guerrilla war. They used their knowledge of the terrain and dug 48,000 kilometres of underground tunnels. They carried out surprise attacks and then disappeared into the jungle. They easily merged with civilians and US troops found it difficult to identify the Vietcong. Despite huge losses the Vietcong were resilient: one journalist described the US tactics as 'using a sledgehammer on a floating cork'.

The Tet Offensive, January 1968

While the Vietcong used guerrilla tactics in their fight against US forces, they also carried out some major attacks, such as the Tet Offensive during the Tet religious festival. South Vietnamese towns and US bases as well as the US embassy in Saigon were attacked. They were eventually driven back with 50,000 dead but they had struck at the heart of US-held territory and while losing this battle they had won a psychological victory.

US tactics

The Americans fought a modern high-tech war using B52 bombers, helicopters and rocket launchers. Science played a sinister part with chemicals like Agent Orange, a defoliant used to prevent the Vietcong hiding in the jungle, and napalm, a type of burning jelly that sticks to the skin. 'Search and destroy' tactics were used to flush out the elusive enemy, or 'Charlie' as the Americans called the Vietcong.

Opposition to the Vietnam War

The war was televised and millions of Americans saw its horrific results from their living rooms. In 1969, CBS television showed shocking images of a massacre of 504 men, women and children by US troops at My Lai in 1968. This turned middle America against the war. Lieutenant William Calley who led the attack was sentenced to life imprisonment but served only three days of his sentence.

An anti-war protest movement gained support: leading figures like Martin Luther King, Muhammed Ali and Jane Fonda spoke out. There were an increasing number of protests across the USA.

Young men burned 'draft cards' and Johnson was taunted with chants of 'Hey, hey LBJ, how many kids did you kill today?' Johnson did not seek re-election and Richard Nixon became President in 1969.

Vietnamisation: 'giving the war back'

Nixon's solution to the increasing reluctance of the US public to be part of the war was to strengthen the South Vietnamese army and make it strong enough to defend the country itself, giving him the excuse to withdraw US troops. As the process of Vietnamisation began, peace talks were held to try to end the war. By 1973 a ceasefire had been agreed and, by the end of the year, all US troops had left.

The war started up again in 1974 and the USA sent supplies but no troops. Communist forces overran much of South Vietnam in 1975 and in 1976 Ho Chi Minh succeeded in uniting Vietnam as a single communist country. Cambodia and Laos became communist – the dominoes had fallen and the US policy of containment had failed.

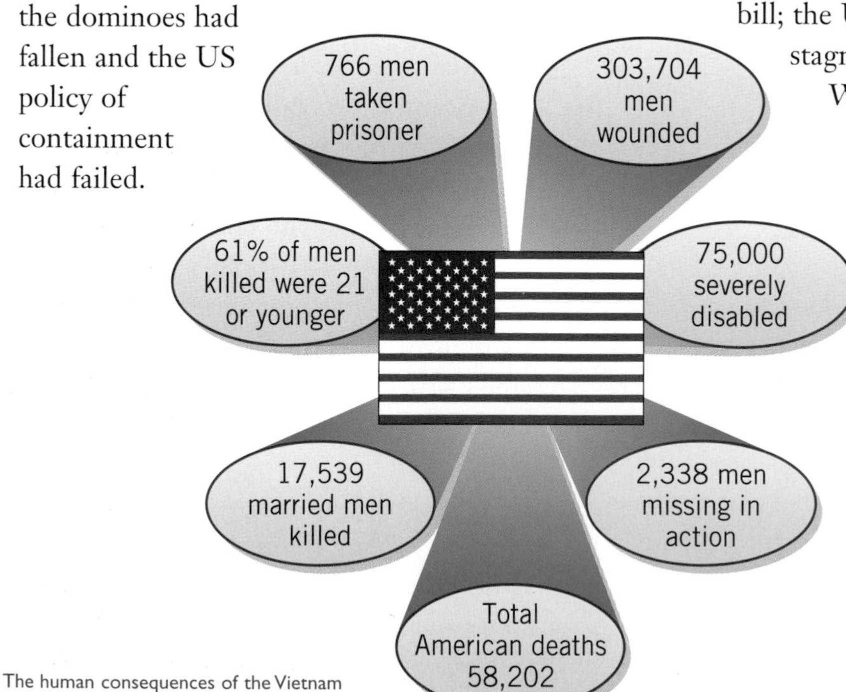

The human consequences of the Vietnam War to the USA.

Questions

1 Why did the USA become involved in Vietnam?

2 Why has the Vietnam War been described as unwinnable?

CHANGES IN COLD WAR RELATIONSHIPS

Détente

Détente is a French word, meaning relaxation, which has been used to describe periods of thaw in Cold War relations. It applies mainly to the years between 1971, when the USA and USSR began a number of summit meetings, and 1979 when the Soviets invaded Afghanistan. Détente was restored after Mikhail Gorbachev became Soviet leader in 1985. The superpowers wanted détente for several reasons:

- To reduce the risk of nuclear war.
- To reduce the massive cost of the arms race – the USA had a huge Vietnam War bill; the USSR's economy was stagnating and trade with the West was needed.
- The Vietnam War had greatly affected American foreign policy. The USA sought better relations with the USSR and China. Though China had no nuclear weapons at the time its huge army posed a threat in Asia.

Improved relations with China

Nixon was a staunch anti-communist yet he secured friendly relations with the USSR and China in the 1970s and 1980s. Much of his success was due to his adviser Dr Henry Kissinger. US aims were to limit the arms race and discourage Soviet and Chinese expansion, particularly in the Third World.

The USA and China were each still distrustful of the USSR but were prepared to 'hold their noses' and improve relations with one another. In 1971 the USA agreed that communist China should take its seat in the United Nations. The US table tennis team played matches in Peking, giving rise to the term 'ping-pong diplomacy', and in 1972 Nixon made his historic 'journey for peace' visit to China.

Number of soldiers

USA	2,100,000
USSR	4,200,000
China	3,000,000

Inter-continental missiles

USA	1054
USSR	1590
China	0

Submarine-launched missiles

USA	656
USSR	700
China	0

Bomber aircraft

USA	498
USSR	160
China	0

A 1970's military balance sheet.

Détente with the USSR: Salt I

In 1972 Nixon flew to Moscow (the first President to do so since Roosevelt in 1944) in a landmark in Russo-American relations. The Strategic Arms Limitation Talks (SALT) started in 1969, leading to the SALT I agreement of 1972. The agreement, which was to run for five years, limited the number of intercontinental (ICBMs) and anti-ballistic missiles (ABMs) and agreements were made not to test ICBMs and submarine-launched missiles.

The Helsinki Accords, 1975

In 1975, 35 countries including the USA and the USSR signed an agreement that has been seen as the high point of détente. The USA recognised the frontiers of Eastern Europe and Soviet dominance there. This was linked to a promise by all countries to respect basic human rights of speech, religion and movement.

The impact of the war in Afghanistan

US President Carter attempted to get further agreement on arms limitations through SALT II talks but progress with the Soviet leader, Brezhnev, was slow. SALT II was never ratified (agreed) by the US Senate due mainly to the Soviet Union's invasion of Afghanistan in 1979. Diplomatic links were broken and Carter withdrew the US Olympic team from the 1980 Olympic Games in Moscow.

In January 1981 Reagan replaced Carter as President and the USA returned to an aggressive anti-Soviet foreign policy.

SOURCE G This cartoon was published in a British newspaper in 1976. It shows Kissinger of the USA on the left and Brezhnev of the Soviet Union on the right.

Despite arms reduction talks both sides had been developing new weapons. Reagan vastly increased his defence budget and announced that the USA had developed a new type of bomb – the neutron bomb, which had the capacity to kill many people without much damage to property. In 1983 US scientists began work on the Strategic Defense Initiative (SDI) or 'Star Wars', a kind of giant shield in space which would use lasers to shoot down enemy missiles. One of the reasons for this was to bring down communism in the USSR by forcing the USSR to spend huge sums of money on arms rather than on other investments.

Despite the build-up of arms, talks for reductions in arms were resumed. The Strategic Arms Reduction Talks (START) aimed to reduce nuclear weapons but little progress was made (the treaty was signed in 1991).

The breakthrough in Russo-American relations came in 1985 when Gorbachev called for a reduction in hostilities. He began talks with Reagan in 1987 and by 1989 Soviet troops had left Afghanistan.

In December 1987 both leaders agreed to destroy all medium- and short-range weapons in Europe within three years. This was called the Intermediate Nuclear Forces Treaty (INF) and represented a turning point in the arms race.

The end of the Cold War

The policies of President Gorbachev resulted in the Soviet grip over Eastern Europe loosening. In 1989, Gorbachev told the leaders of communist-controlled Eastern Europe that Soviet troops would no longer be able to defend them. In other words, the Soviet Union was removing its control from Eastern Europe. During the next twelve months, communist governments throughout Eastern Europe were overthrown. The Cold War had ended; communist control of Eastern Europe had collapsed.

Q Questions

1. How did relations with the USSR and China change after 1970?
2. Who gained the most from détente?

8 EXAM PRACTICE

CHANGE IN THE USA, 1929–90

Study the information below and answer the questions which follow.

INFORMATION

In 1932 Franklin D. Roosevelt was elected President of the USA and immediately set about changing American society.

EQ Exam Questions

1 a What was the New Deal? [2]
  b Describe how the people of America were affected by the Depression. [4]

2 Explain why America became so affluent in the 1950s and 1960s. [6]

3 Why was Ronald Reagan such a popular president? [8]

4 Did life improve for all Americans during the period 1929–90?
In your answer you may wish to consider the Depression, the impact of the Second World War, young people, the situation in 1990 and any other relevant factors. [10]

THE RACE ISSUE, 1929–90

Study the information below and answer the question which follow.

INFORMATION

In 1957, nine black 15-year-old boys and girls tried to enter the whites-only high school at Little Rock, Arkansas. A huge crowd of hostile white people swore and spat at them. Government troops were used to escort the students into the school.

EQ Exam Questions

1 a What is meant by *segregation*? [2]
  b Describe the activities of the Ku Klux Klan. [4]

2 Why were black Americans so badly affected by the Depression of the 1930s? [6]

3 Why was Martin Luther King important in the 1950s and the 1960s? [8]

4 Did life for black people in the US change significantly between 1929 and 1990?
In your answer you may wish to consider segregation, the Civil Rights movement, Martin Luther King, the situation in 1990 and any other relevant factors. [10]

COLEG CYMUNEDOL ABERGELE
ABERGELE COMMUNITY COLLEGE
CANOLFAN ADNODDAU DYSGU
LEARNING RESOURCE CENTRE

THE FOREIGN POLICY OF THE USA, 1929–90

Study the information below and answer the questions which follow.

INFORMATION

The war in Vietnam was part of a series of wars involving the USA during this period.

EQ Exam Questions

1 a What is meant by *isolationism*? [2]
  b Describe how the US contributed to winning the Second World War. [4]

2 Explain the importance of the Cuban Missile Crisis for the US. [6]

3 Why was Vietnam so important in US foreign policy? [8]

4 How important was the US in world affairs during the period 1929–90?
In your answer you may wish to consider the policy of isolationism, the Second World War, the Cold War, the situation in 1990 and any other relevant factors. [10]

INDEX